TRUMAN AND THE 80TH CONGRESS

TRUMAN

UNIVERSITY OF MISSOURI PRESS

AND THE 80TH CONGRESS

Susan M. Hartmann

COLUMBIA, 1971

ISBN 0–8262–0105–9
Copyright © 1971 by
The Curators of the University of Missouri
University of Missouri Press, Columbia, Missouri 65201
Library of Congress Catalog Number 78–149008
Printed and bound in the United States of America
Photographs on end papers reprinted by permission
of United Press-International

TO MY PARENTS

ACKNOWLEDGMENTS

SINCE its inception in 1965, this study has benefited from the help and support of many persons and institutions. Professor Richard S. Kirkendall of the University of Missouri—Columbia has unstintingly given of his time and critical acumen through all stages of the project and has been an important source of inspiration and encouragement to my development as a historian.

A number of institutions allowed me access to the sources upon which this study rests and gave me an opportunity to work with kind, knowledgeable people. I am especially grateful to Philip C. Brooks, Director of the Harry S. Truman Library, and his expert staff, particularly Harry Clark and Philip Lagerquist, who greatly facilitated my extended research at the Library. The Bureau of the Budget kindly allowed me to use papers of the Bureau still in its possession. I must also thank the archivists at the Library of Congress, the National Archives, the Memphis Public Library, the Sam Rayburn Library, the state historical societies of Kansas, Nebraska, and Ohio, the South Carolina Department of Archives and History, the Franklin D. Roosevelt Library, and the libraries of the University of Michigan, the University of Nebraska, the University of Oklahoma, the University of Kentucky, the University of North Carolina, the University of West Virginia, Cornell University, and the University of Missouri. I am also grateful to Clark M. Clifford for sharing with me some of his experiences as Truman's special counsel.

Grants from the University of Missouri—St. Louis and the Truman Library Institute of National and International Affairs provided me with the time and financial assistance essential to my research.

I am also indebted to Professors Mary H. Blewett of Lowell State College, Lyle W. Dorsett of the University of Missouri—St. Louis, Richard M. Dalfiume of the State University of New

York—Binghamton, Monte M. Poen of Northern Arizona University, and William O. Wagnon of Washburn University, who, as fellow graduate students, shared my interest in Harry S Truman and who have continued to offer ideas and encouragement. Special thanks are due Professor Alonzo Hamby of Ohio University for carefully reading the entire manuscript and offering insightful criticism. I am deeply indebted to Professor James Neal Primm of the University of Missouri—St. Louis. His moral support got me past temporary difficulties, and his sharp eye produced many improvements in style and substance. Finally, I am grateful to Charles J. Hartmann, Jr., who offered continuous interest and encouragement in my research and writing. The dedication of this book acknowledges my special appreciation to my parents, Mr. and Mrs. Herbert R. Meckfessel, for the many ways in which they made the book possible.

S.M.H.

St. Louis, Missouri
January, 1971

CONTENTS

TRUMAN AND THE 80TH CONGRESS

UNCERTAIN before November, 1946, the course of the United States after World War II became even more so after the Republicans' success in the elections of that year. Republican gains meant a divided government for the next two years and probable Republican dominance in 1948. Their victory also gave rise to several questions: Could the United States and the Soviet Union reach an accommodation that would make peace a reality? Would the social and economic reforms of the New Deal be preserved and pushed forward, or would a conservative reaction ensue? Finally, did the 1946 elections foreshadow a major political realignment from which the GOP would emerge again as the dominant national party? The history of the Eightieth Congress illuminates the ways in which the President, Congress, and the public began to determine the answers and set patterns in foreign policies and domestic policies and politics that would affect events in the United States for the next twenty years.

Although U.S. foreign policy had been moving the nation toward a confrontation with the Soviet Union since at least 1945, it was during the Eightieth Congress that the Cold War began. For the first time, in 1947 and 1948, the United States employed substantial economic and military power to support its tough diplomatic stance toward Russia; for the first time, U.S. leaders used militant rhetoric and singled out the Soviet Union as the primary threat to world peace; and for the first time, the Administration had to marshal congressional support for its containment policy. This study focuses on Truman's major legislative goals in the area of foreign policy, his efforts on their behalf, and the ways they were influenced, modified, and implemented by the Republican-dominated Congress.

In domestic policy the Eightieth Congress is best known for its attack on New Deal programs and its refusal to expand the

1

welfare state. A close examination, however, reveals the limited nature of the attack as well as the considerable lack of agreement among Republicans—and Democrats—about desirable legislative goals. Moreover, an analysis of Truman's legislative leadership should determine his contributions to the record of the Eightieth Congress. To what extent was he responsible for blunting the assault on the New Deal? Conversely, how did his behavior contribute to the modification, limited though it was, of New Deal programs and the failure to expand them? Presidential power, especially in domestic affairs, is limited, and this study seeks to assess the external and personal obstacles to Truman's success as a legislative leader.

Finally, the Eightieth Congress was the arena in which the battle for the Presidency in 1948 was waged. While political candidates usually run on or against the record of the incumbent government, the campaign of 1948 was unique in the degree to which candidates concentrated on the record of the past Congress, and it was one of the few times that an incumbent President has been able to put his opponents on the defensive. Truman's campaign for re-election began shortly after the Democratic debacle of November, 1946. He adjusted legislative goals and strategy to meet changing circumstances, but the dominant influence on his behavior throughout the Eightieth Congress was the forthcoming election. Thus, Truman's use of the record of the Eightieth Congress was the crucial factor in the Democratic victory of 1948.

CHAPTER 1

REACTION TO THE ELECTION RETURNS

SHORTLY AFTER the congressional elections of November, 1946, Howard Spencer returned from a self-imposed exile in the Bahamas. Spencer, who had been one of Franklin D. Roosevelt's wealthy neighbors in Hyde Park, had left the United States in 1936, after an overwhelming majority of voters had ratified the New Deal by electing Roosevelt to another four-year term.[1] Now, Spencer believed, it was safe to return. Fourteen years of Democratic ascendancy had ended when the Republicans captured both houses of Congress. For Howard Spencer, and for a substantial number of successful candidates, the opportunity had arrived to reverse the most repugnant tendencies of the New Deal.

Another, less happy journey also began in the wake of the elections: Even before the polls had closed, a train bearing President Harry S Truman started back to Washington from Independence, Missouri, where he had voted. To newsmen who observed him as he read the latest tabulations, Truman remained noncommittal about the election returns, but to Special Counsel Clark M. Clifford, he seemed "terribly downcast" about the Democratic reversal and its implications for the Administration's legislative program.[2]

The political situation did give cause for gloom. Weaknesses in party organization became apparent when, for the first time in over a decade, Democratic candidates had to run without the support of Roosevelt's popularity. Their attempts to stir the electorate by using recordings of Roosevelt's voice, as well as Truman's, indicated their lack of faith in Truman's voter appeal. Making the recordings was the only direct action Truman took in the

1. William E. Leuchtenburg, *Franklin D. Roosevelt and the New Deal, 1932–1940*, 176–77.
2. Merriman Smith, *A President Is Many Men*, 60; Clark M. Clifford, interview, August 23, 1965, Washington, D.C.

campaign. He made no public statements in support of Democratic candidates, and his advisers rejected drafts for an election-eve speech emphasizing the importance of electing a progressive Congress and appealing for a large voter turnout. During the campaign, only Truman's removal of controls over meat and his statement favoring the admission of 100,000 Jews to Palestine could be construed as attempts to influence the election results. His lack of popularity, as reflected in the polls, discouraged his participation in the campaign and indicated his loss of enthusiastic support from significant blocs of the Roosevelt coalition, particularly liberals and labor.[3]

Both personal and external factors contributed to Truman's ineffectiveness. After four years of war, people in the United States were impatient with restraints and especially eager to use their accumulated savings to buy commodities that had been scarce or nonexistent during the war. But the shortages of meat, sugar, electrical appliances, nylons, and a host of other items continued. Families who had gone without a new car for five years or more were forced to wait longer unless they had connections or were willing to pay black-market prices. An unprecedented housing shortage forced returning veterans to live in basements and boxcars or move in with relatives and friends. Chicago alone reported 100,000 homeless veterans. After the removal of most price controls in June, 1946, as frustrated consumers competed frenziedly for scarce commodities, prices rose precipitately and threatened to cancel out real gains in income that many people had achieved during the wartime boom. In 1946 the consumer price index jumped from 129.6 to 153.3 (1935=100), and the wholesale price index rose from 107.1 to 140.9 (1926=100). The

3. Jack Redding, *Inside the Democratic Party*, 46; Bryson Rash to Candidate, October 10, 1946, Clarence Cannon Papers, 1946 Campaign-Politics; *The New York Times*, October 29, 1946, pp. 1, 14, 17, October 31, 1946, p. 1; "Suggested Radio Speech by the President on the Eve of the Elections," Clark M. Clifford Papers, Speech File; Alfred Steinberg, *The Man from Missouri: The Life and Times of Harry S. Truman*, 286–88; Allen J. Matusow, *Farm Policies and Politics in the Truman Years*, 59–61; J. Joseph Huthmacher, *Senator Robert F. Wagner and the Rise of Urban Liberalism*, 312, 324; Alonzo L. Hamby, "Harry S. Truman and American Liberalism, 1945–1948" (Ph.D. dissertation, University of Missouri—Columbia, 1965), 39–138.

inflation and shortages hurt Truman and the Democratic party at the polls in November. Rising prices also portended difficulties for the future. With the nation's economic health endangered by inflation and with a Congress controlled by the opposition and unfriendly to economic controls, the prospects for Democratic victory in 1948 were threatened. Further, many observers were predicting a sharp decline and possible recession once inflationary pressures had run their course.[4]

Postwar labor disputes also helped to discredit the inexperienced Administration and added to the problems Truman would face in the Eightieth Congress. Convinced that they had made extraordinary sacrifices during the war and determined to maintain workers' incomes at not less than wartime levels despite the reduction of the work week from forty-eight to forty hours, unions pressed for higher wage rates by calling an unprecedented number of strikes. In 1946 a total of 116,000,000 man-days of work were lost because of strikes in the auto, steel, packinghouse, electrical, and communications industries, as well as coal mines and railroads. The work stoppages complicated the problem of scarcities, management added to the price spiral by raising prices to compensate for wage increases, and the public demanded curbs on labor unions. In dealing with labor problems, Truman managed to alienate both sides. He took an extremely punitive approach during the rail dispute in the spring of 1946, demanding that Congress give him emergency authority to draft striking workers. Even Republican Senator Robert A. Taft of Ohio, no great friend of labor, objected to such a curtailment of basic freedoms, and A. F. Whitney pledged the entire treasury of his Brotherhood of Railway Trainmen to defeat Truman in 1948. After the railway dispute, however, Truman resisted pressures for permanent legislative restrictions on organized labor by vetoing the Case bill, which had a requirement of notice for strikes, a sixty-day cooling-off period, the outlawing of secondary boycotts, and other antilabor provisions. Truman's veto ameliorated labor's angry reaction to

4. Eric F. Goldman, *The Crucial Decade—and After: America, 1945–1960*, 25–28; Richard O. Davies, *Housing Reform During the Truman Administration*, 40–41; Council of Economic Advisers, "The Impact of Foreign Aid Upon the Domestic Economy," October, 1947, James E. Webb Papers.

his proposal to draft strikers, but labor remained distinctly apathetic during the 1946 campaign, with the Political Action Committee of the CIO merely going through the motions. The election results indicated that additional trouble would come when a Congress more concerned about what it considered union excesses would attempt to translate into legislation the growing public demand for curbs on organized labor.[5]

Another problem for the President was the increasing disaffection of liberals during his eighteen months in office. This diverse, relatively small, but highly articulate group of middle-class reformers had been an important source of strength for FDR and the New Deal. They had worked for equal opportunities, greater economic security, and racial equality for people in the United States and economic development and increased democracy abroad. After Roosevelt's death, they sought in Truman a source of unity and inspiration and found him spectacularly wanting. Truman—the small-town, Midwestern, machine politician with the country accent and adventurous grammar—could hardly fill the shoes of a sophisticated, charismatic, and seemingly independent statesman, but even more important to liberals was the record of the early Truman Administration. Concerned about the widening breach with the Soviet Union and U.S. support for reaction and imperialism abroad, disheartened by the exodus of New Dealers from the government and their replacement by often-undistinguished personal friends of the President, disgusted by the Administration's ineptitude in handling reconversion, inflation, and labor disputes, and dismayed by congressional failure to pass reform legislation, liberals became convinced that with Truman in the White House, all their hopes for reform at home and abroad were dead.[6]

Progressives had good cause to be disheartened by the record of the Seventy-ninth Congress. While it passed the Employment act

5. Cabell Phillips, *The Truman Presidency: The History of a Triumphant Succession*, 111–18; R. Alton Lee, *Truman and Taft-Hartley; A Question of Mandate*, 15–18, 31–45.

6. Hamby, "Truman and American Liberalism," 39–138; Alonzo L. Hamby, "The Liberals, Truman, and FDR as Symbol and Myth," *Journal of American History*, 56 (March, 1970), 859–62.

—a watered-down version of the reformers' drive for federal machinery to ensure full employment—and the Veterans' Emergency Housing Act, which failed in operation to relieve the housing shortage, the Seventy-ninth Congress refused Truman's requests for reform measures, killed the price-control authority of the government, and almost passed the antiunion Case bill over the President's veto. In giving Truman the major blame, however, the liberals revealed short memories. To be sure, Truman's legislative leadership was weak and inconsistent: He vacillated on some issues and, while calling for general legislation, would rarely commit himself on details of a particular program or support a specific bill already in Congress. But the miring of the reform program had more profound causes than those originating in the White House.[7]

In the first place, Truman faced the same conservative coalition in Congress that had plagued Roosevelt since 1937 and bottled up many of his proposals. Strengthened by Republican gains in 1942, this group of Southern Democrats and conservative Republicans formed a core of anti-Administration votes in the Seventy-eighth Congress, which overrode presidential vetoes of tax and labor legislation, liquidated the National Youth Administration and the Civilian Conservation Corps, and killed the National Resources Planning Board, a federal agency composed of liberal economists who were charting the postwar expansion of reform.[8]

In addition, the Truman Administration faced an economic atmosphere totally different from that of the New Deal years. The climate of severe economic crisis, deflation, and unemployment had permitted the reforms of the 1930's. In a period of an expanding economy, serious inflation, and high employment, Truman could hardly justify increased spending for welfare legislation in Keynesian terms, for his Administration was confronted by the

7. Mary H. Hinchey, "The Frustration of the New Deal Revival" (Ph.D. dissertation, University of Missouri—Columbia, 1965), 103, 148–52; Hamby, "Truman and American Liberalism," 76–79; Barton J. Bernstein, "Economic Policies," in Richard S. Kirkendall, ed., The Truman Period as a Research Field, 98–105; Richard O. Davies, "Social Welfare Policies," ibid., 152–71.

8. James T. Patterson, Congressional Conservatism and the New Deal: The Growth of the Conservative Coalition in Congress, 1933–1939, 331–37; Hinchey, "The Frustration of the New Deal Revival," 38–39.

argument that reduction of federal expenditures was necessary if inflation were to be controlled. The war-induced prosperity had also transformed the electorate. During the Depression, a defeated and frightened populace had been willing to support experiments that might bring relief, but the postwar period witnessed the emergence of a new middle class, people who were relatively satisfied, determined to maintain their social and economic gains of the past decade, but unsympathetic to the needs or demands of other groups that might infringe upon their new status. This changed atmosphere strengthened the conservative coalition in Congress and combined with Truman's own shortcomings to defeat the bulk of his domestic program in the Seventy-ninth Congress and the Democrats in the 1946 elections. Thus, at the beginning of the Eightieth Congress, Truman faced a legislature even more hostile to reform.[9]

A number of Republicans had devoted their campaigns to assaults on the New Deal. The campaign pamphlets of Ohio Representative John M. Vorys, for example, lauded his past record of eight years' opposition to "New Deal incompetence, waste, graft, extravagance and bureaucracy." Senator Kenneth S. Wherry of Nebraska summarized the issues of the 1946 elections in one phrase, "the defeat of the New Deal," and his colleague John W. Bricker of Ohio assailed the Roosevelt programs with equal vigor.[10]

Although Republicans viewed the election returns as a repudiation of the New Deal, there was no electoral mandate for repeal of any particular programs. To contemporary and later observers, the vote reflected primarily the frustrations and stresses that accompanied adjustment to a peacetime economy. Pre-election polls had shown little opposition to the prewar social and economic programs; the public was most concerned about inflation, shortages of food and other commodities, remaining wartime controls,

9. Bernstein, "Economic Policies," 101; Samuel Lubell, *The Future of American Politics*, 1.

10. Campaign pamphlet, John M. Vorys Papers, Election Materials (1946); Wherry, speech draft, "Summing Up the Issues in This Campaign," Kenneth S. Wherry Papers; Ohio Republican Campaign Committee, news release, November 1, 1946, John W. Bricker Papers.

and strikes and other labor problems. Republican Congressman Marion T. Bennett of Missouri reported that scarcities and controls stood out above all other issues in the campaign. Democratic Representative John H. Kerr of North Carolina complained to Acting Secretary of Agriculture Charles F. Brannan that price controls were "making the people most hostile to our Administration," and Democrat Brent Spence of Kentucky was so concerned about voter reaction to meat shortages that he urged the President to eliminate federal controls. Voters blamed inflation and scarcities on confusion and ineptitude in government. While some vented their frustrations by supporting Republican candidates, many who usually voted Democratic simply stayed home on election day.[11]

Republican candidates dealt skillfully with these anxieties. They assailed New Deal "regimentation," "bureaucracy," "extravagance," and "radicalism," but even its most violent opponents did not suggest dismantling the welfare state. Instead, they waged a negative campaign with such slogans as "Had Enough?" "To Err is Truman," and "Under Truman: Two Families in Every Garage." John Vorys typified the Republican approach when he queried voters: "Got enough meat? Got enough houses? Got enough OPA? . . . Got enough inflation? . . . Got enough debt? . . . Got enough strikes? . . . Got enough Communism? . . . Had enough war?" The opposition also capitalized on apprehensions about national security and fears of internal subversion. A pre-election publication of the Republican National Committee Chairman decried "the infiltration of alien-minded radicals" into high federal positions and "THE ADMINISTRATION'S BRAZEN PUBLIC ALLIANCE WITH THE RADICAL-DOMINATED POLITICAL ACTION COMMITTEE [of the CIO]," while individual candidates spoke specifically about Communists. John Taber of New York, ranking Re-

11. Louis H. Bean, "The Republican 'Mandate' and 1948," *The New York Times Magazine* (January 19, 1947), 52; Eugene H. Roseboom, *A History of Presidential Elections*, 494; *The New York Times*, October 6, 1946, p. E10, October 13, 1946, p. E1; Bennett to E. Worth Higgins, October 7, 1946, Marion T. Bennett Papers; Kerr to Brannan, September 26, 1946, John H. Kerr Papers; Spence to Rayburn, October 17, 1946, Sam Rayburn Papers, Miscellaneous File; Walter Johnson, *1600 Pennsylvania Avenue: Presidents and the People Since 1929*, 226; Goldman, *The Crucial Decade*, 40, 44–45.

9

publican on the House Appropriations Committee, charged that the country was imperiled by communist infiltration into the government, universities and even the Army. Other candidates more vaguely equated the Democratic social welfare and other reform programs with communism. Democratic congressional candidate Harry R. Sheppard complained that the Republicans in California were "alleging by indirection that all Democrats are Communists." In Oklahoma, Republican candidate George B. Schwabe shouted about "the imminent danger of communism" and attacked Administration-sponsored legislation as "socialistic, New Deal, communistic schemes," while Senator Hugh Butler of Nebraska berated the Democrats for failing to eject communists from labor unions.[12]

While the negative strategy of appealing to popular frustrations brought victory in 1946, the Republican party needed to develop a positive legislative program in order to win in 1948. Portions of this program emerged in late 1946 and early 1947 in individual legislative proposals. Two themes, consistent with traditional Republican ideology, as well as with specific objections to Democratic tendencies, underlay these proposals: Congress must reassert its authority and strip the executive branch of excessive powers, and the Federal Government must cease its intervention into business and private life. In his radio address on the eve of the first session, Senate leader Robert A. Taft stated, "The main issue of the election was the restoration of freedom and the elimination or reduction of constantly increasing interference with family life and with business by autocratic government bureaus and autocratic labor leaders." House Speaker Joseph W. Martin of Massachusetts urged a return to "the sound philosophy that the Govern-

12. Vorys, speech, "Republican Campaign Opening," October 8, 1946, Vorys Papers; Tris Coffin, *Missouri Compromise*, 294, 296; Johnson, *1600 Pennsylvania Avenue*, 226–28; *The New York Times*, October 13, 1946, p. E3; Republican National Committee, "The Chairman's Letter," August 15, 1946, Hugh A. Butler Papers, Political File; Taber, statement, October 28, 1946, John Taber Papers, Election Material, 1946; Sheppard to John W. McCormack, October 24, 1946, Rayburn Papers, Miscellaneous File; Schwabe to A. E. Bradshaw, February 8, 1947, George B. Schwabe Papers, Legislative File, Correspondence; Butler, speech draft, "Principal Legislative Proposals to be Dealt with by Congress in 1947," Butler Papers, Political File.

ment does not support the people" and argued that "our American concept of government rests upon the idea of a dominant Congress." These themes provided the rationale for the two vital areas of the Republican program—fiscal policy and labor relations.[13]

In the realm of fiscal policy, excessive government interference in the lives of individuals would be curbed through tax reduction and drastic cuts in federal spending. The most vigorous advocate of tax reduction was the new chairman of the House Ways and Means Committee, Harold Knutson of Minnesota, who proposed a 20 per cent across-the-board cut in order to "stop the New Deal practice of using tax laws to punish its enemies and promote social innovations." A preliminary meeting of the House Republican Steering Committee endorsed the 20 per cent figure, and most Republican leaders, including Taft and Martin in speeches on January 3, supported some kind of tax reduction. The tax burden on individuals could be lightened, Republicans maintained, because the new Congress would restore economy in federal expenditures. House Appropriations Committee Chairman John Taber promised to use a "sledge hammer" on budget estimates and predicted that $9 billion could be saved. Although Taft was more cautious, he believed that $5 billion or $6 billion could be subtracted from totals for the current fiscal year, bringing the budget down to $30 billion.[14]

The second area requiring legislative action was the field of labor relations, where, according to Republicans, the balance of power had swung too far over to the side of labor. While Taft predicted a revival of the Case bill, other Republicans favored even harsher legislation, including abolition of the closed shop and limitations on industry-wide bargaining.[15]

Other domestic proposals receiving rather wide support among

13. U.S. *Congressional Record*, 80th Cong., 1st sess., 1947, XCIII, Part 1, p. 36; Part 10, p. A7.

14. *The New York Times*, November 7, 1946, p. 1, November 10, 1946, p. 5, November 15, 1946, p. 1, November 16, 1946, p. 10; The Office of Joseph W. Martin, news release on the meeting of the House Republican Steering Committee, November 14, 1946, Taber Papers; Butler, speech draft, "Principal Legislative Proposals to be Dealt with by Congress in 1947," Butler Papers, Political File.

15. U.S. *Congressional Record*, 80th Cong., 1st sess., 1947, XCIII, Part 10, p. A7; *The New York Times*, November 12, 1946, p. 1.

Republicans included constitutional amendments limiting presidential tenure to two terms and eliminating the poll tax, legislation limiting employers' liability for back wages from portal suits based on the Fair Labor Standards Act, and the termination or drastic limitation of all remaining government wartime controls. Prospects for legislation in the area of social and economic welfare seemed slim. Few Republican senators had advocated such measures in the Seventy-ninth Congress, and they were not joined by colleagues in the House. For example, Senators Taft, George Aiken of Vermont, Wayne Morse of Oregon, and H. Alexander Smith of New Jersey had supported legislation for federal aid to education, but the committee-approved bill did not reach the Senate floor because leaders saw no chance of House action. Similarly, the federal housing bill cosponsored by Taft passed the Senate, but it could not be pried out of the House Banking and Currency Committee. The new Republican chairman of this committee, Jesse P. Wolcott of Michigan, was a vigorous opponent of public housing. Finally, increasing the minimum wage was well down on Taft's list of possibilities for congressional action, and he suggested only contemplation of the matter. Republicans in general seldom mentioned social and economic measures as they outlined legislative goals.[16]

The new majority gave relatively slight consideration to foreign policy. In his radio address of January 3, Taft devoted only three paragraphs to the subject; he predicted congressional resistance to large-scale foreign assistance and substantial tariff reductions, but he also favored continuation of bipartisan support for the Administration's European policy. Arthur H. Vandenberg of Michigan, the Republican foreign-policy spokesman, pledged cooperation with Secretary of State James F. Byrnes and suggested closer scrutiny of legislation dealing with tariff cutting and international trade.[17]

The more conservative wing of the party managed the Repub-

16. *Ibid.*, November 15, 1946, p. 17, December 27, 1946, p. 1; U.S. *Congressional Record*, 80th Cong., 1st sess., 1947, XCIII, Part 10, pp. A7–A8; The Office of Joseph W. Martin, news release, November 14, 1946, Taber Papers; *Congressional Quarterly*, 2 (1946), 643–51; 3 (1947), 30.

17. *The New York Times*, January 20, 1947, p. 1.

lican program in Congress. Wallace H. White of Maine was Senate majority leader in name only. On the Senate floor, he often openly turned around to receive signals from Taft, which led sympathetic reporters to offer him a rearview mirror. The powerful Senator from Ohio had first come to Washington in 1938, fresh from a campaign based on an all-out fight against the New Deal and pledges to end the "rubber stamp" role of Congress. He returned to the Capitol in 1947 convinced that the Republicans had a mandate to reverse or alter parts of the New Deal. Although his rhetoric often made him seem a constant opponent of social and economic reform, Taft actually accepted some aspects of the New Deal and even sought to expand federal programs for disadvantaged groups. He believed that able-bodied adults should determine their own destinies without government interference but that the government should aid society's unfortunates who were unable to help themselves. Where states and local governments could not meet this responsibility, then the Federal Government should act. Thus, Taft advocated federal aid to education, public housing where private enterprise could not do the job, and public charity for hardship cases. He hoped to use his strategic position as chairman of the Senate Labor Committee, chairman of the Senate Republican Policy Committee, and unofficial floor leader to make a record in the Eightieth Congress upon which the party could stand in 1948, and upon which he could base his claim to the presidential nomination.[18]

Taft's leadership did not extend to foreign policy. The dominant spokesman on that topic was President Pro Tem Vandenberg, who assumed the chairmanship of the Senate Foreign Relations Committee. Taft's relative lack of interest and inexperience in foreign affairs, combined with Vandenberg's expressed confidence in Taft's leadership on domestic questions, was a major reason for Taft's willingness to share his power. Furthermore,

18. William S. White, *The Taft Story*, 49–52, 57–58, 62–63; Caroline T. Harnsberger, *Man of Courage*, 130; Richard O. Davies, " 'Mr. Republican' Turns 'Socialist': Robert A. Taft and Public Housing," *Ohio History*, 73 (Summer, 1964), 135–43; Charles C. Brown, "Robert A. Taft, Champion of Public Housing and National Aid to Schools," *Bulletin of the Cincinnati Historical Society*, 26 (July, 1968), 227; Goldman, *The Crucial Decade*, 55–56. Goldman overemphasized Taft's opposition to the New Deal.

13

Taft did not wish to provoke intraparty conflict now that the Republicans were the majority. Vandenberg's adherence to the party line in domestic matters and his cautious preservation of a degree of independence from the Administration strengthened his prestige. His earlier isolationism and his gradual shift to internationalism enhanced his influence among Republicans who were under pressure to make a similar transition. Vandenberg's counterpart in the House was Charles A. Eaton of New Jersey, who was also an internationalist, but John M. Vorys of Ohio, whose record on foreign affairs was mixed, sometimes challenged Eaton's power and influence.[19]

The conservatism of the House leadership made Taft seem to be a middle-of-the-roader. Speaker Martin, first elected to the House in 1924 and floor leader since 1939, dominated House Republicans. His opposition to reciprocal trade, the Employment Act of 1946, farm parity payments, and extension of rural electrification, and his support of restrictive labor legislation, exemplified Martin's consistent record of isolationism and opposition to the New Deal. Chairmanship of the powerful Rules Committee went to Leo E. Allen, who faithfully mirrored the conservatism and isolationism of his predominantly rural district in northwestern Illinois. Majority Leader Charles A. Halleck of Indiana was of a similar Old Guard stripe, but he broke ranks occasionally to support the Administration on foreign policy.[20]

Major committee chairmanships went to men who agreed with the Republican leaders. John Taber, Chairman of the House Appropriations Committee, reflected the attitudes of his upstate New York constituents who needed no major federal assistance and to whom urban problems were remote. Taber's singleminded, and often reckless, determination to reduce federal spending won him the epithet "Meat-Axe." Relative moderation, however, reigned in the Senate committee, whose chairman, Styles Bridges

19. Malcolm E. Jewell, *Senatorial Politics and Foreign Policy*, 69, 118, 119; Arthur H. Vandenberg, Jr., ed., *The Private Papers of Senator Vandenberg*, 318–19; Holbert N. Carroll, *The House of Representatives and Foreign Affairs*, 97–98.

20. Tris Coffin, "A Man of the Good Old Days," *New Republic*, 116 (February 17, 1947), 28–30; "People of the Week," *U.S. News*, 21 (November 8, 1946), 64; *Congressional Quarterly*, 3 (1947), 84; "News in Focus," *New Republic*, 116 (January 6, 1947), 5.

of New Hampshire, abjured what he called sledge-hammer tactics in favor of reductions based on a close scrutiny of needs. Tax legislation was managed in the House by Chairman Knutson of the Ways and Means Committee, who had promised a 20 per cent across-the-board cut. Again, a slightly more cautious approach prevailed in the Senate, where Eugene D. Millikin of Colorado headed the Finance Committee. His views were slightly to the right of his friend Taft.[21]

In the Senate, Taft tried to promote the Republican objective of equalizing labor-management relations. He had a difficult task, for on his Committee on Labor and Public Welfare sat three of the more liberal Republicans—Wayne Morse, Irving Ives of New York, and George Aiken. These men, whom one representative described as "New Dealers who have infiltrated the Republican Party," held the balance of power between Republicans and Democrats. Taft's counterpart in the House was Fred A. Hartley, Jr., of New Jersey, whose record had earned him the opposition of organized labor in his recent campaigns.[22]

The distribution of committee assignments revealed divisions within the majority that would create problems for the Republican leaders throughout the Eightieth Congress. Congressman Richard J. Welch of San Francisco, a perennial nominee of both parties and the favorite of the AFL and CIO in his district, was the ranking Republican on the House Labor Committee. The leaders shifted this prolabor Republican to the chairmanship of the Public Lands Committee to ensure conservative direction of the Labor Committee. Senate leaders faced a similar situation but were unable to prevent an open rupture. Senator Aiken ranked below Taft on the Labor and Public Welfare Committee, but since Taft was also ranking Republican on the Finance Committee, Aiken assumed that Taft would take Finance and that the Labor chairmanship would be his. Taft, however, maneuvered

21. J. Lacey Reynolds, "Taber: 'The Third House of Congress,'" *The New York Times Magazine* (February 15, 1948), 10; *Congressional Quarterly*, 3 (1947), 16; Frank McNaughton, "Report from Washington," January 17, 1947, Frank McNaughton Papers.

22. Marion T. Bennett to F. G. Campbell, March 25, 1947, Bennett Papers; *Congressional Quarterly*, 3 (1947), 34; "People of the Week," *U.S. News*, 22 (February 14, 1947), 66.

Eugene Millikin into chairmanship of the Finance Committee and took the Labor post himself, thereby achieving two objectives —an important committee assignment for his friend and a position of direct control over labor bills for himself. Aiken's anger about being deprived of the chairmanship was exacerbated when Taft did not select him as one of four Republicans to work on a draft of a labor bill. Reporters quoted Aiken as saying, "I don't intend to be sidetracked—not without a fight." If there was a fight, it took place behind closed doors, and the Senator from Ohio won. For the time being, the party closed ranks.[23]

Recovering from the shock of defeat, the Administration began preparations for its own legislative program. In developing his early strategy, President Truman relied heavily on a report prepared by James H. Rowe, Jr., of the White House staff. Based on the assumption that conflict with the new Congress was inevitable, the memorandum prescribed an approach for the attainment of presidential objectives. Rowe insisted that the President should recommend legislative measures he deemed necessary. These proposals, however, should be as general as possible, phrased in conciliatory rhetoric, and limited to major issues likely to be popular with the public. The President should not offer detailed specific recommendations or draft bills that would only be rejected or substantially altered by the opposition. The exceptions to this general approach were in a few areas where the President felt it necessary to "make a record": "In such cases—which should be very few as distinguished from the many-pointed program submitted to the last Congress—it may be advisable to send up a message, either because the weight of public opinion may force the Congress to accept it, or because making the record is in itself of sufficient importance." Rowe emphasized the potential of the presidential veto but urged that it be used only on legislation involving the "public interest *and* on which public opinion has clearly solidified." Finally, the President should show interest in bipartisan cooperation and refrain, for the time being, from

23. *Ibid.*, 79; Hugh A. Butler to Kirk Coulter, November 15, 1946, Butler to Taft, November 16, 1946, Butler Papers, Research File; *The New York Times*, November 25, 1946, p. 4.

16

pointing out differences between the Administration and the congressional majority.[24]

While these recommendations accurately foreshadowed presidential strategy during the early months of the Eightieth Congress, other advice from Rowe, which was not heeded, stressed Truman's failure to marshal all available techniques for legislative and political success. The presidential aide urged regularly scheduled meetings with the minority leaders to encourage exchange of views and information. He also suggested specifically that former Speaker of the House, Sam Rayburn of Texas, and former Secretary of the Senate Leslie Biffle serve as unofficial liaison men with the opposition leaders and provide Truman with political intelligence at weekly, private meetings.[25]

Truman's conduct between the November elections and the convening of Congress exemplified his legislative strategy. The President adhered to his determination to defend and expand New Deal reforms but avoided a bold, crusading stance. He planned to conciliate the new Congress, beat the Republicans to the punch wherever he could without compromising Administration policy, and toss ticklish problems to the new majority. The Administration would not retreat from the reforms Truman had been espousing since 1945, but proposals would be mild and general. Finally, the Administration would strive to maintain bipartisanship in foreign policy and keep this area of legislative concern carefully separated from domestic matters.

Although publicly conciliatory, Truman was skeptical of prospects for nonpartisan cooperation, expressing to James Forrestal his view that politics and political maneuvering were inevitable. He was also aware of the political advantage that might be gained

24. Rowe, memo to Clifford, " 'Cooperation'—or Conflict?—The President's Relationship with an Opposition Congress," December, 1946, Clifford Papers.

25. The President's appointment calendar indicates no regular meetings. During the first session, the President saw Rayburn eight times—twice in January, twice in February, once in April, once in May, and twice in July. Five of these meetings were off the record; three were at Rayburn's request; at least two dealt with nonlegislative matters. The President saw Senate Minority Leader Alben Barkley only three times during the period. The President's Appointment Calendar, 1947, Matthew Connelly Files.

because the Republicans controlled Congress. As he wrote to one pro-Administration Senator in November, 1946, "If the Democrats really go after it, as they should, the Republican responsibility can really be made their responsibility as it should be." Republican control of Congress could not only obscure the significant role that conservative Democrats played in obstructing the Administration's domestic policies, but also smother politically embarrassing factionalism within the Democratic party. Indicative of this factionalism and of the lack of respect for Truman among some Democratic congressmen was the suggestion of Senator J. William Fulbright of Arkansas that Truman appoint a Republican Secretary of State and then resign. Democratic dissension also threatened to surface in the House when Sam Rayburn announced that he did not want the minority leadership. The logical alternative to the Texan was John W. McCormack of Massachusetts, but Southern Democrats predicted that the nomination of this Northerner who supported the New Deal would produce open conflict within the party. Responding to persuasion by his Southern colleagues and pressure from the White House, Rayburn agreed to take the post. Truman's decision to present a moderate legislative program would further help to conceal intraparty conflict.[26]

On November 11, the President's silence that had followed the elections was broken at a press conference. A cocky and contentious statement drafted by Truman had been refined by Clifford so that it accurately reflected the Administration's strategy of adhering to basic Democratic policies while emphasizing conciliation and cooperation. Announcing that he accepted the election returns in good faith, Truman remarked, "I do not claim for

26. James Forrestal, *The Forrestal Diaries*, Walter Millis and E. S. Duffield, eds., 218; Truman to Joseph O'Mahoney, November 26, 1946, Harry S. Truman Papers, PPF 820; Wilbur D. Mills (Arkansas) to Rayburn, November 23, 1946, Rayburn to Mills, November 25, 1946, John H. Kerr (North Carolina) to Rayburn, December 10, 1946, Rayburn to Kerr, December 16, 1946, Estes Kefauver (Tennessee) to Rayburn, November 19, 1946, Harold D. Cooley (North Carolina) to Rayburn, December 5, 1946, Edward Hebert (Louisiana) to Rayburn, November 22, 1946, John J. Sparkman (Alabama) to Rayburn, November 11, 1946, E. E. Cox (Georgia) to Rayburn, December 30, 1946, Rayburn Papers, Miscellaneous File; *The New York Times*, January 5, 1947, p. 1.

myself and my associates greater devotion to the welfare of our Nation than I ascribe to others of another party." At the same time, he did not acknowledge any mandate for major change: "The change in the majority . . . does not alter our domestic or foreign interests or problems." His executive duty consisted in doing what he considered best for the public welfare, but, "our search for that welfare must always be based upon a progressive concept of government." After praising those Republicans who had abandoned partisanship in order to cooperate with the Administration in foreign affairs, he concluded by pledging cooperation and good will in all matters.[27]

Even before his press conference, Truman had begun to implement his strategy of stealing some of the Republicans' thunder. Recognizing the political capital that the opposition had made from the public's antipathy to controls, he issued on November 9 an order terminating most of the remaining wage and price controls. Ceilings were left only on sugar, rice, and rent. At the same time, he placed the responsibility for rising prices squarely outside the Administration: "The real basis of our difficulty is the unworkable law which the Congress gave us to administer. The plain truth is that, under this inadequate law, price control has lost the popular support needed to make it work." Henceforth, Truman pointed out, elimination of controls would make industry and labor responsible for preventing inflation by maintaining a high rate of production.[28]

The Administration was moving toward elimination of other wartime powers. Early in December, department and agency heads were asked to submit recommendations for the liquidation of temporary powers under their jurisdiction to enable "the Executive branch to take the initiative in a coordinated fashion in eliminating temporary powers." On December 18, representatives from various departments met and recommended to Truman that he proclaim the termination of hostilities. They also suggested

27. Truman's notes for postelection message, Clifford Papers, Speech File; The President's News Conference of November 11, 1946, *Public Papers of the Presidents of the United States: Harry S. Truman, 1946*, 477–79.

28. Statement by the President Upon Terminating Price and Wage Controls, November 9, 1946, *ibid.*, 475–77.

that the President might demonstrate his commitment to cooperation by informing congressional leaders in advance. Truman,
however, believed that there was a psychological advantage in
unilateral action. Thus, his announcement on December 31 that
20 government powers were ended immediately and 33 others
would follow in the next few months took the Republicans by
surprise. The political implications of the proclamation were twofold. Republicans had been arguing the necessity of Congress to
force the President to relinquish war and emergency powers; now
he had shown his willingness to give them up without pressure
from Congress and had eliminated a Republican issue. Also,
because the proclamation meant that the federal farm price-
support program would end in December, 1948, the Republicans
would have to enact a new program or take the consequences of
inaction.[29]

The President moved in other ways to strengthen the Administration against attacks from the new majority. In the summer of
1946, a subcommittee of the House Civil Service Committee, in
its investigation of loyalty among federal employees and government procedures for determining it, found no uniform policy
and suggested the establishment of a commission to make a more
extensive evaluation. Responding to this report, and mindful of
recent Republican exploitation of the communism issue, Truman
on November 25 appointed the Temporary Commission on Employee Loyalty to consider the findings and recommendations of
the subcommittee, to examine existing loyalty standards, inves-
tigative, and removal procedures, and to make recommendations
for strengthening the loyalty program.[30]

This same technique was used to fortify the Administration's
offensive strategy. No result had come from Truman's 1945 pro-

29. John R. Steelman to Department Heads, December 14, 1946, U.S. Bureau
of the Budget Files, Record Group 51, Series 47.1; Richmond B. Keech to Clark
Clifford, December 19, 1946, Clifford Papers; The President's News Conference
on the Termination of Hostilities of World War II, December 31, 1946, *Public
Papers: Truman, 1946*, 512–13; Dewey Short, press release, March 24, 1947,
Clifford Papers, Political File; *The New York Times*, January 1, 1947, pp. 25, 32.

30. Earl Latham, *The Communist Controversy in Washington: From The
New Deal to McCarthy*, 364–65; Eleanor Bontecou, *The Federal Loyalty-Security
Program*, 23.

20

posal for enacting a universal military-training program, so in December, 1946, he appointed an advisory commission to examine the need and various plans for such a program. This commission included prominent persons from industry, science, and public service, as well as from education and the clergy, two groups who had most vigorously opposed universal military training. The Seventy-ninth Congress had also rejected presidential proposals for abolition of the poll tax and a permanent Fair Employment Practices Commission. Pressured by civil-rights advocates for more vigorous presidential efforts, especially to end the terror and violence suffered by Southern blacks, Truman appointed the President's Committee on Civil Rights to investigate and report to him.[31]

Finally, the President was careful to see that the Republicans received no help from people within the Administration for those portions of their program that he opposed. In a memorandum to department and agency heads, and directly at a Cabinet meeting, Truman urged Administration officials to support the budget as submitted in order to avoid exposing the Administration "to sniping from the Republicans, particularly in the House." The President also suggested that Secretary of Commerce Averell Harriman delete from a proposed speech a section that advocated curbing the powers of organized labor.[32]

More puzzling was the President's request for a private meeting in December with Hugh Butler, Republican Senator from Nebraska. A conservative, self-styled "states rights man from start to finish," ideologically close to Harry F. Byrd, Democratic Senator from Virginia, Butler was unlikely to be persuaded to support Administration programs, and the President did not directly try. Rather, he sought to express personally his desire for cooperation and to convince a rather influential Republican of his strong convictions on a few specific issues. The two agreed on two do-

31. Harry S. Truman, *Memoirs*, Vol. II, *Years of Trial and Hope*, 53–54, 180; Barton J. Bernstein, "The Ambiguous Legacy: The Truman Administration and Civil Rights" (MS, Truman Library, 1966), 8–13.

32. Truman to James E. Webb, November 15, 1946, Truman Papers, OF 79; Forrestal, *The Forrestal Diaries*, Millis and Duffield, eds., 237; Clark Clifford to Averell Harriman, December 3, 1946, Truman Papers, OF 3.

mestic questions: Both opposed immediate tax reduction and favored congressional support of conservation and agriculture.[33]

Truman outlined his legislative program more specifically in his State of the Union message on January 6, 1947. The address clearly reflected the strategy adopted earlier. He warned against wholesale dismantling of the New Deal labor program: "We must not . . . adopt punitive legislation." He heavily stressed two policies that found support among Republicans—a balanced budget, and a large-scale housing program. The President stayed with his proposals for expanding New Deal reforms, but he played down the more controversial items, and his recommendations looked toward consideration and study by Congress. In comparison, his 1946 message had been much more vigorous and emphatic. Finally, he reasserted his confidence that bipartisanship in foreign policy would continue.[34]

Specifically, Truman recommended a five-point, short-range program and a more extensive long-range program. The first immediate recommendation dealt with labor-management relations, and the President made four suggestions: legislation to prohibit jurisdictional strikes, secondary boycotts, and the use of force to resolve conflicts over the interpretation of existing contracts; measures to expedite the settlement of labor disputes by expanding facilities within the Department of Labor; steps to "alleviate the causes of workers' insecurity," including congressional consideration of "the extension and broadening of our social security system, better housing, a comprehensive national health program, and provision for a fair minimum wage"; and the establishment of a commission of representatives from Congress, labor, management, and the general public to make a broad study of labor-management relations.[35]

33. The meeting is described in a memo from Butler to Roy Welsh and John Comstock, December 16, 1946, Butler Papers. For Butler's political views, see Butler to Clayton Rand, March 9, 1948, Butler to Wray M. Scott, June 25, 1948, Butler to Wallace White, November 7, 1946, Butler Papers.

34. Richard E. Neustadt, "Presidency and Legislation: Planning the President's Program," *American Political Science Review*, 49 (December, 1955), 999; Richard E. Neustadt, "Congress and the Fair Deal; A Legislative Balance Sheet," *Public Policy*, 5 (1954), 360.

35. Annual Message to the Congress on the State of the Union, January 6,

Truman next proposed that Congress seek to reverse the trend toward economic concentration by strengthening antimonopoly legislation, providing federal assistance to encourage new industry, and giving special attention to the stimulation of small business. The third major request dealt with housing, and he urged enactment of legislation similar to the bipartisan Taft-Ellender-Wagner bill that had passed the Senate during the previous session. A balanced budget and debt reduction, combined with a specific request for the extension of the wartime excise taxes that were due to expire June 31, formed the fourth major objective, and a long-range agricultural program was the fifth.[36]

The President singled out three other domestic policy areas for special mention. He repeated his recommendation for a national health-insurance program and establishment of a department of welfare, promised detailed recommendations for civil-rights legislation as soon as his special committee reported to him, and emphasized the importance of protecting and expanding natural resources.[37]

In the areas of foreign policy and national defense, the President looked forward to speedy ratification of the peace treaties with Italy, Bulgaria, Rumania, and Hungary and stressed the necessity for early legislation for admittance of displaced persons into the United States. He also advocated free trade among nations, international control of atomic energy, and reduction of its military significance, and he promised to re-examine his universal military-training proposal after he received the report of his recently appointed commission.[38]

Congress responded favorably to the moderate tone of the address. Republicans thought it demonstrated the President's sincere commitment to cooperation. Wrote Congressman Vorys, "The President sounded mostly like a Republican yesterday and if he continues that way, we can put through a mighty good program." Political observers described the message as "cautious,"

1947, *Public Papers of the Presidents of the United States: Harry S. Truman, 1947*, 4–5.

36. *Ibid.*, 6–7.
37. *Ibid.*, 8–9.
38. *Ibid.*, 9–12.

"mild," "a tacit acknowledgement of Republican triumph in the last election," "non-political," "far to the right of that sent to Congress a year ago," and "dominated by a persuasive spirit." Reporters noted, however, that in extending the olive branch, the President had not surrendered his own prerogatives. Truman still had two more formal reports to present to Congress, both more strongly indicating his commitment to the New Deal and demonstrating that a break still existed between the Administration and the Republican majority.[39]

On January 8, the President submitted his Economic Report. Emphasis on the decline of real wages and mass purchasing power contrasted with the statement that "business in general is receiving exceptional profits" did not delight conservatives. Neither did they favor such specific proposals as voluntary price reduction by business, extension of rent control, upward revision of the minimum wage and expanded coverage, increases in social security benefits, and abstention from tax reduction. These, with a reiteration of the President's request concerning housing and labor, formed the short-range program for which he asked immediate attention. Long-range goals included legislation to end discrimination in employment; an agricultural program based upon the principle of plenty rather than scarcity, preservation of the family-sized farm, greater attention to rural health, education, and welfare, and an expanded school-lunch program; attention to flood control and development of low-cost hydroelectric power; expanded assistance in health and education; increased and extended social security coverage; and further implementation of the reciprocal trade program.[40]

Two days later, Truman submitted to Congress the budget for fiscal 1948. The Administration estimated expenditures at $37.5 billion and receipts at $37.7 billion. The President carefully demonstrated that the figures were at rock bottom and could not be cut further without jeopardizing the Federal Government's ability

39. *The New York Times*, January 7, 1947, p. 1, January 12, 1947, p. E7; Vorys to Steve A. Stack, January 7, 1947, Vorys Papers; reports of January 7 and January 8, 1947, Assistants, Aides, and Counsels to the President, Files.

40. Special Message to the Congress: The President's First Economic Report, January 8, 1947, *Public Papers: Truman*, 1947, 15–16, 28–30, 32–38.

to fulfill its foreign and domestic responsibilities. He was determined that taxes should not be reduced at the moment, but when it was possible, tax revision should benefit the lower-income groups. The inflationary situation, as well as the need to reduce the national debt of $260 billion, justified maintaining existing revenues. In addition, Truman again urged reforms in social security, national health insurance, housing, education, agriculture, and conservation.[41]

As expected, congressional reaction to these two messages was less favorable than it had been to the State of the Union address. The press reported Republicans' doubts that they were being appeased and signs of encouragement among liberals. Senator Taft viewed the Economic Report "as a vehicle to recommend a complete social welfare program" and spied "the whiskers of the New Deal peeking around all the corners of the report." Southern Democrats disliked the proposal for legislation to end job discrimination. The Budget message brought on even louder protests from both groups. Senator Byrd of Virginia professed regret that Truman had not followed what Byrd considered a mandate for stringent government retrenchment, while Republicans termed the budget estimates "shockingly disappointing" and "astounding" and predicted cuts ranging from $3.8 billion to $8 billion. Senator Vandenberg felt that Truman had made substantial budget reductions, partially to co-opt Republican efforts in this area, but even he felt that there was room for congressional budget cutting.[42]

Now that their positions on the issues were somewhat clarified, the gulf between the Administration and Congress seemed narrower than it had in the wake of the November elections. The President had pledged cooperation with Congress, had taken steps to relinquish government emergency powers, and had toned down many of the most controversial parts of his program. The

41. Annual Budget Message to the Congress: Fiscal Year 1948, January 10, 1947, *ibid.*, 55, 57–60; The President's News Conference on the Budget, January 8, 1947, *ibid.*, 40–41, 56–60, 71–73, 76, 81, 89.

42. *The New York Times*, January 12, 1947, p. E7, January 9, 1947, p. 15, January 10, 1947, p. 15, January 11, 1947, pp. 1, 18; Vandenberg to John M. Bush, April 23, 1947, Arthur H. Vandenberg Papers, William L. Clements Library, University of Michigan.

Republicans, despite their verbal assaults on the New Deal, promised to reverse the policies of the past fourteen years only in fiscal policy and labor legislation. Furthermore, Republican leaders had promised general cooperation with the Administration on foreign policy.

Nevertheless, if both sides adhered to their stated positions, a clash was inevitable. Both advocated strict economy in government spending, yet the Republicans felt that Truman had not gone far enough. The new majority—51 Republicans to 45 Democrats in the Senate and 245 Republicans to 188 Democrats and 1 American Laborite in the House—was determined to effect a major tax cut; the President said to wait. The Republicans' proposals for labor legislation went beyond Truman's program, and they gave little attention to measures to enhance workers' security. Moreover, some influential Republicans were sharply critical of the reciprocal-trade program and weary of appropriating funds for European relief. The extent of the executive-legislative breach would depend upon how far the Republicans could go in enacting legislation at odds with Administration policy and upon how vigorously the President would pursue his own program.

CHAPTER 2

THE CONCILIATORY PHASE

FROM JANUARY to mid-May of 1947, Congress and the President were on good terms. Contributing to harmony was the inability of the congressional majority to enact the more controversial parts of their program—tax and labor legislation—until late in the session. President Truman continued to be conciliatory, refraining from attacks on Congress or demands for action on his more liberal proposals. When the Republicans did attempt some limited forays against New Deal programs, either the President chose not to fight or the Republicans found themselves too divided to carry through the attack. During these months Truman's prestige was on the rise, while the congressional majority was hampered by intraparty discord.

Truman's appointments during the early part of the first session reflected his desire to placate Congress. For Under Secretary of the Treasury, Truman named A. L. M. Wiggins, a banker and businessman from North Carolina. Wiggins had criticized many New Deal programs, particularly those that dealt with finance, and observers thought his selection marked a conservative tendency in the Administration and an attempt to cultivate the good will of Southern Democrats. Lewis W. Douglas, a New Deal critic who had supported Republican presidential candidates Alfred M. Landon and Wendell L. Willkie, was nominated as ambassador to Britain, but the most spectacular effort toward cooperation with Congress was the choice of General George C. Marshall to replace James F. Byrnes as Secretary of State. While there were many reasons for the nomination, the President was keenly aware of Marshall's tremendous prestige with the public and with Congress, as well as his "thorough knowledge and appreciation of the role of Congress." The Senate's quick confirmation of the nomination demonstrated the correctness of Truman's assessment.[1]

The President also moved to strengthen the Administration where it was vulnerable to Republican attack. His Temporary Commission on Employee Loyalty reported on March 30, and following its recommendations, Truman issued an executive order outlining a new loyalty program. To head the Loyalty Review Board, which was responsible for coordinating various agency policies and which heard appeals of lower-level decisions, Truman appointed a prominent conservative Republican, Seth Richardson. This program temporarily deprived the Republicans of a political issue and forestalled for a time a more severe attack on constitutional liberties. In exchange, however, Truman sanctioned a program that disregarded fundamental concepts of justice—including due process—destroyed many reputations, and damaged morale among federal employees.[2]

Truman also sought to undercut the opposition by sending to Congress on February 19 a special message recommending the repeal of more than one hundred war and emergency statutes. Although legislation was not finally enacted until July, the Administration again had taken the initiative in relinquishing powers. The Congress, in turn, complied with presidential requests for the extension of some controls that the Administration felt were still necessary. Although Truman preferred later expiration dates than provided for in the legislation, Congress authorized the extension of allocation and priority regulations over various commodities as well as controls on rubber, exports and sugar.[3]

1. *The New York Times*, December 31, 1946, p. 24; "People of the Week," *U.S. News*, 22 (January 10, 1947), 53–54; *The New York Times*, February 27, 1947, p. 1; Harry S. Truman, *Memoirs*, Vol. II, *Years of Trial and Hope*, 115; *U.S. Congressional Record*, 80th Cong., 1st sess., 1947, XCIII, Part 1, p. 272.

2. Truman, *Years of Trial and Hope*, 279–81; Eleanor Bontecou, *The Federal Loyalty-Security Program*, 237–55.

3. Special Message to the Congress on the Termination of Emergency and Wartime Powers, February 19, 1947, *Public Papers of the Presidents of the United States: Harry S. Truman, 1947*, 134–36; Douglas McGregor to James E. Webb, July 22, 1947, U.S. Bureau of the Budget Files, Record Group 51, Series 47.1a; Special Message to the Congress on Extension of the Second War Powers Act, January 31, 1947, *Public Papers: Truman, 1947*, 107–13; *The New York Times*, March 25, 1947, p. 20; Special Message to the Congress Recommending Extension

The President's willingness to cooperate with the new Congress contributed to the rise of his popularity rating, which a Gallup poll placed at 51 per cent in March, 1947. Republican Congressman Clifford R. Hope of Kansas noted Truman's conciliatory and moderate demeanor and concluded that his increase in popularity was the result of his "becoming more of a Republican every day." The significant increase in popular support for Truman rested largely upon the Administration's strong stand against the coal strike called by John L. Lewis in defiance of a court injunction, the President's nomination of Marshall, and his initiative on decontrol of the economy. The image of the confused, uncertain, accidental President was changing to one of a confident, self-assured leader. No embarrassing episodes like the firing of Wallace or the speech advocating that strikers be drafted happened in 1947. In all, Democratic hopes for 1948 were much brighter in March than they had been since November.[4]

At the same time, Republicans were discovering that the fruits of victory were not entirely sweet: Majority status illuminated disagreements that had been more easily concealed when the party had not been responsible for enacting a program. While House leaders experienced little difficulty in controlling their members, in the Senate a small but vociferous group of Republicans obstructed tight party control. Senator Bricker of Ohio complained to Congressman Bennett that some of his colleagues had "read the election returns differently than I do." Bennett noted specifically that Senators Aiken, Morse, and Charles W. Tobey of New Hampshire voted so often with the minority that they "give the Democrats a majority though we have one on paper." John

of the Second War Powers Act, May 22, 1947, *Public Papers: Truman, 1947*, 252–54; Statement by the President Upon Signing the Second Decontrol Act, July 19, 1947, *ibid.*, 333; Special Message to the Congress on Rubber, February 7, 1947, *ibid.*, 123–35; Special Message to the Congress on Export Controls, March 19, 1947, *ibid.*, 181–82; Statement by the President Upon Signing the Sugar Control Extension Act, March 31, 1947, *ibid.*, 188.

4. "The Upswing for Mr. Truman," *U.S. News*, 22 (March 21, 1947), 15–16; Hope to Frank E. Ferris, April 10, 1947, Clifford R. Hope Papers, Legislative Correspondence; "Washington Wire," *New Republic*, 116 (January 27, 1947), 11; "Washington Whispers," *U.S. News*, 22 (February 7, 1947), 68; *The New York Times*, April 13, 1947, p. E7.

Taber also noted the difficulties of working with men like Tobey and Morse, but he felt that Taft "could work [it] out if he would be a little smoother."[5]

Republican differences were aired as individual senators publicly challenged the leaders. Senator Morse issued the first public warning, when in a speech commemorating Wendell Willkie, he urged his party to adopt a progressive stance. Stronger and more specific demands came from George Aiken. In debate about the legislative budget on February 19, the Vermont Senator disputed the leaders' claims to a mandate and maintained that the Republican campaign had been a negative one. Thus, he rejected the view that there was a mandate to cut taxes 20 per cent, to enact harsh labor legislation, to weaken the government's financial structure by preventing debt reduction, to withdraw aid to starving people, and to weaken REA or TVA. Strict adherence to this manufactured mandate, Aiken warned, would threaten Republican chances in 1948. At the close of his speech, Aiken received enthusiastic approval from three other Republicans—Morse, Tobey, and William Langer of North Dakota.[6]

Intraparty sniping erupted again in March, and this time the Republican leaders got it from both sides. B. Carroll Reece, chairman of the Republican National Committee, touched off the trouble when he called for teamwork in Congress and said, "A successful team is one which executes the signals called by the duly chosen quarterback. Differences of opinion as to the choice of a particular play are ironed out in the huddles before the plays are called. Team play is the first essential of success; and it is just as important, if not more so, in the second half as in the first." At this, Wayne Morse blew up. He called Reece's statement "a brazen demand for reactionary control of the Republican party" and asserted that the leaders were attempting to take the party back to the 1920's. A demand from twelve freshman senators for greater participation in policy planning indicated the possibility

5. Bricker to Bennett, April 7, 1947, Bennett to Dr. Leslie R. Webb, March 29, 1947, Marion T. Bennett Papers; Taber to Rufus C. Homan, March 10, 1947, John Taber Papers.

6. U.S. *Congressional Record*, 80th Cong., 1st sess., 1947, XCIII, Part 10, p. A599, Part 1, pp. 1164–67. See also George D. Aiken, "Senator Aiken Warns His Party," *The New York Times Magazine* (March 22, 1947), 10, 71.

of additional support for the Morse-Aiken-Langer-Tobey group among such newer members as Ralph E. Flanders of Vermont, Irving M. Ives of New York, John Sherman Cooper of Kentucky, William F. Knowland of California, and Milton R. Young of North Dakota. Republican leaders were also criticized by conservative Senator Harlan J. Bushfield of South Dakota for not moving faster in making good the party pledges of 1946. On the Senate floor, Bushfield identified himself as spokesman for "a lot" of conservative Republicans and charged his party with failure to effect tax reduction, a budget cut of $6 billion, and a "sensible" solution to the labor situation.[7]

Such conflict hampered many of the Republican attacks on the Administration's policies. One notable exception was the constitutional amendment limiting presidential tenure, a retrospective assault against Roosevelt. Republican supporters and Democratic opponents alike attempted to submerge its political aspects. Republicans justified the amendment by arguing that without it a dictator might arise; Democrats maintained that it would tie the hands of future generations and that it indicated a lack of faith in the people. Despite disavowals of partisanship, the debate occasionally reverted to attacks on and defense of Roosevelt. This evidence of partisanship was especially apparent in the House, where Democratic Congressman Adolph J. Sabath of Illinois asserted that Republicans viewed the amendment as an anti-Roosevelt resolution. Sabath himself called the amendment a "pitiful victory over a great man now sleeping on the banks of the Hudson," while Republican Mitchell Jenkins of Pennsylvania maintained that "the tenure of Franklin D. Roosevelt proved that Washington and Jefferson were wise" in retiring after two terms. Every Republican voted for the measure, joined by 13 Democratic senators and 47 Democratic representatives, most of them from Southern states.[8]

Controversy surrounding the confirmation of David E. Lilienthal to head the Atomic Energy Commission gave Republicans

7. *The New York Times*, March 3, 1947, pp. 1, 19, March 4, 1947, p. 19, March 10, 1947, p. 30, March 9, 1947, p. E2; U.S. *Congressional Record*, 80th Cong., 1st sess., 1947, XCIII, Part 2, p. 1781.

8. *Ibid.*, Part 1, pp. 841–44, 849, 872, Part 2, pp. 1867, 1945, 1978.

another opportunity to strike back at the New Deal. It also indicated the viability of vocal anticommunism, raised again the issue of military versus civilian control of atomic energy, and revealed for the first time a split among Republican leaders.

On November 1, 1946, the President had given Lilienthal and four other men recess appointments to the AEC. Lilienthal had distinguished himself as chairman of the Tennessee Valley Authority, and the five appointments were well received by the press. The opposition to Lilienthal in the Joint Committee on Atomic Energy was instigated by Senator Kenneth D. McKellar of Tennessee, who was not even a member of that committee. The Senator's quarrel with the nominee had begun in 1941, when Lilienthal as head of TVA had failed to include McKellar in major policy and patronage decisions. Since then, McKellar had waged a relentless attack on Lilienthal. He considered Truman's naming Lilienthal without consulting him an "intentional affront" and was so enraged that he refused to attend a meeting called by the President to discuss the crucial issue of aid to Greece and Turkey. McKellar told Truman that he opposed Lilienthal because of his "inefficiency, incompetence, untruthfulness and dishonesty," but his public attack centered on Lilienthal's alleged communist sympathies and charges that he had employed communists and fellow travelers in the TVA.[9]

Although committee members were disgusted by McKellar's personal invective—Senators Vandenberg and Tom Connally even stopped attending the hearings—the opposition broadened. One by one, influential Republicans and an occasional Democrat issued statements opposing Lilienthal. As Republicans took up the battle, the emphasis shifted away from communism toward charges of Lilienthal's New Dealism and supposed softness toward Russia. Republican Senators Styles Bridges, Majority Whip Kenneth Wherry, E. H. Moore of Oklahoma, Majority Leader Wallace White, C. Wayland Brooks of Illinois, and Owen Brewster

9. Joseph P. Harris, *The Advice and Consent of the Senate; A Study of the Confirmation of Appointments by the United States Senate*, 155–58; David E. Lilienthal, *The Journals of David E. Lilienthal*, Vol. I, *The TVA Years, 1939–1945*, 396, 457, 482, 584–85; McKellar to Truman, March 7, 1947, Kenneth D. McKellar Papers.

of Maine came out in rapid succession against confirmation during the early part of February, and on February 22, Taft denounced Lilienthal as "temperamentally unfit" to head an executive agency in a democracy. He called the nominee a "power-hungry bureaucrat" who had defied Congress and who had tolerated a communist cell within the TVA. If this were not enough to disqualify him, Taft continued, one could point to his willingness to surrender the atomic bomb to international control without adequate safeguards, as evidenced in the Acheson-Lilienthal report on atomic energy.[10]

With most of the Republican leaders opposed to him, Lilienthal doubted that he could be confirmed. Other observers believed that the crucial vote was that of Senator Vandenberg. On March 10, Vandenberg joined seven other members of the Joint Committee on Atomic Energy in recommending confirmation. Although he made no public statement, the Michigan Senator had considered the arguments against Lilienthal and dismissed them. In a letter to B. E. Hutchinson, Vandenberg expressed his belief that the procommunist charges were "fantastic fabrication." Lilienthal's record on public ownership was to Vandenberg an asset, because the latter believed that government control of atomic energy was essential until its uses were controlled by international agreement. Finally, the Senator feared that rejection of Lilienthal would alienate scientists from the atomic energy enterprise and delay development of "the 'super bomb' which will still leave us 'out in front' despite what happens elsewhere." While thus expressing himself privately, Vandenberg gave no indication whether he would defy his Republican colleagues with an all-out floor fight for Lilienthal.[11]

For Truman, the confirmation issue marked the limits of his

10. *The New York Times*, February 6, 1947, p. 7, February 10, 1947, p. 13, February 11, 1947, p. 10, February 13, 1947, p. 1, February 14, 1947, p. 1, February 15, 1947, p. 4, February 21, 1947, p. 18; Taft, statement inserted into U.S. *Congressional Record*, 80th Cong., 1st sess., 1947, XCIII, Part 3, p. 3021.

11. David E. Lilienthal, *The Journals of David E. Lilienthal*, Vol. II, *The Atomic Energy Years, 1945–1950*, 143; Arthur H. Vandenberg, Jr., ed., *The Private Papers of Senator Vandenberg*, 353–54; *The New York Times*, March 11, 1947, p. 1; Vandenberg to B. E. Hutchinson, February 17, 1947, Arthur H. Vandenberg Papers, William L. Clements Library, University of Michigan.

strategy of conciliation. On February 10, Lilienthal had offered to withdraw, but the President had already decided that "he was in this fight to the finish . . . [and] that if they [the opposition in the Senate] wanted to make an issue of this matter, he would carry the issue to the country." On February 13, Truman announced his determination to stay with the nominee, terming McKellar's accusations "absolutely unfounded," and he reaffirmed his support in two subsequent press conferences. He expressed to the Senator from Tennessee his sorrow that "you felt it necessary to jump all over David Lilienthal" and told McKellar that the appointee was "one of the best administrators" in the Federal Government. Meanwhile, the Administration prepared a substantial brief supporting Lilienthal with point-by-point refutations of the charges made against him.[12]

When Senate debate began on March 24, the opposition stated its case against Lilienthal. Styles Bridges emphasized the lack of safeguards for the United States in the Acheson-Lilienthal recommendations and charged that Lilienthal had not worked closely enough with the military since the AEC had taken over the atomic energy program. Republican Senator Harry P. Cain of Washington opposed confirmation of a "New Dealer," stating that Truman had selected Lilienthal before he realized, as the result of the November elections, "that America once more wanted to place its faith and confidence in men . . . who understand that the authoritarian philosophy . . . of the New Order—call it New Deal if you will—had been sincerely and vigorously tried and found wanting." He was amazed that senators who had recently come from campaigns "waged against what they conceived the big Government radicalism of the New Deal to be" could support confirmation. Hugh Butler contended that the Senate should not confirm a "dictator." The issue of communism appeared when Senators Brewster and Byrd argued that Lilienthal's indifference

---

12. Lilienthal, *Atomic Energy Years*, 144; The President's News Conference of February 15, 1947, *Public Papers: Truman, 1947*, 131; The President's News Conference of February 20, 1947, *ibid.*, 148; The President's News Conference of February 28, 1947, *ibid.*, 158; Truman to McKellar, March 11, 1947, McKellar Papers; Unsigned mimeographed report, "Lilienthal—Materials in Support of Confirmation," March 8, 1947, Clark M. Clifford Papers, Atomic Energy File No. 2.

and tolerance about communism was no less dangerous than if he were himself a party member. Finally, some resorted to the assertion that no controversial figure should be confirmed and that senators should support no one whom they would not themselves appoint.[13]

Lilienthal's supporters spent most of their time answering attacks and urging speed so as not to disrupt the work of the AEC. The nominee found able advocates in Republican Senators Knowland, Morse, Leverett Saltonstall of Massachusetts, Tobey, and Aiken, as well as in most of the Democrats, led by Minority Leader Alben Barkley of Kentucky and Carl A. Hatch of New Mexico. In the end, however, Vandenberg clinched the victory. At the close of the debate, the Senator from Michigan, in what the New Republic called "his highest hour in nineteen years as Senator," rose to Lilienthal's defense and vigorously disposed of every objection that had been raised against the nominee. He concluded with a call for confirmation, the galleries roared with applause, and Republicans Tobey, Aiken, and Ives rushed to congratulate him. All else was anticlimactic. After 18 Republicans joined 34 Democrats, Bricker's motion to recommit was defeated, 52 to 38. On April 9, the Senate voted to confirm, 50 to 31. The votes of 20 Republicans who defied Taft to support Lilienthal and the votes of nearly all the Democrats—only five Southern Democrats voted against the Administration—gave the President victory in his first test of strength with Congress.[14]

More direct attacks upon New Deal programs developed as the appropriations bills began to grind through Congress. In accord with his strategy of conciliation, President Truman tried to avoid antagonizing Congress while standing behind his budget esti-

---

13. U.S. Congressional Record, 80th Cong., 1st sess., 1947, XCIII, Part 2, pp. 2534–36, 2594, Part 3, pp. 2860, 2861, 2865, 2953–56, 3011; Butler to Austin Brown, April 4, 1947, Hugh A. Butler Papers, Legislation.

14. Harris, Advice and Consent of the Senate, 164; U.S. Congressional Record, 80th Cong., 1st sess., 1947, XCIII, Part 3, pp. 2850–55, 3095–97, 3100–3101; "News in Focus," New Republic, 116 (April 14, 1947), 5–6; U.S. Congressional Record, 80th Cong., 1st sess., 1947, XCIII, Part 3, pp. 3108–11, 3116, 3241. Democratic Senators O'Daniel (Texas), Byrd (Virginia), McKellar (Tennessee), Stewart (Tennessee), and McClellan (Arkansas) voted against confirmation, and Overton (Louisiana) and McCarran (Nevada) were paired against.

mates. Leaving to aides the burden of defending the Administration's estimates, Truman intervened only occasionally and carefully refrained from attacking Republicans or engaging in sharp recrimination. Forceful presidential action was not as vital as it might have been because the Administration found powerful Republican allies who opposed drastic cuts.

The skirmish over the budget began in early February, weeks before Congress acted on specific appropriations. The Legislative Reorganization Act of 1946 had provided for the establishment of a Joint Congressional Committee on the Budget, which was to consider Administration estimates and determine early in the session a maximum figure for federal expenditures. Since this figure was to be established before action on specific appropriation bills, most people conceded that it would be largely guesswork. Nonetheless, heated controversy surrounded the issue.

The Republicans' determination to slash the budget was based upon three considerations. In the first place, taxes were to be reduced, and Congress would have to reduce proposed federal expenditures by several billion dollars in order to cut taxes without adding to the federal debt. Also, by cutting government funds, the Republicans could curtail various New Deal programs to which they objected, and eliminate thousands of "bureaucratic spenders" who had infiltrated the government in the past fourteen years. According to Congressman Earl Wilson of Indiana, "A new philosophy of government is going to be initiated and that is that it is the people's duty . . . to support its Government rather than the New Deal parasitic philosophy of the Government supporting the people." The "New Deal's philosophy of 'tax and tax; spend and spend and spend; elect and elect,' " he said, was dead. Congressman George B. Schwabe was more specific. Complaining that "I sit from four to six hours a day and listen to these bureaucrats attempt to justify their socialistic, New Deal, communistic schemes," the Oklahoman maintained that Congress should refuse appropriations "for these unnecessary and obnoxious, if not wholly un-American bureaus." The school-lunch program was "one of the New Deal fly traps and catch-alls" that the Republicans should abolish. Less important than tax reduction and curtailing of New Deal programs, but of some significance in the case for cutting appropriations, was the desire for substantial reduction of the national debt.[15]

Intraparty differences prevented agreement on the legislative budget. The Senate, whose members reflected broader constituencies than their House colleagues did, favored less drastic reductions, and the President, recognizing that the Senate was likely to take a more cautious approach, met with Republican members of the Senate Appropriations Committee in an effort to strengthen the Administration's position. Although Committee Chairman Bridges indicated that no agreement had been reached and maintained that Senate Republicans would continue to insist on "drastic cuts," the President probably influenced some committee members to oppose extreme slashes and to fight to restore cuts that the House was expected to make. On February 13, the President held a press conference in which he gently reaffirmed his opposition to any cuts in Administration figures.[16]

Notwithstanding the President's position, the Joint Committee voted on February 14 to cut $6 billion from the Administration's figures. Voting with the majority of Republicans were 7 Democrats, all but 1 from the South. In the Joint Committee, Taft and a substantial number of other Senate Republicans, supported by most of the Democrats, attempted to reduce the cut to $4.5 billion, failed, and carried their efforts to the Senate floor. House Republicans, with only Margaret Chase Smith of Maine defecting, and 12 Democrats from the South and border states quickly confirmed the committee's action. In the Senate, however, the Republicans were divided. The Senate rejected the Joint Committee's recommendation, voting 51 to 33 for an amendment supporting the committee minority's figure of $4.5 billion. In supporting the lesser cut, 21 Republicans joined 30 Administration Democrats, who accepted it as the best that could be obtained. The Republican leaders split again; Taft, Vandenberg,

15. *Ibid.*, Part 2, p. 2636. See also comments by Rich (Republican, Pennsylvania) and Hoffman (Republican, Michigan), *ibid.*, pp. 1621, 2389. Schwabe to A. E. Bradshaw, February 8, 1947, Schwabe to M. W. Bottomfield, June 3, 1947, George B. Schwabe Papers, Legislative File, Correspondence.

16. *The New York Times*, February 6, 1947, p. 16; The President's News Conference of February 13, 1947, *Public Papers: Truman, 1947*, 130.

White, and Millikin voted for the amendment, and Wherry and Bridges voted for the larger figure. The Senate also amended the report to provide for a mandatory debt reduction of $2.6 billion, a provision that would make tax reduction difficult. The resolution was then sent to conference, where neither House nor Senate conferees would budge, and Congress adjourned without acting on the legislative budget.[17]

As expected, House and Senate Republicans disagreed on individual appropriation bills. The general pattern was for the House to make drastic cuts over the protests of Democrats and a few liberal Republicans. In response to public and official protests against House action, the Senate would then restore some of the more extreme cuts, and the two houses would compromise the differences in conference. Most controversial were the appropriation bills for the Interior and Agriculture departments.

The House Appropriations Committee reported a bill slashing Administration estimates for the Department of Interior by almost 50 per cent. The cuts were justified on two grounds: (1) that during a period of inflation it was unwise for government to spend millions for construction when private enterprise "is anxiously seeking . . . the same commodities for which government will be priority buyer" and (2) that appropriations in general must be cut in order to fulfill campaign promises for tax reduction. Hardest hit were reclamation and power projects, and Western Republicans were quick to protest. Senator Morse warned Republicans that they were not "entitled to the support of the West in a national campaign if this Congress and its leaders cut the heart out of the reclamation program," and Congressman Lowell Stockman of Oregon attacked Appropriations Chairman Taber for relentlessly crushing attempts within the committee to increase appropriations. House supporters of reclamation were able to restore only $4,875,000 of the cut of $138,881,907. However, Senate Republicans suggested a cut of about 27 per cent, and the compromise bill appropriated a total of $194,587,589, about two-thirds of the Administration's estimate of $296,135,420.[18]

17. *The New York Times*, February 12, 1947, pp. 1, 3, February 21, 1947, p. 1; U.S. *Congressional Record*, 80th Cong., 1st sess., 1947, XCIII, Part 2, p. 1438.

18. U.S. House of Representatives, Committee on Appropriations, *Interior De-*

In its attack upon New Deal agricultural programs, the House Appropriations Committee suggested that the states assume more responsibility for alleviating farm problems. Agriculture should turn away from "the paternalistic road along which there are subsidies and grants coupled with more and more direction from Washington." The committee realized the need to prevent soil erosion but was even more anxious "to prevent the erosion of that rugged individual character" of the farmer. Accordingly, the committee cut the budget estimates for conservation and use payments from $267 million to $150 million for 1947 and eliminated the authorization for 1948 completely. The school-lunch program was cut from $75 million to $45 million, funds for farm-tenant loans were eliminated completely, production and subsistence loans were cut from $90 million to $60 million, crop insurance from $9 million to $2 million, and tenant-mortgage insurance from $15 million to $1 million. The aggregate reduction amounted to 32 per cent of the Administration's estimates. The Senate was more generous in the more sensitive areas, including soil-conservation payments, the school-lunch program, and farm-tenant loans, although the final appropriation was almost $200 million below the Administration's request of $805,141,608.[19]

In his only substantial comment on congressional budget cutting—his Jefferson Day speech of April 5—the President stuck by his original figures but showed reluctance to create animosity among Republicans. Truman was following the advice of Secretary of Commerce Averell Harriman, who maintained that proposals that would permit the President to make political capital by lambasting the Republicans should be put off until 1948. The Secretary argued that extremely partisan rhetoric would severely

partment Appropriation Bill, Fiscal Year 1948, House Report 279 to accompany H.R. 3123, 80th Cong., 1st sess., 1947, 2, 6–7; U.S. Congressional Record, 80th Cong., 1st sess., 1947, XCIII, Part 3, pp. 3749, 3977, 4088, 4092, 4093, 4095; John R. Waltrip, "Public Power During the Truman Administration" (Ph.D. dissertation, University of Missouri—Columbia, 1965), 55.

19. U.S. House of Representatives, Committee on Appropriations, Department of Agriculture Appropriation Bill, Fiscal Year 1948, House Report 450 to accompany H.R. 3601, 80th Cong., 1st sess., 1947, 4–5, 23, 26–27, 29, 32; James E. Webb to M. C. Latta, July 29, 1947, U.S. Bureau of the Budget Files, Reports to the President on Pending Legislation.

damage the national interest by jeopardizing budget prospects, as well as foreign policy measures, and would not really help the Democrats. Harriman wrote, "Our working margin is thin enough at best in Congress that we must continue to maintain an environment in which all responsible leaders on both sides of the aisle will be encouraged to cooperate with the President. Otherwise there is little hope of any success in the executive program." The Secretary believed that in a time of grave national and international problems, a "display of narrow partisanship" was out of character and would only injure the President's prestige.[20]

In accord with Harriman's urgings, Truman emphasized national responsibility and refrained from sniping at Republicans. He acknowledged that no party "has a monopoly on Jefferson's principles" and while, stressing the nation's international responsibilities, praised men in both parties who had contributed to a united front in foreign policy. The President also affirmed the importance of a sound domestic economy if the United States were to meet its international obligations. Commending the projected budget surplus for fiscal 1947, he injected the only partisan note when he pointed out that the surplus was achieved "without any Republican help!" The President then recounted the painstaking process of trimming budget requests within the Administration before they were presented to Congress. Since departmental estimates had been cut to the very minimum, any further reductions would mean "false economy," particularly in the areas of reclamation, soil conservation, water resource development, and functions of the Labor Department. In cautioning against budget reductions, Truman used the pronoun "we" and refused to single out the opposition party. "To the extent that we countenance any such substantial reduction," Truman concluded, "we shall weaken our own house by our refusal to keep it in basic repair."[21]

The second kind of legislation exemplifying the early presidential strategy dealt with portal-to-portal claims based on the Fair Labor Standards Act. Truman again defended New Deal reforms

20. Harriman to Clark Clifford, March 27, 1947, Clifford Papers, Speech File.
21. Address at the Jefferson Day Dinner, April 5, 1947, *Public Papers: Truman, 1947*, 193, 195.

but refrained from attacking Congress. He demonstrated, as he did repeatedly throughout the Eightieth Congress, an unwillingness to provide leadership in drafting bills and working with sympathetic Democratic legislators.

The portal-to-portal question went back to a decision in 1943 by a United States district court awarding overtime claims of $2,400 to 289 union workers at the Mount Clemens Pottery Company in Michigan. These claims, based on the Fair Labor Standards Act, covered time spent on the job location in nonproductive but necessary activity before and after actual work, such as changing clothes, assembling tools, and traveling within the plant. A June, 1946, Supreme Court decision upholding the lower court resulted in a deluge of similar suits, brought mainly by CIO unions, involving approximately $5 billion. At the same time, the Supreme Court ordered the lower court to determine the exact amount of the claims in the light of the *de minimis* doctrine; that is, if the claims were deemed trivial, they should be rejected.[22]

While Republicans prepared legislation to invalidate these portal-to-portal claims, the Administration attempted to forestall legislation. The Attorney General submitted an *amicus curiae* brief asking the district court to dismiss the claims against the Mount Clemens Company on the *de minimis* principle. In addition, the Treasury Department issued a ruling that the government would be liable for 60 per cent of any claims for back pay made against companies if government contracts were involved, thus indicating the disastrous effects that could result from the Supreme Court's decision. On February 8, the district court dismissed the Mount Clemens claims and also decided that no claims based on violations antedating the Supreme Court ruling of June, 1946, could be honored.[23]

Recognizing that Republican leaders remained determined to enact legislation dealing with portal claims, Administration officials worked out a plan to eliminate unjustifiable claims while preserving the substance of the Fair Labor Standards Act. J. Donald Kingsley, a White House aide, suggested that the Administra-

22. *The New York Times*, January 26, 1947, p. E1.
23. *Ibid.*, p. E3, February 9, 1947, p. 1.

tion support legislation providing for a federal statute of limitations on employees' claims and for authority to enable the Wage and Hour administrator to issue decisions on what constituted a workday. Although an informal Cabinet committee supported this recommendation, Administration officials who testified before congressional committees were unable to commit the President. Both William C. Foster, Under Secretary of Commerce, and L. Metcalfe Walling, administrator of the Fair Labor Standards Act, advocated authority for the administrator to make binding interpretations, but they inisted that they were presenting their own views without knowing the President's. Likewise, Democratic legislators felt the lack of presidential leadership as they attempted to modify the Republican bill in the absence of guidelines from the White House. After portal legislation had passed both houses, J. Howard McGrath of Rhode Island, a member of the Senate Judiciary Committee, was still trying to discover Truman's position so that he could determine his line of action in the conference committee.[24]

In the absence of presidential leadership, Congress prepared legislation drastically curtailing portal claims. The final bill invalidated all past claims except those founded on contract or custom, absolved employers from all claims if they could show they had acted in good faith, invalidated future claims for preliminary and postliminary activities not based on contract or custom, and provided for a two-year statute of limitations.[25]

Liberal Democrats and a few Republicans fought the bill strenuously. In the House, Minority Leader Rayburn remained silent —He ultimately voted for the bill—and Democrats Emanuel Celler of New York, Adolph Sabath of Illinois, Estes Kefauver of Tennessee, and Helen Gahagan Douglas of California led the opposition while Republicans Jacob Javits of New York and Richard Welch of California supported them. Senate Democrats James E.

---

24. J. Donald Kingsley to John R. Steelman, January 16, 1947, Harry S. Truman Papers, OF 407; Informal Cabinet Committee to study the Portal-to-Portal problem, mimeographed report, undated, John W. Snyder Papers; *The New York Times*, January 23, 1947, p. 8; William S. Tyson to Keen Johnson, March 26, 1947, Clifford Papers.

25. Tom Clark to James E. Webb, May 14, 1947, Bureau of the Budget, Reports to the President on Pending Legislation.

Murray of Montana, Patrick McCarran of Nevada, McGrath, Barkley, Claude Pepper of Florida, Olin D. Johnston of South Carolina, and Republican George Aiken launched major attacks against the bill. Their basic objection was that the measure went far beyond a mere attempt to deal with portal claims; it would undermine the very foundation of the Fair Labor Standards Act. The minority report on the House bill queried, "Why do not the proponents of the bill honestly say they want to kill the Fair Labor Standards Act?" The measure's vague definitions, provisions based on good faith and custom or practice, and its two-year statute of limitations, opponents maintained, would limit the protection afforded to employees under existing laws and enable employers to undermine wage standards without risking substantial liability. Moreover, the measure would punish the unorganized workers, whose real wages were already in a state of decline.[26]

Despite these objections, the bill passed by huge majorities. The record vote in the lower house was 345 to 56, with 50 Democrats, 5 Republicans, and 1 American Laborite voting No. In the Senate, the Administration's forces attempted to pass a more moderate substitute, but they lost, 53 to 35, with 45 Republicans and 8 Southern Democrats opposing and 33 Democrats and Republicans Langer and Aiken supporting the substitute. On the final vote, an additional 10 Southern and border-state Democrats joined the majority, and the bill passed, 64 to 24.[27]

Passage of the portal measure finally forced the President to take a stand, but only after a painstaking survey of all shades of opinion. He used the full ten days to make up his mind and di-

26. U.S. *Congressional Record*, 80th Cong., 1st sess., 1947, XCIII, Part 2, pp. 1485, 1493–96, 1507–10, 1513, 1565–69, 2235–38, 2243–60, 2301–8, 2349–55, 2371–74; U.S. House of Representatives, Committee on the Judiciary, *Regulating the Recovery of Portal-to-Portal Pay and for Other Purposes*, House Report 71 to accompany H.R. 2157, 80th Cong., 1st sess., 1947, 18; U.S. *Congressional Record*, 80th Cong., 1st sess., 1947, XCIII, Part 2, pp. 1485, 1495, 1503, 2243–60, 2301–8.

27. *Ibid.*, p. 1573. The 5 House Republicans voting against the bill were Welch (California), Meade (Kentucky), Javits (New York), Brophy (Wisconsin), and Hull (Wisconsin). *Ibid.*, p. 2366. The 8 Senate Democrats voting for the bill were Holland (Florida), Overton (Louisiana), Eastland (Mississippi), Hoey (North Carolina), McKellar (Tennessee), O'Daniel (Texas), Byrd (Virginia), and Robertson (Virginia). *Ibid.*, p. 2375.

rected the White House staff to obtain views from all executive bodies even remotely concerned with the legislation. In addition, the President met twice with Cabinet officials and aides to discuss the bill while his decision was pending. Two questions dominated Truman's deliberations: To what extent would the portal bill weaken the Fair Labor Standards Act, and What was the likelihood of Congress' passing a favorable bill if Truman vetoed the measure pending? Clifford at first tried to commit Truman to vetoing the bill and then specifying the kind of measure he wanted. Subsequent discussions with Administrative Assistant George M. Elsey and a survey of major labor legislation since 1906 convinced him that Congress traditionally rejected presidential leadership in labor matters. Moreover, Barkley insisted that Congress would not approve more favorable legislation if Truman vetoed the bill. Persuaded that a veto would be unproductive, Truman then made sure of the bill's effect on existing legislation. He was concerned about unorganized workers who needed government protection and asked his advisers for assurance that the little man would not be hurt badly by the portal bill. Lewis B. Schwellenbach, Secretary of Labor, and Leon Keyserling of the President's Council of Economic Advisers continued to press for disapproval, and Keyserling even prepared a draft veto message, but most of Truman's advisers, including Attorney General Tom Clark, Secretary of Commerce Harriman and Secretary of the Navy James Forrestal urged approval. Harriman and the Bureau of the Budget, however, suggested that Truman sign the bill and at the same time set forth his objections to certain provisions.[28]

Truman accepted the advice of the majority. He sought to build into his approval message guarantees that the measure im-

28. Elsey to Clark Clifford, "Major Labor Legislation Since 1906," Elsey, notes on Cabinet meeting, May 12, 1947, George M. Elsey Papers, Subject File; Richard E. Neustadt to F. J. Bailey, May 5, 1947, Bureau of the Budget, Record Group 51, Series 47.1a; Nourse, memorandum, February 23, 1948, Edwin G. Nourse Papers, Daily Diary; The President's Appointment Calendar, May 12, May 13, 1947, Matthew Connelly Files; Nourse to Truman, May 8, 1947, Nourse Papers, Daily Diary; Leon Keyserling, draft of veto message, Clifford Papers, Subject File; Philip B. Fleming to James E. Webb, May 7, 1947, Schwellenbach to Webb, May 7, 1947, Clark to Webb, May 4, 1947, Harriman to Webb, May 7, 1947, Forrestal to Webb, May 7, 1947, Bureau of the Budget Staff to Webb, May 8, 1947, Bureau of the Budget, Reports to the President on Pending Legislation.

posed no severe limitations on the Fair Labor Standards Act. Specifically, Truman attempted to ensure a favorable interpretation of the portal bill in the courts. In urging approval, Clark had argued that 74 per cent of the federal judges were Roosevelt appointees and would protect workers' interests in cases involving the measure. To make this more certain, Truman followed the advice of Supreme Court Justice William O. Douglas, who stressed the importance of presidential interpretation of key provisions. The courts, Douglas said, would consider Truman's message in determining the intent of the law.[29]

Truman's approval of the bill surprised the many who had expected a veto or at least sharp criticism of the bill. Instead, the President, in a unique action, reviewed the objections that had been made to the legislation and, ignoring or dismissing criticisms of the bill by almost all his advisers, disclosed at length his own interpretations of the questionable provisions. He concluded, "It is not the purpose of this Act to permit violation of our fundamental wage and hour standards, or to allow a lowering of these standards." In closing, he recommended that Congress increase the minimum wage to at least sixty-five cents and extend the provisions of the Fair Labor Standards Act to large numbers of workers who were at that time excluded.[30]

This moderate and restrained message sharply contrasted with Truman's ringing disapproval of legislation removing price controls in June and July, 1946, and his later criticism of the Eightieth Congress in June and July, 1947. As late as mid-May, 1947, the President's initial design was still intact. He was convinced that the portal bill contained no serious limitations on the protection of workers. Moreover, the issue was not one on which substantial public opinion demanded a veto. Unorganized workers were politically inarticulate, and a large part of the population, forgetting about the unorganized workers whom the bill affected,

29. Elsey, notes on Cabinet meeting, May 12, 1947, Elsey Papers, Subject File. A study made in 1950 showed that the courts in a number of cases had used Truman's message as part of the legislative history of the portal act. *Ibid.*

30. Special Message to the Congress Upon Signing the Portal-to-Portal Act, May 14, 1947, *Public Papers: Truman, 1947,* 243–44. For Administration views, see Bureau of the Budget, Reports to the President on Pending Legislation, Portal-to-Portal Pay.

viewed the extravagant portal claims as another attempt by powerful unions to line their pockets at the expense of consumers. Thus, Truman found no compelling reason to abandon his conciliatory posture. Since Congress had yet to act on crucial foreign-policy legislation (Greek-Turkish aid), this was no time to antagonize legislators. In addition, the Administration was in a poor position to veto legislation for which it had failed to provide an alternative. Finally, as his aides pointed out, by accepting the portal bill the President would be better able to cope with Congress if he felt compelled to veto the even harsher labor bill upon which Congress would soon take final action.[31] Nonetheless, affirmative presidential leadership before the bill was passed might have prevented this challenge, limited though it was, to a major New Deal program.

Truman's approval of the portal bill marked the end of his appeasement strategy. In succeeding months, Republicans overcame the intraparty disunity that had hindered drastic appropriation cuts and had permitted the Lilienthal confirmation. Ensuing legislation, unlike the portal bill, represented too great a threat to the Administration's policies, and Truman was constrained to take a stand against Congress. It was also becoming increasingly apparent to the President that political advantages could be gained by assumption of the role of vigorous defender of the common man against a reactionary Congress. This new attitude, however, did not emerge until Congress had acted on the Administration's major foreign-policy proposals of the first session.

31. Adrian Fisher to Harriman, May 8, 1947, Bureau of the Budget Staff to Webb, May 8, 1947, Bureau of the Budget, Reports to the President on Pending Legislation.

CHAPTER 3

CONSENSUS ON FOREIGN POLICY

TRANQUIL RELATIONS between President and Congress in the early months of 1947 extended also into foreign affairs, where the Administration won support for new proposals and deflected attacks against existing programs. Working closely with Senator Vandenberg, the Administration headed off congressional attempts to thwart the the Geneva tariff-reduction negotiations, a crucial element in the reciprocal-trade program. In the most significant foreign-policy legislation of the first session, the Administration gained legislative approval for economic and military aid to Greece and Turkey, the beginning of its containment policy. In addition, Congress authorized $350 million for continued relief to war-devastated Europe, and the Senate ratified peace treaties with Italy, Hungary, Bulgaria, and Rumania. Finally, in the area of national defense, Congress enacted the President's proposal for unification of the armed services.

At the start of the Eightieth Congress, such legislative-executive accord seemed unlikely. The Administration's policy was in a state of flux as decision makers discarded original premises and sought to chart a new course for United States foreign policy. Inherited from Roosevelt, the initial postwar design rested on the assumption that the Allies, led by the United States, would manage international peace and order within the framework of the United Nations. In addition, most U.S. political and business leaders agreed on the necessity to expand international trade, and to this end the Administration devised programs to reduce trade barriers, provide direct relief for war-devastated countries, and contribute to the rebuilding of Europe through a system of loans. Such a design would increase the possibilities for peace and stability and safeguard as well supplies of raw materials and markets for investment capital and for excess goods deemed essential for the domestic economy. These economic objectives endured, but the

47

original hopes for postwar cooperation were shattered, partly, to be sure, because of these objectives and the Soviet Union's refusal to acquiesce in a world order geared to the imperatives of U.S. capitalism. As the Soviet Union ruthlessly, when necessary, consolidated control over Eastern Europe, the United States did not accept Russia's legitimate concern for friendly—that is, pro-Soviet —governments in neighboring countries, stressed self-determination, and interpreted Soviet action as the first step in communist expansion into more crucial areas. The Soviet Union, suspicious of the most powerful and avowedly anticommunist country in the world, refused to concur in U.S. plans for the postwar settlement and often proved intransigent in the United Nations and peace conferences, while its leaders fed U.S. fears with the communist rhetoric of world revolution. By late 1946, the Administration had developed a policy of verbal and diplomatic firmness toward the Soviet Union but had reached no decisions about deploying U.S. power to bolster this approach.[1]

While seeking to adjust its foreign policy to its view of the changing international situation, the Administration had also to remember domestic requirements. Specifically, it needed congressional support and cooperation. Most Republicans, notably Vandenberg, welcomed the tougher approach. In a Senate speech of February, 1946, he posed the question, "What is Russia up to now?" and insisted that it be answered. He was optimistic about the chances for reasonable harmony, but he called for drawing a line beyond which there would be no compromise and standing firmly behind it. In the privacy of his diary, the Senator was more candid:

> Byrnes gives every evidence of *"no more appeasement"* in his attitudes, however; and I am *certain* that this is the way (if there *is* one) to reach common ground with the Soviets. I want to be scrupulously

1. The economic imperatives of U.S. postwar foreign policy are cogently argued by Gabriel Kolko, *The Politics of War: The World and United States Foreign Policy, 1943–1945,* and Thomas G. Patterson, "The Quest for Peace and Prosperity: International Trade, Communism, and the Marshall Plan," in Barton J. Bernstein, ed., *Politics and Policies of the Truman Administration,* 78–112. Barton J. Bernstein, "American Foreign Policy and the Origins of the Cold War," *ibid.,* 15–77, surveys the development of U.S. policy from 1944 to 1947.

fair and reasonable with them; but I want to be relentlessly firm in our insistence upon these American positions. No more Munichs! If it is impossible for us to get along with the Soviets on such a basis, the quicker we find it out the better.

Taft, too, was critical of previous appeasement of Russia and credited Republican criticism for stiffening U.S. policy.[2]

Important businessmen and lawyers in the Republican Eastern establishment—men like Henry Stimson, Robert Lovett, Paul Hoffman, John Foster Dulles, and Paul Nitze—generally supported and often helped design the Administration's foreign policy. Most Republican legislators, however, were simultaneously politically interventionist and economically isolationist. They were loudly anticommunist and urged the Administration to take a stronger stand against Russia, but they were extremely hesitant when it came to spending money abroad. In implementing its postwar economic program, the Administration had faced substantial Republican opposition to the Export-Import Bank legislation, the authorization of a loan of $3.75 billion to Britain, and the establishment of the International Bank and Monetary Fund. Legislators in the Eightieth Congress who were especially concerned about federal spending were even more reluctant to authorize the economic props of the Administration's foreign policy and thereby jeopardize such domestic objectives as tax reduction and a balanced budget. Moreover, most Republicans had voted against the reciprocal-trade program in its original authorization and subsequent extensions.[3]

It was, in fact, Republican opposition to the reciprocal-trade program that brought the first congressional challenge to Administration foreign policy. Although the United States in practice often deviated from the ideal of eliminating trade restrictions, that goal was central to U.S. postwar policy, because the expan-

2. U.S. *Congressional Record,* 79th Cong., 2d sess., 1946, XCII, Part 2, pp. 1694–95; Vandenberg, Paris Diary, April 28, 1946, Vandenberg to Clarence H. Booth, July 31, 1946, Arthur H. Vandenberg Papers, William L. Clements Library, University of Michigan; Taft, keynote speech at Ohio Republican Convention, *The New York Times,* September 12, 1946, p. 4.

3. John K. Galbraith, "Who Needs the Democrats?" *Harper's Magazine,* 241 (July, 1970), 48–50; Joseph M. Jones, *The Fifteen Weeks (February 21–June 5, 1947),* 96.

sion of international trade seemed vital to world peace and prosperity, as well as essential to the health and growth of the U.S. economy. While most U.S. businessmen enthusiastically supported the concept of freer trade, some powerful industrial and agricultural interests wanted to maintain their own tariffs, subsidies, and restrictive arrangements. Opposition to the reciprocal-trade program came from congressmen who represented these interests, those who were protectionist in principle, and those who were eager to reduce what they considered excessive executive encroachment on congressional authority. On November 9, 1946, William L. Clayton, Under Secretary of State for Economic Affairs, announced a forthcoming meeting in Geneva, where representatives of eighteen countries would enter into tariff negotiations. Candidly admitting the political vulnerability of this subject, Clayton said that he had witheld his announcement until after the elections in order to prevent the reciprocal-trade program from becoming a partisan issue in the campaign. Republican Senator Hugh Butler, however, argued that the voters had delivered a mandate against the program. Asking Clayton to delay the negotiations until the new Congress could scrutinize thoroughly the entire reciprocal-trade program, Butler wrote, "The attempt to use the authority of the Trade Agreements Act, previously wrested from a Democratic Congress, to destroy our system of tariff protections, seems to me a direct affront to the popular will expressed last month." The opposition materialized early in January, when Ohio Congressman Thomas A. Jenkins, a high-ranking member of the Ways and Means Committee, introduced a resolution embodying Butler's demands. It received support from many Republicans, including Senators Butler and Brewster and Congressmen Bertrand W. Gearhart of California, Daniel A. Reed of New York, and Ross Rizley of Oklahoma. The adoption of Jenkins' resolution would have prevented U.S. participation in negotiations for which the United States was the principal sponsor and undermined the Administration's foreign economic program.[4]

4. Kolko, *The Politics of War*, 245–54; Patterson, "The Quest for Peace and Prosperity," 81–85; *The New York Times*, November 11, 1946, p. 1; Butler to Clayton, December 19, 1946, Congressman Ross Rizley to Butler, January 29,

As other bills to sabotage the Geneva meeting were introduced, the Administration began to take steps to head off congressional action. In his first appearance before the Senate Foreign Relations Committee, Secretary of State Marshall expressed deep concern about the recent attacks on the reciprocal-trade program, and he made it known that any manifestations of economic isolationism in Congress would severely handicap him at the forthcoming Moscow Foreign Ministers Conference, where postwar settlements for Germany and Austria were to be discussed.[5]

Even before Marshall delivered his warning, other State Department officials and Republican supporters of reciprocal trade were working to save the program. William Clayton's concern about Republican opposition prompted him to meet with Vandenberg, who favored tariff reductions but felt that the State Department, which was necessarily prompted by considerations of foreign policy, often ignored the consequences of tariff cuts for the domestic economy. Clayton and Vandenberg included in these discussions Under Secretary Dean Acheson and Eugene D. Millikin, a consistent foe of the reciprocal-trade program and chairman of the Senate Finance Committee, which handled tariff legislation. Throughout the meetings, Clayton and Vandenberg continued to look for a way to limit executive authority to reduce tariffs without jeopardizing the entire program, and on February 10, the senators issued a joint statement outlining the results of the discussions. They argued that there was no immediate need for restrictive legislation—Modification of the program, if necessary, could wait until 1948, when the current act expired. They also insisted that it would be undesirable to postpone or abandon the Geneva negotiations. In deference to opponents of the program, they recognized the serious concern for protection of the domestic economy. The economy, however, could be protected by executive order. Vandenberg and Millikin offered four specific suggestions: (1) the Tariff Commission should recommend to the President

---

1947, Rizley to George C. Marshall, January 27, 1947, Hugh A. Butler Papers; U.S. *Congressional Record*, 80th Cong., 1st sess., 1947, XCIII, Part 1, pp. 385, 477.

5. *The New York Times*, February 14, 1947, p. 1.

points below which reductions would endanger the domestic economy, (2) escape clauses should be written into agreements, (3) the Tariff Commission should inform itself of the operations of all agreements, hold public hearings to determine if the escape clause should be invoked, and make recommendations to the President, and (4) the recommendations of the Tariff Commission should be made public. As a result of their discussions with State Department officials, the two senators were "encouraged to hope that improvements by executive order along the lines suggested will be seriously considered by the President and the State Department."[6]

On February 25, the President issued an executive order incorporating most of Vandenberg's and Millikin's suggestions. In an accompanying statement, Truman reaffirmed the Administration's commitment to the reciprocal-trade program: "I wish to make clear that the provisions of the order do not deviate from the traditional Cordell Hull principles. They simply make assurance doubly sure that American interests will be properly safeguarded." Concluding, he stressed that bipartisanship in economic foreign policy was just as essential as bipartisanship in other matters of international concern.[7]

The executive order and the cooperation of Vandenberg and Millikin thwarted, for the time being, the attack on the reciprocal-trade program, but there were indications that trouble might reappear. Vandenberg and Millikin noted that the order did not incorporate their suggestion that the Tariff Commission make recommendations *before* agreements were signed. Taft had said earlier that even if the President put all of the senators' suggestions into effect, substantial objections to the program would remain. Legislators Butler, Reed, Jenkins, and Knutson, die-hard opponents of reciprocal trade, used the executive order to launch another attack, and the House Ways and Means Committee be-

---

6. Vandenberg to Sinclair Weeks, January 3, 1947, Vandenberg Papers; *The New York Times,* January 26, 1947, p. 5; U.S. *Congressional Record,* 80th Cong., 1st sess., 1947, XCIII, Part 1, p. 912.

7. Statement by the President Upon Issuing Order on the Administration of the Reciprocal Trade Agreements Program, February 25, 1947, *Public Papers of the Presidents of the United States: Harry S. Truman,* 1947, 151–52.

gan intensive hearings to examine closely the State Department's intentions concerning the Geneva meeting and to prepare for major revision of the program in 1948.[8]

While cooperating with Republican leaders to modify the reciprocal-trade program, the President also wanted to strengthen public support for the program and to assure other nations that Congress would not repudiate any agreements negotiated at Geneva. Accordingly, he devoted a speech at Baylor University on March 6 to the topic of international trade. In it, Truman declared that domestic interests would be safeguarded, outlined the economic benefits of tariff reduction, and tied the reduction of trade barriers to freedom of enterprise. On a more lofty plane, he explained the integral relationship of economic policy and world peace, associated the reciprocal-trade program with objectives of the United Nations, and proclaimed to the world, "Our people are united. They have come to a realization of their responsibilities. . . . They are determined upon an international order in which peace and freedom shall endure."[9]

At the same time it was negotiating with Congress to preserve an old element of its foreign policy, the Administration was moving toward a major restatement of its position toward the Soviet Union. This change of direction, which would be known as the Truman Doctrine, thrust the United States into the role of dominant power in the Mediterranean and verbally committed the United States to using its power to stop communism everywhere. As such, it provided the basis for future U.S. interventions abroad to maintain the *status quo*. The Truman Doctrine and the specific aid to Greece and Turkey represented no abrupt departure in U.S. policy; rather, they marked the culmination of trends that had begun as early as 1945. However, there were two novel elements: For the first time, the United States stated explicitly that communist gains were a threat to world peace and pledged its

8. U.S. *Congressional Record*, 80th Cong., 1st sess., 1947, XCIII, Part 2, pp. 1413, 1417, 1469–73; *The New York Times*, February 9, 1947, p. 1; Albert W. Hawkes to Millikin, February 26, 1947, Butler to Millikin, March 7, 1947, Butler Papers; Holbert N. Carroll, *The House of Representatives and Foreign Affairs*, 44.

9. Unsigned memo to Dean Acheson, February 10, 1947, Clark M. Clifford Papers, Speech File; Address on Foreign Economic Policy, Delivered at Baylor University, March 6, 1947, *Public Papers: Truman*, 1947, 167–72.

power to check such developments everywhere, and also for the first time, the Administration needed congressional cooperation and support to implement its new approach.

Great Britain, the traditional guarantor of Western interests in the Mediterranean, had attempted to continue her role at the close of the war, but as British economic and military weakness became increasingly apparent, the United States stepped up its activity in the area. In March, 1946, Anglo-American diplomacy thwarted Soviet attempts to maintain troops in Iran and to alienate one of her northern provinces. Russian designs on Turkey and control of the Dardanelles, the crucial link between the Black Sea and the Mediterranean, were similarly opposed by firm diplomacy and the sending of a U.S. task force to the Mediterranean. Britain, however, had provided the economic and military assistance required to strengthen the Turkish army.[10]

The situation in Greece was more complex. The harsh Nazi occupation had virtually destroyed the economy and had permitted new forces to gain power, notably indigenous leftists led by the Greek National Liberation Front (the EAM), by far the strongest resistance group. After the occupation, British troops, with Stalin's acquiescence, put down a revolt against the monarchist government that Britain had installed, but the insurgents kept many of their hand weapons and continued to harass the government. A plebiscite in September, 1946, restored King George II, but EAM supporters, many of whom were not communists, suspected fraudulence and refused to vote. Thus, the government rested on a narrow base of support. Moreover, it engaged in repressive activities against its opponents, continued ex-Nazi collaborators in army and police posts, and failed utterly to solve the country's economic problems. By late 1946, the government continued to rely heavily on British military and economic aid, but it still could not deal effectively with the guerrillas, who received increasing support from their Balkan neighbors—Yugoslavia, Bulgaria and Albania.[11]

10. Walter LaFeber, *America, Russia, and the Cold War, 1945–1966*, 28–29.

11. Richard J. Barnet, *Intervention and Revolution: The United States in the Third World*, 107–11. The most detailed account is in Stephen G. Xydis, *Greece and the Great Powers, 1944–1947*.

54

Until 1947, the U.S. role in Greece had been primarily one of support for Britain and gradual expansion of its own activities. The United States had sent observers to the Greek elections. In addition, it had committed funds, indirectly through the loan of $3.75 billion to Britain and the United Nations Relief and Rehabilitation Aid (about $160 million in 1946) and directly through a loan of $25 million from the Export-Import Bank, a credit of $45 million for military surplus stocks, and a credit of $50 million for maritime equipment. By the fall of 1946, the State Department was considering ways to increase U.S. aid to Greece if British resources failed. At the same time, it recommended general economic measures to the Greek government, and in January, 1947, it sent a mission to study economic conditions and advise the government. The most significant indicator of the extent to which U.S. interest in Greece had intensified was a confidential message from President Truman that was transmitted to the Greek government in October, 1946. In it, Truman acknowledged that Greece was of vital interest to the United States and promised substantial aid to maintain its independence. But, the President insisted, it was up to the Greek government to demonstrate to the U.S. public that democracy survived there and that the people, with the exception of the communists, were united. He urged that the government be broadened and that it avoid excesses against political opponents. Thus, the Administration had already committed itself to greater assistance and a strong role as adviser in Greek internal affairs. In addition, it began to consider the problem of persuading the U.S. public and Congress that such a program was desirable.[12]

The expected British withdrawal from Greece and Turkey materialized on February 21, when the British first secretary informed the State Department that Britain's crippled economy made it impossible for her to maintain her presence in those two countries past March 31, 1947. The Administration's response was a dramatic but logical extension of the United States' develop-

12. *Ibid.*, 146, 227, 356, 372, 453; Dean Acheson to Arthur Capper, November 8, 1946, Arthur Capper Papers; James Forrestal, *The Forrestal Diaries*, Walter Millis and E. S. Duffield, eds., 210, 216; Xydis, *Greece and the Great Powers*, 317, 400–402; Barnet, *Intervention and Revolution*, 112–13.

ing position: the assumption of Britain's responsibilities in the Mediterranean. The rationale was simple. The Soviet Union was bent on unlimited expansion, which the United States alone was sufficiently powerful to check. If Greece and Turkey should fall under communist control, the Soviet Union could easily expand its influence into North Africa and South Asia. These developments would have an immensely injurious psychological effect on Western Europe, which was facing overwhelming economic difficulties and challenges from strong domestic communist parties.[13]

Opinion within the Administration was practically unanimous on the course U.S. policy should take. Although there was ample evidence to the contrary—Many of the Greek insurgents were not communists, and Stalin, in fact, opposed the revolution—the Administration chose to assume that success for the rebels meant the automatic extension of Soviet power. Social revolution and Russian expansion were held to be identical and to call for a strong response from the United States. The lone dissenter in the Administration was George Kennan, Russian expert in the State Department. He conceded that Turkey was vulnerable to Soviet pressure but argued that since the threat was primarily political, the United States should not provoke the Soviet Union by sending military aid to her neighbor. On the other hand, he supported economic and political assistance for Greece, where he thought the situation less serious than did his colleagues. Overruling Kennan's objections on the Turkish question, the Administration decided to begin immediately to give Greece and Turkey whatever aid could be granted under existing authority and to seek congressional authorization for a full-scale program of assistance.[14]

The Administration then mobilized to win congressional support. Previous attempts to win Republican approval of major foreign policies had consisted of bringing important Republicans into the early stages of the decision-making and planning processes, as in the formation of the United Nations and the writing

13. Jones, *The Fifteen Weeks*, 46–47.
14. Kolko, *The Politics of War*, 182–93; Barnet, *Intervention and Revolution*, 120–22; George F. Kennan, *Memoirs, 1925–1950*, 313–19; Jones, *The Fifteen Weeks*, 136–38.

of the peace treaties. This time, however, the strategy was one of vigorous presidential initiative in a crisis atmosphere. In deciding not to involve Republicans in the decision-making process, the President may have chosen to avoid a premature rebuff by confronting legislative leaders with the situation in such a way that they could not resist going along. In any case, Truman had already made his decision when he called congressional leaders to the White House on February 27.

Invited to this briefing were Senators Vandenberg; Styles Bridges, chairman of the Appropriations Committee; and Tom Connally, ranking Democrat on the Foreign Relations Committee. The House delegation consisted of Speaker Martin; Minority Leader Sam Rayburn; Charles Eaton, chairman of the Foreign Affairs Committee; and Sol Bloom, ranking Democrat on the committee. Secretary of State Marshall opened the meeting with a statement describing Britain's withdrawal and its implications, but the legislators remained unpersuaded. Alarmed by the unresponsiveness of the congressmen and convinced that Marshall had "flubbed his opening statement," Dean Acheson urgently requested the floor. Believing that it was essential to "pull out all the stops," he outlined the situation in bold, threatening terms. The stakes in the Middle East were so high, Acheson asserted, that failure of the United States to act decisively would open three continents to Soviet penetration and strike an irreparable blow to freedom everywhere. Certain that the threat was acute, Acheson also knew that Congress would act only if confronted with a crisis. He was right. The congressional leaders were impressed by his plea, but Vandenberg insisted that the President present the crisis and its requirements to the public in the same frank way. He felt it was necessary to "scare hell" out of the people in order to win their support. Truman agreed and promised another meeting with a larger group of legislators to outline in detail the requirements of the program.[15]

Further steps were necessary to sell the program to the Congress

---

15. *Ibid.*, 138–44, 168–69; Dean Acheson, *Present at the Creation: My Years in the State Department*, 219. House Appropriations Committee Chairman John Taber was necessarily absent and received a separate briefing.

and the public. State Department officials helped draft the official request from the Greek government, preparing the text "with a view to the mentality of Congress . . . in order to obtain a decision for the speedy strengthening of Greece." To inform and persuade the public, Acheson held a series of off-the-record meetings at which he briefed the press on all aspects of the Greek-Turkish situation. The President heeded Forrestal's advice that business support was crucial and appointed a special Cabinet committee, headed by Secretary of the Treasury John Snyder, to communicate to public leaders, especially businessmen, the necessity for the Greek-Turkish program and its implications.[16]

The Administration's endeavor to gain support—and the one with massive long-range implications—lay in its manner of presentation. As Acheson had done privately, the Administration exaggerated the extent of the crisis and bluntly portrayed its proposals in bold, crusading, ideological terms. In part, this endeavor was necessary to win approval from the Republican-controlled Congress. The anticommunist tone of the proposal would delight Republicans who had been pressing the Administration for a tougher approach toward Russia. The crisis atmosphere might convince economy-oriented legislators that financial sacrifices were necessary. But the tone of the proposal also faithfully portrayed the way in which most policy makers viewed the situation. Secretary of the Navy Forrestal agreed with Acheson's analysis and joined Clark Clifford in an attempt to prepare a statement that would focus sharply on the central problem: "which of the two systems currently offered the world is to survive, and what practical steps need to be taken to implement any policies that the government may establish." Under Secretary of State Will Clayton expressed a similar attitude. Insisting that the United States should assume "world leadership quickly," he maintained that the people of the United States had to be "shocked into doing so." Therefore, the Administration had to tell them the "whole truth" that "in every country in the Eastern Hemisphere and most of the . . . Western Hemisphere Russia is boring from within."[17]

16. Xydis, Greece and the Great Powers, 479; Jones, The Fifteen Weeks, 144, 168; Forrestal, The Forrestal Diaries, Millis and Duffield, eds., 248, 251–52.

17. H. Bradford Westerfield, Foreign Policy and Party Politics: Pearl Harbor

A few foreign-policy advisers objected to the tone of the speech. Marshall and Charles Bohlen were "somewhat startled" when they received a draft in Paris while en route to the Moscow Foreign Ministers Conference. They objected to the message's anticommunist emphasis, and Marshall expressed to Truman his view that the President was "overstating his case a bit." The objection was to no avail. Truman replied that his contacts in the Senate convinced him that without such a dramatic statement, there was no chance of congressional approval. George Kennan was similarly overruled when he took issue with "the sweeping nature of the Administration's proposal and the commitments which it implied." Truman, in fact, sought to embolden further the rhetoric of his statement. Asking for more emphasis on the implications of the decision for U.S. foreign policy in general, he rejected speech drafts that seemed to him uninspiring and coldly statistical. On later drafts, he scratched out the word "should" and penciled in "must." Looking back on his message, Truman explained, "I wanted no hedging in this speech. This was America's answer to the surge of expansion of Communist tyranny. It had to be clear and free of hesitation or double talk."[18]

On March 12, the President read his speech to a joint session of Congress. He did not mention the Soviet Union by name, but he placed the Greek-Turkish crisis within a broad framework of world peace and national security. After explaining the circumstances that threatened each country, he traced the results which would ensue if they fell.

> If Greece should fall under the control of an armed minority, the effect upon its neighbor, Turkey, would be immediate and serious. Confusion and disorder might well spread throughout the entire Middle East.
>
> Moreover, the disappearance of Greece as an independent state

---

to Korea, 206-12; Jones, *The Fifteen Weeks*, 118, 120, 124; Forrestal, *The Forrestal Diaries*, Millis and Duffield, eds., 249; Clayton, handwritten memorandum, March 5, 1947, William L. Clayton Papers, Speech File, 1946.

18. Charles E. Bohlen, *The Transformation of American Foreign Policy*, 87. Acheson, *Present at the Creation*, maintains that Marshall approved the message and that Acheson, in fact, used Marshall's approval to dissuade Clifford, who wanted an even stronger speech. Kennan, *Memoirs*, 319–20; Harry S. Truman, *Memoirs*, Vol. II, *Years of Trial and Hope*, 105.

would have a profound effect upon those countries in Europe whose peoples are struggling against great difficulties to maintain their freedom and their independence while they repair the damages of war. . . .

Should we fail to aid Greece and Turkey in this fateful hour, the effect will be far reaching to the West as to the East.

Truman then outlined a course of action for the United States. He requested $400 million to strengthen Greece and Turkey militarily and economically; authorization to send U.S. economic and military missions to supervise the use of the aid and to assist the governments' reconstruction efforts; and authority to facilitate the sending of the aid. At the close of his speech, he again emphasized the critical nature of the situation and the consequences of inaction:

This is a serious course upon which we embark. I would not recommend it except that the alternative is much more serious. . . .

If we falter in our leadership, we may endanger the peace of the world—and we shall surely endanger the welfare of the nation.[19]

The President's message confronted Congress with an inflexible either-or situation. By presenting its proposal as the only solution to a crisis situation, the Administration offered Congress the choice of either approving it or repudiating the President and thereby crippling the United States internationally. Nonetheless, many congressmen had serious misgivings about the proposed program, although outright opposition was limited. These objections centered on five major concerns: (1) that in approving the Administration's program, Congress would commit the United States to a broad policy of intervention and foreign aid, (2) that unilateral intervention in the Greek-Turkish situation would weaken the United Nations, (3) that the Soviet Union would be provoked to war, (4) that undemocratic governments would be strengthened in Greece and Turkey, and (5) that the program would place too heavy a strain on the U.S. economy.

The global implications of the new policy appeared in Truman's widely quoted assertion that the United States must "sup-

19. Special Message to the Congress on Greece and Turkey: The Truman Doctrine, March 12, 1947, *Public Papers: Truman, 1947,* 178–80.

port free peoples who are resisting attempted subjugation by armed minorities or by outside pressures." This declaration reflected not only the Administration's decision that it was necessary to employ American power to contain communism, but also its belief that a bold and dramatic statement was necessary to stir an apathetic public to what the Administration considered to be its world-wide responsibilities. However, the declaration, promptly termed the Truman Doctrine by the press, alarmed such students of foreign policy as Walter Lippmann, as well as certain congressmen, and for a time seemed to jeopardize the specific program of aid to Greece and Turkey. The issue was clearly drawn during the public hearings before the Senate Foreign Relations Committee. Closely questioned by Senators Connally, Smith, and Vandenberg, Dean Acheson, the Administration's spokesman, limited the current proposal to specific objectives concerning Greece and Turkey but reaffirmed the Administration's intention to respond in other situations in which a country's independence was threatened. Senator Vandenberg also sought to meet objections on this point. In his speech presenting the bill to Congress, he disclaimed any close parallel between Truman's pronouncement and the Monroe Doctrine, and he clearly defined the limits of the program when he stated, "I do not view it as a universal pattern but rather as a selective pattern to fit a given circumstance."[20]

The ranking members of the Senate Foreign Relations Committee took the initiative in disposing of a second important objection to Greek-Turkish aid. Although Vandenberg was convinced that "Greece could collapse fifty times before the United Nations itself could ever hope to handle a situation of this nature," he viewed the Administration's failure to link the program with the international organization as a "colossal blunder." Public expressions of concern about this issue came from firm supporters of the President's policy, as well as from those who simply used

20. Walter Lippmann, columns in *Washington Post*, April 8, April 22, 1947; James W. Pratt, "Leadership Relations in United States Foreign Policy Making: Case Studies, 1947–1950" (Ph.D. dissertation, Columbia University, 1963), 30–31; Jones, *The Fifteen Weeks*, 190–93. Jones quotes Acheson: "It cannot be assumed, therefore, that this government would necessarily undertake measures in any other countries identical or even closely similar to those proposed for Greece and Turkey."

the question of the United Nations as a means of attacking the whole program. Senators Vandenberg and Connally quickly dispelled much of the concern by drafting an amendment providing for the United Nations to terminate the program—The United States in this instance would waive its veto power—whenever it found that action by the United Nations would make U.S. assistance unnecessary or undesirable. Then, in his major address on the bill, Vandenberg emphasized the relationship of the program to the objectives of the United Nations and maintained that to have dumped the Greek-Turkish problem into the lap of this new organization would have destroyed its prestige and authority by giving it a job at which it could only fail.[21]

In response to congressional and public concern about the nature of the governments to be supported, Dean Acheson admitted to Cabinet officials that the Greek government was unsatisfactory because it contained many reactionary elements and tolerated internal corruption and inefficiency. Vandenberg, too, conceded that the monarchy was decadent, chosen in an election only because it seemed the only answer to communism. Publicly, Administration officials emphasized the government's legal basis in the 1946 plebiscite and insisted that the choice for Greece was "between a totalitarianism and an imperfect democracy." Vandenberg countered objections by arguing that the United States was not necessarily condoning the Greek monarchy by extending aid to the Greek people. Supporters of the program also predicted that proper administration of the aid by U.S. officials would liberalize the governments. But to most policymakers and congressmen, the nature of the governments was beside the point. As Republican Representative Albert M. Cole of Kansas put it, the decision should not be based on whether Greece was democratic, but on whether "Russia is a threat to the peace of the world . . . and whether Greece is the military strategic point at which to stop such aggression."[22]

21. Arthur H. Vandenberg, Jr., ed., *The Private Papers of Senator Vandenberg*, 340–41, 345–46; Jones, *The Fifteen Weeks*, 181–83; Forrestal, *The Forrestal Diaries*, Millis and Duffield, eds., 257; U.S. *Congressional Record*, 80th Cong., 1st sess., 1947, XCIII, Part 3, p. 3197.

22. Forrestal, *The Forrestal Diaries*, Millis and Duffield, eds., 251; Vanden-

Opposition to Greek-Turkish aid came from both liberals and conservatives, but for different reasons. In addition to denouncing U.S. support for reaction abroad, those on the left stressed the provocative and belligerent tone of the President's proposal. Claude Pepper, Democratic Senator from Florida, feared that it would "destroy any hope of reconciliation with Russia" and objected to allying the United States with the "reactionary and corrupt regimes of the world." Henry A. Wallace, who had been Vice President and Secretary of Commerce and who was a major spokesman for internationalist liberals, charged the President with "whipping up anti-Communist hysteria." Opponents on the right tended to stress the program's domestic implications, insisting that it would bankrupt the United States and necessitate detested wartime controls and executive powers. These conservatives were as vehemently anticommuist as the Administration, but they proposed to support their position by ensuring the fiscal solvency of the United States and ridding the country of communists within.[23]

Despite the strength of various objections, most congressmen apparently came to consider the cost of repudiating the President prohibitive. The Senate passed the bill on April 22 by a vote of 67 to 23. The opposition consisted of 7 Democrats and 16 Republicans who represented three shades of opinion. Senators Byrd of Virginia and McKellar of Tennessee opposed the bill on grounds of economy and overcommitment. Senators Pepper and Glen H. Taylor of Idaho agreed with Henry Wallace. Most of the 16 Republican opponents were Midwesterners who wanted to limit U.S. involvement abroad, as well as government expenditures. Members of the House divided along similar lines, and on May 9,

---

berg to Jones Luther Risk, May 7, 1947, Vandenberg Papers; Labor Department, press release of speech by Lewis Schwellenbach before the Commonwealth Club of San Francisco, March 20, 1947, Clifford Papers; U.S. *Congressional Record*, 80th Cong., 1st sess., 1947, XCIII, Part 3, p. 3196; Harley Kilgore to Tom Connally, April 9, 1947, Harley M. Kilgore Papers, General File, University of West Virginia Library; Cole to George W. Maxwell, April 21, 1947, Albert M. Cole Papers, Legislative Correspondence.

23. U.S. *Congressional Record*, 80th Cong., 1st sess., 1947, XCIII, Part 3, pp. 3281, 3468, 3737–38, 3774; Henry Wallace, "The Fight for Peace Begins," *New Republic*, 116 (March 24, 1947), 13; Marion T. Bennett to Ray L. Schubert, May 10, 1947, Marion T. Bennett Papers; John Taber to Carter Woods, March 18, 1947, John Taber Papers.

the bill passed by a vote of 287 to 107, with 93 Republicans, 13 Democrats, and 1 American Laborite voting No.[24]

Legislative support for Greek-Turkish aid had been achieved by various means. Both Acheson and Vandenberg had helped to make the proposal more palatable by promising that the global scope of the Truman Doctrine would be limited in practice, a pledge that the Administration subsequently broke. Opposition had been diluted by the Administration's acceptance of the Vandenberg-Connally amendment to tie the program more closely to the United Nations. Vandenberg's prestige and authority contributed greatly to the Senate's approval, and once the Senate had endorsed it, the House could only with great difficulty reject the program. Ultimately—and this perhaps accounted for Vandenberg's initial support—the Administration had fabricated a crisis atmosphere and made its proposal in terms of U.S. security from communist expansion. Congressman Francis Case of South Dakota pointed out to Truman the reluctance with which legislators voted approval: "The situation was regarded as an accomplished fact. You had spoken to the world. The Senate had acted. At least 75 members, I judge, would have voted against final passage, myself included, had it not been that we thought it would be like pulling the rug out from under you or Secretary of State Marshall." Vandenberg expressed the same view to the Senate: "To repudiate the President of the United States at such an hour could display a divisive weakness which might involve far greater jeopardy than a sturdy display of united strength. We are not free to ignore the price of noncompliance."[25]

The proposal to aid Greece and Turkey had interrupted congressional study of the Administration's second important request. This measure—direct relief for war-ravaged Europe—did not contain the anticommunist potential of the Greek-Turkish program, and the Administration found it much more difficult to

24. U.S. *Congressional Record*, 80th Cong., 1st sess., 1947, XCIII, Part 3, p. 3793, Part 4, p. 4975.
25. Pratt, "Leadership Relations in Foreign Policy Making," 45–46; Cecil V. Crabb, Jr., *Bipartisan Foreign Policy: Myth or Reality?* 61, 68; Case to Truman, May 10, 1947, Harry S. Truman Papers, OF 426; U.S. *Congressional Record*, 80th Cong., 1st sess., 1947, XCIII, Part 3, p. 3198.

wrest the funds from a Congress bent on economy. At the close of the war, the United States had assumed responsibility for helping to repair war damage in the liberated countries through its contributions to the United Nations Relief and Rehabilitation Administration. The aid from UNRRA was going to expire in 1947, and Truman proposed that the United States help to fill the gap for countries whose peoples still needed the basic essentials of life. Specifically, he asked for $350 million to be administered by the United States.[26]

Most of the opposition to the President's request came from inland Republicans and Southern Democrats. In the House Foreign Affairs Committee, Midwestern Republicans attempted to cut the authorization and to place burdensome restrictions upon the administration of the aid. These Republicans were only partly successful in changing the Administration's draft. Congressmen Robert Chiperfield of Illinois, Bartel J. Jonkman of Michigan and Lawrence Smith of Wisconsin signed a minority report and expected other committee Republicans to support their efforts to revise the bill on the floor of the House. The opposition recommended that the amount be cut to $200 million because, they asserted, aid would be necessary only until the end of the year. They also attacked the State Department for refusing to make public the specific amounts for each country, and they pointed out the inconsistency of aiding Poland and Hungary, which had communist governments, while simultaneously providing assistance to Greece and Turkey to enable them to resist communism.[27]

On the House floor, Foreign Affairs Chairman Eaton encountered the wholesale desertion of Republican committee members and lack of support from the House leaders. Jonkman's amendment to cut the amount to $200 million was adopted, 225 to 165. Those who voted for the amendment were 190 Republicans and 35 Democrats (all but 2 from the South); those who voted against

26. Special Message to the Congress Requesting Appropriations for Aid to Liberated Countries, February 21, 1947, *Public Papers: Truman, 1947*, 149–50.

27. Pratt, "Leadership Relations in Foreign Policy Making," 50–57; U.S. House of Representatives, Committee on Foreign Affairs, *Relief Assistance to the People of Countries Devastated by War*, House Report 239 to accompany H. J. Res. 153, 80th Cong., 1st sess., 1947, Part II, "Minority Views," 7–10; *The New York Times*, March 19, 1947, p. 1.

it were 128 Democrats, 36 Republicans (all but 5 from the coasts), and 1 American Laborite. The emasculated bill then passed by a large majority, 333 to 66.[28]

In the Senate, the Administration, working through Vandenberg, sought to cut its losses. After consulting State Department representatives, the Foreign Relations Committee redrafted the bill in the light of objections raised in the House. The committee added five amendments to tighten up the administration of the aid and bolstered the justification for the full $350 million. During the debate, Vandenberg made it clear that this was the last foreign aid authorization he expected to support during the session. An attempt on the floor to add amendments paralleling the House action was defeated, 64 to 19, and the committee bill passed, 79 to 4. The bill then went to the conference committee, which sustained the Senate's action, except that it included the names of recipients.[29]

The Senate accepted the committee action, but a motion in the House to recommit the report precipitated another floor fight on May 21. This time, 33 House Republicans (20 from coastal states), all of whom had voted earlier for restrictive amendments, switched to support the conference report, and the recommittal motion was defeated.[30]

The Administration thus recorded a second substantial achievement in legislation concerning foreign policy. It had had a more difficult time with parsimonious Republicans in the House because there was not the atmosphere of crisis that had affected the

28. U.S. *Congressional Record*, 80th Cong., 1st sess., 1947, XCIII, Part 3, p. 4292.

29. Pratt, "Leadership Relations in Foreign Policy Making," 70–71; Westerfield, *Foreign Policy and Party Politics*, 273; U.S. *Congressional Record*, 80th Cong., 1st sess., 1947, XCIII, Part 4, p. 5245.

30. Pratt, "Leadership Relations in Foreign Policy Making," 76–77. The Republicans who switched were Anderson, Bradley, Bramblett, Fletcher, Gearhart, and Welch of California; Foote and Seely-Brown of Connecticut; Goff of Idaho; Dirksen and Stratton of Illinois; Cole and Hope of Kansas; Hale of Maine; Herter of Massachusetts; Devitt of Minnesota; Kean of New Jersey; Gamble, E. A. Hall, L. W. Hall, Latham, McMahon, Nodar, and Ross of New York; Bolton, Burke, Lewis, and Vorys of Ohio; Case and Mundt of South Dakota; Holmes and Jones of Washington; and Kersten of Wisconsin.

Greek-Turkish proposal and because the Administration was unable to place the measure in an anticommunist framework—Indeed, the Soviet satellites Poland and Hungary were among the aid recipients. The State Department's willingness to agree to amendments restricting the way in which it would administer the relief contributed to gaining legislative support, but even more crucial was Vandenberg's support (the result of two years of painstaking cultivation by the Administration), the force of the Senate's action, and Vandenberg's assurance that these were to be the final dollars spent on foreign aid during the session.

In another important area, the Administration had all but secured Senate support for the peace treaties with Italy, Hungary, Rumania, and Bulgaria long before they were presented for ratification. Assuring this support was accomplished by including Vandenberg and Connally, the ranking members of the Senate Foreign Relations Committee, in the delegation that negotiated the treaties at the Paris Foreign Ministers Conference in April and May, 1946. Thus, Vandenberg's experience at the negotiations supported his argument that although the treaties were not completely satisfactory, they were the best that could be obtained.[31]

Only the Italian treaty met opposition, which was based on three arguments that reflected concern about a communist threat and a belief that the terms were overly harsh toward Italy. Senator J. William Fulbright believed that ratifying the treaty and thus providing for withdrawal of U.S. troops would leave Italy vulnerable to a communist takeover similar to the one that had occurred in Hungary on May 30. Senator Styles Bridges of New Hampshire spoke for those senators whose large Italian constituencies made the issue politically ticklish. Recalling that the United States had promised generous terms to the Italian people if they would overthrow Mussolini and support the Allies, he contended that the treaty was excessively punitive. Finally, a few senators, led by Kenneth Wherry, objected because the Soviet Union had de-

31. U.S. *Congressional Record*, 80th Cong., 1st sess., 1947, XCIII, Part 5, pp. 6227–32.

manded reparations that the United States and Britain had forsworn. Thus, they envisioned a weakened Italy turning to the United States for economic aid, which would go right through Italy and into Russian hands in the form of reparations.[32]

Neither Republicans nor Democrats, however, were willing to repudiate their leaders on this point. The Senate defeated, 76 to 22, a motion sponsored by Senator Fulbright to delay consideration for six months, and then it ratified the treaty, 79 to 10 (7 Republicans and 3 Democrats opposed). Approval of the other treaties came by voice vote without debate.[33]

The final measure involving foreign policy, as well as national defense, that the first session considered was unification of the armed services into a single Department of Defense. Although Truman had requested such action in December, 1945, opposition by the Navy barred legislation. Finally, in January, 1947, the Secretaries of the Army and the Navy advised the President that they had reached agreement on a unification plan. Truman immediately informed Congress of the agreement, and an Administration bill was ready by February 26. Although the Armed Services committees amended the measure to provide less flexibility for the President and the new department, the final enactment was approved by the President and passed both houses by voice vote with little debate.[34]

Legislative-executive cooperation on matters of foreign policy and national defense during the first session was limited primarily by the enduring strains of isolation and by pressures to reduce Federal Government expenditures. The reciprocal-trade compromise proved to be only a delaying action. Major difficulties were experienced in securing congressional approval for the $350 mil-

32. *Ibid.*, pp. 6248, 6327, 6330.
33. *Ibid.*, pp. 6408–9, 6415, 6420, 6427.
34. Truman, *Years of Trial and Hope*, 49–52; Letter to the President of the Senate and to the Speaker of the House Concerning Creation of a Department of National Defense, January 18, 1947, *Public Papers: Truman*, 1947, 101–2; Letter to the President of the Senate and to the Speaker of the House Transmitting Draft of National Security Act, February 26, 1947, *ibid.*, 153; James E. Webb to M. C. Latta, August 4, 1947, Truman Papers, OF 1285; *The New York Times*, July 10, 1947, p. 1.

lion for post-UNRRA relief, and the House especially demonstrated great reluctance to go along with the Administration's proposals. While the Administration's presentation of the situation gave congressmen little choice but to support the President's proposal to aid Greece and Turkey, legislators had serious misgivings, and many rejected the wider implications of the Truman Doctrine.

Attempts in the House to modify the proposal for post-UNRRA relief indicated that the Administration might face future difficulties with this body. Unlike the Senate, the House did not have a traditional role of responsibility in foreign policy. Its Foreign Affairs Committee lacked the prestige of its Senate counterpart, and the lower body lacked a powerful internationalist leader like Vandenberg. Moreover, House leaders refused to support vigorously the decisions of the Foreign Affairs Committee, which allowed representatives to reflect localistic concerns. Finally, the House procedure of limited debate often led to quick decisions based upon inadequate discussion.[35]

Nonetheless, the Administration's successes in the areas of foreign policy and national defense were considerable. Unification of the armed forces and ratification of the four peace treaties were obtained with little difficulty. The reciprocal-trade compromise enabled the Administration to enter into the General Agreement on Tariffs and Trade, which the President called a "landmark in the history of international relations."[36] Enough Republicans supported the Administration on post-UNRRA relief to fulfill the U.S. commitment to European countries shattered by war. And, in the most crucial action during the first session, large congressional majorities approved Greek-Turkish aid, thereby supporting a major reorientation of U.S. foreign policy.

Any explanation of these developments must give substantial credit to the Administration's cultivation of Republican leaders and its willingness to make concessions on its proposals, as well

35. Carroll, *The House and Foreign Affairs*, 8, 90–91, 243, 251, 267.
36. Statement by the President on the General Agreement on Tariffs and Trade, October 29, 1947, *Public Papers: Truman*, 1947, 480.

as to Vandenberg's ability to persuade Republicans to support his commitments. The paramount factor, however, was the Administration's emphasis on the presumed direct threat to U.S. security posed by the expansion of communism, a threat that could be countered only by congressional support of the Administration's international programs.

CHAPTER 4

CONFLICT OVER DOMESTIC POLICY

HAVING PASSED the major foreign-policy bills, Congress began to put the final touches on its domestic program. The tenuous lines of legislative-executive cooperation broke at this point, and Truman abandoned his conciliatory posture. Presented with tax and labor legislation inimical to his views, the President responded with vigorous vetoes. In addition, he assumed the offensive, criticizing the Republican leadership, demanding action on reform legislation, and strenuously attacking appropriations cuts. By the end of the session, congressional leaders were bitterly assailing the President, and although he was less acrimonious, Truman had dealt a series of sharp blows to the Republican majority.

A number of factors dictated the shift in presidential strategy. Congressional attempts to alter tax and labor policies gave Truman no choice but to defend the position he had taken in January. Moreover, his cooperative attitude had produced little firm support for his domestic proposals, for the Republicans seemed determined to press for their own program and to ignore the President's requests. Just as important, however, were political considerations, and they hold the reasons for Truman's moving beyond a mere defense of existing programs and toward an offensive strategy.

Since the defeat of November, 1946, a small, tightly knit group of liberals within the Administration had been endeavoring to commit the President to a consistent and coherent program of domestic reform and at the same time improve his chances for re-election in 1948. This group included Clark Clifford, Federal Security Agency Director Oscar R. Ewing, Leon Keyserling of the Council of Economic Advisers, Assistant Secretary of Labor David A. Morse, and Charles S. Murphy, an administrative assistant. They met each week to establish positions on various domestic issues, and then each would work independently to commit the President to the agreed-upon course of action. This group clearly influenced several actions of the President during the remainder of the first session. At the same time, Truman's political advisers became increasingly aware of threats to his renomination. On June 2, Gael Sullivan, executive director of the Democratic National Committee, submitted a confidential memo demonstrating the popularity of Henry A. Wallace as a possible presidential candidate. The report dealt with Wallace's speaking campaign against Greek-Turkish aid, pointed out that Democratic leaders throughout the country now took him seriously, and recommended action to appease Wallace or undermine his strength. Thus, by early June, 1947, Truman was made increasingly aware of the political advantages—even necessity—of his assumption of a new role: vigorous defender of the common man against a reactionary Congress dominated by special interests.[1]

Truman took the offensive in domestic policy on May 19, when he sent a special message urging Congress to give immediate attention to a national health-insurance program. Although the President had first proposed such a program in November, 1945, he had failed to exert himself in its behalf, and the Democratic-controlled Seventy-ninth Congress had taken no action. In 1947 there was little likelihood that a Republican majority would be any more sympathetic. However, when Senator James E. Murray of Montana, an original sponsor of the program, indicated that he would introduce a new version of the bill, Truman decided to reassert his commitment to health insurance and asked Murray to delay introduction of his bill until the President could send a special request to Congress. The primary objective was to delineate clearly between the President's program of nationwide insurance and a measure introduced by Republican Senators Taft, Smith, Joseph H. Ball of Minnesota, and Forrest C. Donnell of Missouri, which provided federal assistance in medical care only for the poor. In a radio speech on June 3, Democratic Senator J. Howard

1. Cabell Phillips, *The Truman Presidency: The History of a Triumphant Succession*, 162–65; Patrick Anderson, *The President's Men; White House Assistants of Franklin D. Roosevelt, Harry S. Truman, Dwight D. Eisenhower, John F. Kennedy, and Lyndon B. Johnson*, 93, 94, 116–17; Gael Sullivan, "Memo re. Wallace Situation," June 2, 1947, Clark M. Clifford Papers, Subject File. Keyserling's draft of a veto message on the portal bill suggests that this group of Administration liberals tried unsuccessfully to persuade the President to reject the measure.

McGrath, who supported the Administration, emphasized the differences in the two programs, and in July, 1947, a group of Democratic senators began to take steps to turn the issue of medical care to advantage in the 1948 campaign.[2]

Truman continued the offensive in his press conference of June 5 by reading a statement that attacked Republican leader Taft's "fallacious and dangerous" economic views. Notably, two members of the liberal group in the Administration—Clifford and Keyserling—drafted the statement. The occasion for Truman's criticism was a reported statement by Taft that "apparently the President and the administration are abandoning talk of keeping prices down in favor of heavy spending abroad that will keep them up." In response to Taft's charges, Truman maintained that the Administration realized that foreign aid would contribute to inflationary pressures but that such aid was paramount to the effects it might have on the domestic economy. Noting that the Administration had no authority to control prices, he went on to blast Taft for his "defeatist economic philosophy" that followed "the old idea of boom and bust."[3]

The President's speech of June 7 at the reunion of the 35th Division at Kansas City further indicated the differences between the Administration and the congressional majority. Besides repeating his demand for a national health-insurance program, Truman also called for action to raise the minimum wage, extend social security, provide adequate housing, and follow "prudent

2. Monte M. Poen, "The Truman Administration and National Health Insurance" (Ph.D. dissertation, University of Missouri—Columbia, 1967), 73–80, 112–19; Special Message to the Congress on Health and Disability Insurance, May 19, 1947, *Public Papers of the Presidents of the United States: Harry S. Truman*, 1947, 250–52; Murray to J. Howard McGrath, May 14, 1947, J. Howard McGrath Papers, Senatorial File; Summary of the National Health Act of 1947 (S.545), U.S. Federal Security Agency (Office of the Administrator), Files, Record Group 235, File 011.4 (Health Insurance); J. Howard McGrath, radio speech, "What Should the Congress do About Health Insurance," June 3, 1947, McGrath Papers, Senatorial File. McGrath called the Republican bill an "attempted fraud on the public. . . . It *pretends* to solve *your* medical care problems but actually doles out help only if *you* are willing to publicly ask for charity." Senators Wagner, Murray, Chavez, Taylor, Pepper, and McGrath to Gael Sullivan, July 23, 1947, McGrath Papers, Senatorial File.

3. The President's News Conference of June 5, 1947, *Public Papers: Truman*, 1947, 263–64; Keyserling to Clifford, undated, Clifford Papers, Subject File.

fiscal and tax policies." But the major part of his speech was devoted to natural resources and agriculture, specifically the House appropriations cuts in these programs. He warned of the grave danger facing conservation programs if Congress failed to provide adequate funds for their administration, and he called upon the Senate to restore House cuts in conservation, reclamation, and power programs. Concerning agriculture, Truman warned, "We should guard against all efforts to destroy the program designed to carry out soil conservation practices on our farms." Truman used such statements in an attempt to bring public pressure to bear on the Congress and at the same time to make his position on these federal programs absolutely clear.[4]

Meanwhile, the Republican tax bill was making its way through the final stages of legislation. The Administration had consistently opposed tax reduction. Responding to the advice of his Council of Economic Advisers, who rejected a tax cut primarily on inflationary grounds, the President had counseled against tax reduction in his message on the budget in January, in his Jefferson Day speech of April 5, and in his press conference of May 13. In addition, Secretary of the Treasury John Snyder argued the Administration's case against lowering taxes before the House Ways and Means Committee on March 13 and the Senate Finance Committee on April 22. To strengthen his case, Snyder conferred with the ranking Democrat on the House committee, Robert L. Doughton of North Carolina, and asked for suggestions on his presentation.[5]

Nonetheless, the Republicans persisted in their determination to enact a tax cut. The efforts of Harold Knutson, chairman of the Ways and Means Committee, to commit his party to a 20 per cent across-the-board cut in personal income taxes was only partially successful. In order to meet the demands of other Repub-

4. Address in Kansas City at the 35th Division Reunion Memorial Service, June 7, 1947, *Public Papers: Truman, 1947*, 269–71.

5. Council of Economic Advisers to Truman, April 4, 1947, Harry S. Truman Papers, OF 985; Address at the Jefferson Day Dinner, April 5, 1947, *Public Papers: Truman, 1947*, 195–96; The President's Special Conference with the Association of Radio News Analysts, May 13, 1947, *ibid.*, 241; *The New York Times*, March 14, 1947, p. 1, April 23, 1947, pp. 1, 15; Snyder to Doughton, March 10, 1947, Robert L. Doughton Papers.

licans for greater relief in the lower income brackets and to assure united Republican support for a tax measure, the House leaders forced Knutson to compromise. The result was a committee bill that provided for a 30 per cent cut on incomes below $1,000; 30 to 20 per cent in the $1,000–$1,396 bracket; 20 per cent in the $1,396–$302,000 bracket; and 10 per cent on incomes above $302,000. For persons over sixty-five, the personal exemption was increased from $500 to $1,000, and the tax reduction was to be retroactive to January, 1947. A vigorous statement of minority views was signed by 9 of the 10 Democrats on the committee.[6]

Arguments in support of the measure cited its long-range and short-range economic implications and the political principle upon which it was based. In the long run, maintained its advocates, the kind of tax reduction provided in H.R. 1 would contribute to a high level of employment and business activity by strengthening managerial and investment incentive. In the short run, the bill would serve as a "hedge against recession and cumulative deflation." Finally, some Republicans justified the bill as a means of reversing the spending policies of the New Deal by forcing government retrenchment and reversing the New Deal's policy of income redistribution through a progressive income tax.[7]

Opponents of the bill attacked its timing and the form of relief provided. Balancing the budget and providing for substantial debt reduction, they asserted, should receive the highest priority, and it was much too early to determine what total government expenditures would be. Since labor and material shortages, not lack of venture capital or markets, were limiting production, tax reduction would not contribute to substantial economic expansion. Indeed, its probable effect would be to add to the already danger-

6. *The New York Times*, March 19, 1947, p. 21; Clifford Hope to Bruce Richardson, March 22, 1947, Clifford R. Hope Papers, Legislative Correspondence; John M. Vorys to William Schneider, March 29, 1947, John M. Vorys Papers; U.S. House of Representatives, Committee on Ways and Means, *Individual Income Tax Reduction Act of 1947*, House Report 180 to accompany H.R. 1, 80th Cong., 1st sess., 1947.

7. *Ibid.*, 1; U.S. Senate, Committee on Finance, *Individual Income Tax Reduction Act of 1947*, Senate Report 173 to accompany H.R. 1, 80th Cong., 1st sess., 1947, 9; A. E. Holmans, *United States Fiscal Policy, 1945–1959: Its Contributions to Economic Stability*, 68.

ous inflationary pressures. Furthermore, premature tax cuts would jeopardize a much-needed thorough revision of the whole tax structure that could be carried out when economic conditions warranted reduction. Finally, opponents argued, the kind of reduction provided for in H.R. 1 was inequitable because it discriminated against low-income groups. In short, according to Democratic spokesman Doughton, the bill was "a hurriedly conceived untimely, discriminatory, and unsound patchwork of political expediency."[8]

All of these arguments were voiced in the House, which debated the measure on March 26 and 27. Only one debater did not follow his party's line—Albert J. Engel, Republican from Michigan. He objected primarily to the bill's failure to provide more equitable relief for low-income groups, and he, Howard H. Buffett of Nebraska, and H. Carl Andersen of Minnesota were the only three Republicans who opposed the bill. The votes of 40 Democrats, 33 of them from the South or from border states, and those of the Republican majority passed the measure, 273 to 137.[9]

The Senate Finance Committee delayed consideration of H.R. 1, hoping that the Senate and House might agree on the legislative budget first. By mid-April, however, compromise seemed impossible, and prospects for a substantial budget surplus at the end of fiscal 1947 (July 1, 1947) seemed good. Thus the committee began study of the bill. The draft reported on May 10 made two major changes in the House bill: The effective date was delayed to July, 1947, and a new income bracket was inserted—$79,700–$302,400—for which the reduction was to be 15 per cent instead of the 20 per cent that the House had provided. Prospects for enactment rose as influential Democrat Walter F. George of Georgia voted with Republicans on the committee to report the bill.[10]

Debate on the Senate floor mirrored the arguments advanced in

8. U.S. House, Committee on Ways and Means, *Individual Income Tax Reduction Act of 1947*, 31–33, 38, 42; *The New York Times*, April 23, 1947, pp. 1, 15; U.S. *Congressional Record*, 80th Cong., 1st sess., 1947, XCIII, Part 2, p. 2642.

9. *Ibid.*, pp. 2627–83, 2739–75.

10. *The New York Times*, April 11, 1947, p. 1, May 10, 1947, p. 1; U.S. Senate, Committee on Finance, *Individual Income Tax Reduction Act of 1947*, 1, 3.

the House, but Democratic efforts in the Senate also involved attempts to delay consideration until June 10, when the fiscal situation would be clearer. The minority leaders took extraordinary steps to get solid Democratic support for this approach. Although they were successful and even garnered the votes of Republicans Wayne Morse and George A. Wilson of Iowa, the motion was defeated, 48 to 44. Another Democrat, John L. McClellan of Arkansas, then moved to amend H.R. 1 to allow husbands and wives in all states to split their income for federal tax purposes, a privilege that only persons in community-property states could then enjoy. Republicans opposed this amendment, contending that a proposal for major revision did not belong in a simple tax reduction bill, but they promised that it would be given consideration next year. Neither the White House nor Democratic leaders supported the amendment, and it was defeated, 51 to 29. The 29 votes were cast by 8 Republicans and 21 Democrats. The third Democratic effort to modify the Republican plan for tax revision was a substitute plan introduced by Democratic Whip Scott W. Lucas of Illinois, again without the support of the President or Democratic leaders. Lucas' amendment, which would have become effective in January, 1948, provided for an increase of $100 in personal exemptions, extension of the community-property principle for federal taxes to all states, and reduction of the surtax rates by 2 per cent in all brackets. This measure offered more relief for low-income groups than did H.R. 1, won the support of 27 Democrats and Republican Langer, but was defeated, 58 to 28.[11]

Having disposed of these amendments, the Senate passed the bill, 52 to 34, a tally that was 6 votes short of the two-thirds majority necessary to override a veto. Roll calls on the bill and proposed amendments indicated much Republican cohesion and Democratic disunity on this politically sensitive issue. Only two Republicans, Langer and Cooper, voted No, and a third, Wayne Morse, was paired against. On the other hand, 7 Democrats, 6 of

<hr/>

11. Alben Barkley, telegram to Elbert D. Thomas, May 22, 1947, Thomas to H. L. Marshall, May 28, 1947, Elbert D. Thomas Papers, General File; Scott W. Lucas to Burnet Maybank, May 23, 1947, Burnet R. Maybank Papers, Legislative File; U.S. *Congressional Record,* 80th Cong., 1st sess., 1947, XCIII, Part 5, pp. 5803, 5839, 5865, 5930–31, 5935.

them Southerners, voted for the Republican bill. The large number of Democratic votes for the McClellan and Lucas amendments, 21 and 28 respectively, revealed that many Democrats favored tax reduction in some form and that the Republicans might enact a tax cut in spite of Truman's opposition if they could compromise by providing more relief for lower income groups and including an income-splitting provision.[12]

The conference committee that was appointed to adjust differences between the House and Senate versions did little to win additional Democratic support. It accepted the Senate provision for making the effective date July 1, 1947, and made a token gesture toward more equitable relief by decreasing the amount of the tax reduction from the House figure of 20 per cent to 15 per cent for incomes between $136,720 and $302,400. In the House, Robert Doughton and 36 other Democrats voted for the bill, which passed, 220 to 99. The Senate passed H.R. 1, 48 to 28, with Democratic desertions remaining consistent.[13]

Sentiment within the Administration was almost unanimous. Of the executive officials polled, only Federal Works Director Fleming approved of the bill, while the Bureau of the Budget, Council of Economic Advisers, governors of the Federal Reserve Board, and secretaries of the Treasury, Commerce, State, and War all recommended disapproval. On June 16, President Truman issued his first veto of legislation enacted by the Eightieth Congress. He insisted that since inflationary pressures were still high, the time was not right for tax reduction, that there was no indication that a recession was imminent, that tax cuts were not necessary to promote economic expansion, and that all efforts should be made to preserve the integrity of the public debt by reducing it while levels of employment and income were high.

12. *Ibid.*, pp. 5945, 5949. Democrats voting for H.R. 1 were George (Georgia), Hoey (North Carolina), McCarran (Nevada), O'Conor (Maryland), O'Daniel (Texas), Stewart (Tennessee), and Umstead (North Carolina). McKellar (Tennessee) was paired for. Burnet R. Maybank to George E. Dargan, July 18, 1947, Maybank Papers; Robert L. Doughton to J. R. Fain, May 1, 1947, Doughton to C. A. Cannon, July 28, 1947, Doughton Papers.

13. *The New York Times*, May 30, 1947, pp. 1, 2, June 3, 1947, p. 19, June 4, 1947, p. 25.

Furthermore, the kind of reduction in H.R. 1 was "neither fair nor equitable" because it granted savings of less than $30 in the $2,000 bracket and almost $5,000 in the $50,000 bracket.[14]

The House attempt to override the veto failed to obtain a two-thirds majority by two votes. Those who voted to override were 35 Democrats, including 26 Southerners, and 233 Republicans. Republican Representatives H. Carl Andersen of Minnesota and Merlin Hull of Wisconsin voted with 134 Democrats and 1 American Laborite to sustain. The President's opposition influenced 8 Democrats—7 of them Southerners—to vote to sustain the veto. Doughton, who had supported the conference report, was one of the Southerners who voted to sustain.[15]

While Republicans debated whether to make another attempt to reduce taxes, the President was reaching a decision on labor legislation, the Republicans' other major goal. Some form of legislation to restrict organized labor was almost inevitable. Employer associations had been trying to obtain amendments to the Wagner act since 1937, and they stepped up their endeavors after the war ended. They received support from the public after the wave of postwar strikes that caused much inconvenience and after the wage increases that seemed to account for rising prices. Although work stoppages had decreased substantially by 1947, a series of strikes in the maritime, coal, and telephone industries kept the labor issue in the news. Unions themselves were partly responsible for the climate favoring restrictions on organized labor. Arbitrary rule by union leaders, jurisdictional strikes, strikes in violation of contract, and denial of equal membership to Negroes had incurred public criticism, but the criticism had produced no efforts to reform labor from within, but only a defensive reaction against all proposals for labor reform. Congress was not alone in feeling the pressures for antiunion legislation; in 1947, more

14. Letters on H.R. 1, U.S. Bureau of the Budget Files, Reports to the President on Pending Legislation; Letters on tax reduction, Clifford Papers, H.R. 3950; Veto of Bill to Reduce Income Taxes, June 16, 1947, *Public Papers: Truman, 1947,* 279–81.

15. U.S. *Congressional Record,* 80th Cong., 1st sess., 1947, XCIII, Part 6, p. 7143.

than twenty state legislatures enacted laws to restrict union activities of one kind or another.[16]

Following the elections of 1946, the Administration began to prepare its position on labor legislation. Formulation of a policy was not easy. If the President sent up a draft bill that Congress could use as a basis for much harsher legislation, Clark Clifford and David Morse argued, the public might think that the Administration endorsed "whatever monstrosity might result." If the President made no recommendations and then vetoed labor legislation, he would be accused of negativism. The dilemma, as Clifford expressed it, was, "How to be positive and yet not do any group any harm." In fact, the Administration could offer no program guaranteed to eliminate major strikes without seriously crippling labor's newly won power. The Administration resolved the dilemma by letting the initiative pass to Congress.

Truman preferred a very general statement that relied on the position he had taken when he vetoed the Case bill in 1946. Then, he had stated that major legislation should await careful and detailed study of the whole area of labor's status in the economy and that he preferred to leave the machinery of such an examination to Congress. To this recommendation, Truman added the Department of Labor's proposals for legislation to prohibit certain unjustifiable practices. Thus the program outlined in his State of the Union message placed Truman in favor of some very mild restrictions on labor. Privately, few people thought that Congress would be receptive to such a limited program. Clifford believed there was only one chance in fifteen that Congress would establish the commission to study labor-management relations. As for the other proposals, he felt that some had little chance of acceptance by the legislature and others were "relatively worthless in the sense of achieving [the] end of big strikes." Truman's failure to exert himself in behalf of his proposals reflected this point of view. He

16. Harry A. Millis and Emily Clark Brown, *From the Wagner Act to Taft-Hartley: A Study of National Labor Policy and Labor Relations*, 290–91, 314–15; R. Alton Lee, *Truman and Taft-Hartley; A Question of Mandate*, 8–11, 28–31; Joel I. Seidman, *American Labor from Defense to Reconversion*, 254; Joseph G. Rayback, *A History of American Labor*, 396.

rejected a suggestion of White House aide John R. Steelman that he defend the National Labor Relations Act and underscore his own position by sending congratulations to its sponsor, Senator Robert F. Wagner on the twelfth anniversary of the law. Moreover, individual congressmen introduced measures embodying the President's recommendations, but no Administration draft reached the Hill until the Taft-Hartley bill was almost through the Senate.[17]

Within the Administration, only the National Labor Relations Board and occasionally the Department of Labor made genuine efforts to encourage those congressmen who were sympathetic to the Administration's point of view. Immediately after the November elections, Chairman of the Board Paul M. Herzog suggested to the President that a bipartisan approach to labor legislation might be worked out. Specifically, Herzog arranged a meeting in Albany, New York, on November 19 with newly elected Republican Senator Irving Ives, who in the New York legislature had been influential in a similar, and successful, approach. After the meeting and conversations with Republican senators, Herzog was optimistic about the possibilities of bipartisanship. Ives did take a moderate approach on the Republican labor bill, but the bipartisanship never materialized, in part because few congressional Republicans sympathized with the Administration's point of view, and in part because Truman failed to push it. The NLRB actively provided information for sympathetic congressmen, including Senators Pepper, Morse, and Ives, and both the Board and the

17. Elsey, notes on the 1947 State of the Union message, undated, December 12, 1946, and January 1, 1947, George M. Elsey Papers, Speech File; Gardner to Julius A. Krug, February 25, 1947, Warner W. Gardner Papers; Bureau of the Budget Staff memo, "Current Problems in Labor Management Relations," undated, James E. Webb Papers; National Labor Relations Board, confidential memorandum to the President on Labor Legislation, December 11, 1946, Clifford Papers, Political File; Annual Message to the Congress on the State of the Union, January 6, 1947, *Public Papers: Truman*, 1947, 4–5; John R. Steelman to Clark Clifford, April 10, 1947, Truman Papers, OF 407; News release, Statement by Sponsors of Substitute Amendment for S. 1126, The Labor Bill in the Senate, Harley M. Kilgore Papers, A & M 967, University of West Virginia Library; Millis and Brown, *From the Wagner Act to Taft-Hartley*, 364, 380; Stephen K. Bailey and Howard D. Samuel, *Congress at Work*, 432.

Labor Department contributed to the House minority report on the Taft-Hartley bill. In the final analysis, however, most of the Administration's efforts in labor legislation were negative and un-coordinated. One political scientist, Seymour T. Mann, has con-cluded that "minority legislators keenly felt the lack of Pres-idential leadership during the legislative struggle. The general statements of January did not suffice. Such leadership did come at the veto state—but then it was too late."[18]

Both the House and Senate held extensive hearings on labor legislation in February and March, although some evidence sug-gests that the House bill was drafted before the hearings were concluded. Almost 140 witnesses appeared before the House com-mittee, and the Senate committee heard testimony from almost 100 representatives of management, labor, the Administration, and the public. Administration officials backed the position out-lined in the State of the Union message, while most of the labor representatives refused to concede that any amendments to the Wagner act were necessary. By April 9, Republicans on the House Labor Committee had prepared a bill that had the approval of the House leaders. The bill, called the Hartley bill, was quickly rammed through the committee, which reported it two days later without change. The majority report maintained that the bill was necessary to decrease industrial strife, to equalize labor-manage-ment relations, and to rescue the worker who had "for the past fourteen years, as a result of labor laws ill-conceived and disas-trously executed . . . been deprived of his dignity as an individual." Although minority members of the committee had only two days to prepare their report, they produced a lengthy and detailed analysis of the bill and concluded that it was "designed to wreck the living standards of the American people" and that it would only bring industrial chaos. Only 6 Democrats signed the minority report; the other 4—Graham A. Barden of North Carolina, O. C.

---

18. Herzog to Truman, November 7, 1946, Truman Papers, OF 407; Herzog to Ives, November, 1946, Paul M. Herzog Papers, Personal Correspondence; Herzog to Truman, December 16, 1946, Clifford Papers, Political File; Seymour T. Mann, "Policy Formation in the Executive Branch: The Taft-Hartley Experience," *Western Political Quarterly*, 13 (September, 1960), 598, 606–7; Bailey and Samuel, *Congress at Work*, 428.

Fisher and Wingate Lucas of Texas, and John S. Wood of Georgia —voted with the Republicans.[19]

The House quickly ratified the work of its committee, adding only three amendments, all of which stiffened the bill's provisions. Most of the opposition to the bill came from Democrats, but a number of Republicans attempted without success to amend the bill. Kenneth B. Keating of New York, Charles W. Vursell of Illinois, Edith Nourse Rogers of Massachusetts, William G. Stratton of Illinois, and other Republicans expressed dissatisfaction with various provisions but indicated their intentions to vote for the bill with the expectation that the Senate would modify harsher parts of it. After defeating a motion to recommit, 291 to 122, the House passed the bill on April 17 by an overwhelming vote of 308 to 107. Voting against were 22 Republicans, 84 Democrats, and 1 American Laborite, while 93 Democrats, including 79 Southerners, voted with the Republican majority.[20]

The Hartley bill provided for sweeping changes in national labor policy. It abolished the closed shop and made the union shop a subject of collective bargaining only if the employer agreed. Jurisdictional strikes and secondary boycotts were outlawed, industry-wide bargaining banned, and unions subjected to anti-trust legislation. The bill provided for federal injunctions against strikes harmful to the public welfare and permitted employers to seek injunctions in other cases. The National Labor Relations Board was replaced by three separate agencies to handle administration, prosecution, and conciliation. Detailed restrictions were imposed upon internal union activity, supervisory employees were excluded from coverage, and bargaining rights were denied unions with communist officers.[21]

19. Lee, *Truman and Taft-Hartley*, 61–63; *The New York Times*, January 29, 1947, p. 1, February 19, 1947, p. 1, February 20, 1947, pp. 1, 3, April 11, 1947, p. 6, April 12, 1947, p. 1; U.S. House of Representatives, Committee on Education and Labor, *Labor-Management Relations Act*, 1947, House Report 245 to accompany H.R. 3020, 80th Cong., 1st sess., 1947, 3–5, 64–65.

20. *The New York Times*, April 18, 1947, pp. 1, 6. See amendments proposed by Landis (Republican, Indiana), Lodge (Republican, Connecticut), and Javits (Republican, New York) in U.S. *Congressional Record*, 80th Cong., 1st sess., 1947, XCIII, Part 3, pp. 3570–75, 3619, 3634–35, 3637–45, 3661, 3671.

21. Millis and Brown, *From the Wagner Act to Taft-Hartley*, 383–84.

While the House took final action on the labor bill, the Senate measure was still in its infancy. As the bill progressed through the Senate, three major groups became discernible. A relatively small group of Administration Democrats, joined by Republicans Morse and Langer, opposed practically the entire measure. These Senators, however, joined a group of moderate Democrats and Republicans to force a third group, led by Taft, to compromise or eliminate some of the bill's harsher provisions.

In the Senate Labor Committee, Taft was unable to push his bill through with the ease experienced by his counterparts in the House. In fact, the committee bill ultimately reflected various ideas of each of the three groups. Democrats Murray, Pepper, Elbert D. Thomas of Utah, and Lister Hill of Alabama, and Republican Wayne Morse represented the Administration and voted against the final version; Republicans Ives, Aiken, and occasionally Smith, were members of the moderates who, with the first group, attempted to eliminate more drastic provisions but who ultimately supported the bill; and Republicans Taft, Ball, Donnell, and William E. Jenner of Indiana belonged to the group that wanted severe restrictions on labor. Democrat Allen J. Ellender of Louisiana shifted from the third to the second group when the bill came to the floor. By votes of 7 to 6 and 8 to 5, the first two groups managed to eliminate four major provisions of the Taft bill: those that would (1) put limitations on industry-wide bargaining, (2) allow private persons to seek injunctions against secondary boycotts and jurisdictional strikes, (3) make "coercion," "restraint," or "interference" unfair union activities, and (4) eliminate the involuntary checkoff of union dues and limit employers' contributions to union welfare funds. An attempt to split the omnibus measure into separate bills, however, failed. According to Aiken, 9 of the 13 committee members supported such an approach, but pressure from Republican leaders persuaded 3 members to switch their votes. Thus, the majority refused to give Truman the opportunity to veto some provisions and approve others. Having eliminated the harsher provisions, 10 committee members supported the bill, but Taft, Ball, Donnell, Jenner, and Smith filed supplemental views and indicated that they would introduce amendments on the floor to reverse the decisions they had lost in committee. They planned to offer four amendments, but Smith favored only three of them. Thomas, Murray, and Pepper filed minority views opposing the bill.[22]

On the Senate floor, the Taft group's efforts to reinsert the harsher provisions received most of the attention. The Senate rejected by a large majority a Ball-Byrd-Donnell-George amendment, which Taft had already abandoned as the result of a private poll of Senate Republicans, to allow private individuals to seek injunctions against secondary boycotts and jurisdictional strikes. By a much narrower margin, 44 to 43, a coalition of 16 Republicans and 28 Democrats voted down an amendment to restrict industry-wide bargaining. If Taft and his supporters had rounded up absentees, the amendment could have passed, but Taft declined to insist on this provision in order not to endanger final passage of the bill. On the remaining amendments, most of the middle group shifted to vote with those who favored greater restrictions. An amendment to require joint administration of union welfare funds and individual authorization for checkoff of union dues was adopted, 48 to 40. After eliminating much of the opposition by striking out the word "interference," Taft secured approval for an amendment to make union coercion or restraint an unfair labor practice by a vote of 60 to 28. Finally, Taft's amendment to allow employers to sue unions for damages in jurisdictional strikes and secondary boycotts passed, 65 to 26. After defeating, 73 to 19, a substitute bill that 10 Northern Democrats introduced and that contained the substance of Truman's recommendations, the Senate passed the Taft bill, 68 to 24.[23]

The Taft bill was a remarkable achievement. It testified to the extraordinary political skill of its sponsor, for unlike the House leaders, Taft had only a slim Republican majority in a Senate that reflected more urban and liberal views than did the House, and the situation was repeated in microcosm in the Senate Labor

22. *The New York Times*, April 15, 1947, p. 1, April 16, 1947, p. 1, April 29, 1947, pp. 1, 20; U.S. Senate, Committee on Labor and Public Welfare, *Federal Labor Relations Act of 1947*, Senate Report 105 to accompany S. 1126, 80th Cong., 1st sess., 1947, 50–56; *ibid.*, Part II, "Minority Views," 42.
23. U.S. *Congressional Record*, 80th Cong., 1st sess., 1947, XCIII, Part 4, pp. 4270–71, 4442, 4676, 4754, 4847, 4874, 5117; *The New York Times*, May 9, 1947, p. 20; Durham to R. T. Amos, July 14, 1947, Carl T. Durham Papers.

Committee. His adroit maneuvering and ability to gauge Senate sentiment, compromising when necessary, enabled him to secure widest possible support for the bill. And getting the bill passed was not the end of his job. As the bill went to conference, he had to keep the Senate bill unencumbered by restrictive House provisions in order to conserve the support in the upper house necessary to override a possible veto.

Many factors favored acceptance of the Senate view. A number of representatives had voted for the Hartley bill with reservations and expectations that the Senate would tone down the bill. Moreover, Hartley himself suggested that the House leaders purposely included harsh provisions, which they intended ultimately to abandon, in order to set an example for the Senate and to diffuse the opposition when he stated, "It is sometimes good legislative practice to include among a bill's provisions at least one that is obviously undesirable, unworkable, or unconstitutional. By doing so, you draw the opposition fire against the particular provision rather than against the measure as a whole." At the close of the conference, Hartley said, "We deliberately put everything we could into the House bill so we could have something to concede and still get an adequate bill in the end."[24]

Taft's announcements to the press at the end of each conference meeting contributed to the impression that the "mild" Senate bill would prevail over the "harsh" House bill. Although the Senate measure was by no means mild and although the compromise bill was more restrictive than the original Senate bill, the House did make most of the concessions. The House receded from the ban on industry-wide bargaining, the limitation on employers' contributions to welfare funds, the virtual outlawing of the union shop, the making of unions subject to the antitrust laws, the authorization for injunctions and triple-damage suits by employers, and the abolition of the National Labor Relations Board. The Senate, on the other hand, conceded to the House proscriptions on strikes by government employees and on political contributions by unions.[25]

24. Fred A. Hartley, *Our New National Labor Policy; The Taft-Hartley Act and the Next Steps*, 67; Millis and Brown, *From the Wagner Act to Taft-Hartley*, 385.
25. *Ibid.*, 383–84; Gilbert Y. Steiner, *The Congressional Conference Commit-*

The House and Senate passed Taft-Hartley by large majorities and sent it to the President, who was also considering the tax-reduction bill. Besides the usual Budget Bureau canvass of interested executive departments, the Administration asked several economists and labor experts to submit their confidential views. Most recommended disapproval because the bill would greatly increase the role of the Federal Government in labor relations and would, by contributing to union insecurity, encourage industrial strife and litigation. Of those Administration officials polled by the Budget Bureau, opposition came from the NLRB, Council of Economic Advisers, and the departments of Labor and the Interior. Only the director of the Federal Works Administration suggested approval.[26]

A number of people reminded the President of the political implications of his decision. To the Clifford-Ewing-Keyserling group, vetoing Taft-Hartley was essential to enhancing Truman's image as defender of the common man, and they worked assiduously to commit the President to this course. From the Democratic National Committee came results of a poll of national committeemen: 103 favored a veto, 66 advised approval, and 4 suggested that Truman allow the bill to become law without his signature. From outside the Administration, Chester Bowles, a liberal Democrat and former director of the Office of Price Administration, exerted similar pressure. Since the Taft-Hartley bill was designed to reduce the power of labor, Truman's opposition was essential to success in the 1948 elections. If the working people lost faith in the liberalism of the Democratic party, Bowles argued, large numbers of them would vote Republican or not vote at all. A veto, however, would do much to unify labor behind the Democrats. Bowles predicted that even if the veto were overridden, the Democrats would gain a "clear political advantage." If the Administration strictly enforced it, he said, workers would

tee: *Seventieth to Eightieth Congresses*, 167–68; *The New York Times*, May 25, 1947, p. E1.

26. William H. Davis to Truman, June 15, 1947, Edwin E. Witte to Clark Clifford, undated, George W. Taylor to Clifford, June 13, 1947, E. Wight Bakke to Clifford, June 14, 1947, William M. Leiserson to Clifford, June 14, 1947, David H. Stowe Papers, Taft-Hartley Veto Message; Letters and memos, Bureau of the Budget, Reports to the President on Pending Legislation.

know in 1948 "exactly what the Republican viewpoint means in terms of their daily life and their livelihood."[27]

Truman solicited advice from Administration and party officials who represented a broad spectrum of opinion, but he did not bring up Taft-Hartley for discussion in a formal Cabinet meeting as he had the portal and tax-cut measures. Rather, he announced at the Cabinet meeting on June 20 that he had decided to veto the bill. Secretary of the Navy Forrestal and Secretary of Agriculture Anderson expressed disagreement, but Truman had already made his decision. The veto message was sent to Congress that same day.[28]

He presented his views to Congress in a detailed, lengthy analysis of the bill. Truman maintained that the bill failed to meet four major tests: (1) a decrease in government intervention in economic life, (2) improvement in labor-management relations, (3) workability, and (4) fairness. In defense of these assertions, he listed and explained nine more specific objections to the measure: (1) it would increase strikes, (2) it restricted the subjects for collective bargaining, (3) it would expose employers to many hazards, (4) it would deprive workers of necessary protections they had under existing legislation, (5) it contained many burdensome or unworkable provisions, (6) its provisions for dealing with strikes affecting the national safety were discriminatory and ineffective, (7) it discriminated against labor, (8) it disregarded the unanimous sentiment expressed at the National Labor-Management Conference in November, 1945, and (9) it raised issues of public policy that went beyond labor-management problems. The President followed his veto message with an appeal to the people in a radio address on the same evening, thereby publicizing and emphasizing his position on labor legislation.[29]

The House quickly and overwhelmingly overrode the veto, 331

27. Phillips, *The Truman Presidency*, 164–65; Keyserling to Clifford, June 3, 1947, Clifford Papers; Lee, *Truman and Taft-Hartley*, 90; Bowles to Truman, May 29, 1947, Clifford Papers.

28. James Forrestal, *The Forrestal Diaries*, Walter Millis and E. S. Duffield, eds., 280.

29. Veto of the Taft-Hartley Labor Bill, June 20, 1947, *Public Papers: Truman, 1947*, 288–97; Radio address to the American People on the Veto of the Taft-Hartley Bill, June 20, 1947, *ibid.*, 298–301.

to 83, but some hope remained that the Senate would sustain it. The initiative for sustaining came not from the White House or the minority leaders, but from organized labor and a few senators. Professing that enough votes could be changed to sustain the veto, labor leaders urged the President and the Democratic National Committee to make additional efforts. First, it was necessary to postpone the Senate vote in order to convince more senators. Democratic leader Alben Barkley was willing to agree with the Republicans to vote at 5:00 P.M. on the day of the veto. Only a filibuster by Democrats Pepper, Taylor, and Kilgore and Republican Morse postponed the vote until the following Monday, June 23. Meanwhile, Philip Murray of the CIO tried unsuccessfully to persuade Democratic leaders to bring two absent senators—Elbert Thomas, who was attending a meeting of the International Labor Organization in Europe, and Robert Wagner, who was ill in New York—back to Washington for the vote. Responding to a plea from Railroad Brotherhood official George Harrison, Truman made his only substantial effort to have the veto sustained. On January 21, he invited Democratic Senators Barkley, George, McClellan, Fulbright, Connally, Hatch, John H. Overton of Louisiana, Burnet R. Maybank of South Carolina, William B. Umstead of North Carolina, Herbert R. O'Conor of Maryland, John J. Sparkman of Alabama, and Republican Milton R. Young to the White House, where he repeated his views on the measure but asked for no commitments.[30]

On June 23, Barkley read to the Senate a last-minute letter from the President reaffirming his opposition to the bill, but the

30. U.S. *Congressional Record*, 80th Cong., 1st sess., 1947, XCIII, Part 6, p. 7489; *The New York Times*, June 21, 1947, p. 1, June 22, 1947, p. 1; Paul L. Badger to Elbert D. Thomas, June 26, 1947, Thomas Papers; Jack Redding, *Inside the Democratic Party*, 78; Truman to Charles Murphy, June 18, 1947, Charles S. Murphy Papers, White House Files; Clark Clifford, memorandum, "Vote on Labor Bill," undated, Clifford Papers; The President's Appointment Calendar, June 22, 1947, Matthew Connelly Files. Lee, *Truman and Taft-Hartley*, agrees with Redding that the Democratic National Committee made firm plans to bring Thomas and Wagner to Washington for the vote but cancelled the plans at the last minute when they found that two additional votes would be insufficient to sustain. Badger's letter indicates that although Les Biffle and Gael Sullivan were under extreme pressure from union leaders, their efforts to contact Thomas were halfhearted.

plea was to no avail. The Senate voted to override the veto, 68 to 25; 48 Republicans and 20 Democrats (17 from the South, 2 from Maryland, and 1 from New Mexico) voted to override, and 22 Democrats and 3 Republicans (Langer, Morse, and George W. Malone of Nevada) voted to sustain.[31]

The circumstances surrounding the passage of Taft-Hartley contained most of the important themes of domestic affairs in the Eightieth Congress. The bill involved a substantial Republican attack, with significant conservative Democratic support, on a major New Deal program. Republicans, however, were also divided, and the efforts of party moderates weakened the assault in the Senate. The threat of a presidential veto also contributed to the dilution of the Republican leaders' original proposals. Truman's liberal rhetoric, unsupported by thorough and vigorous action, was sufficient only to blunt the attack on federal labor policy, not to deflect it. His rhetoric and gestures did serve a crucial political purpose, for they returned labor securely and energetically to the Democratic fold and denied a big domestic issue to a possible third-party movement.

On June 26, the President issued another veto message, his third in two weeks. This veto was the result of an unusual situation in which the goals of domestic and foreign policy conflicted and in which the split within the Administration and within Congress deviated from the usual conservative-liberal pattern. A longstanding conflict in the Administration surfaced between the Department of Agriculture, which was devoted to the support of farm prices through a policy of economic nationalism, and the State Department, which adhered to the belief that the reduction of trade barriers was crucial to world peace. The specific issue was a bill to continue price supports for wool. On April 7, the Senate passed a measure to continue the program originated during the war. The program permitted the Commodity Credit Corporation to support wool prices through its commodity-loan program. Since the beginning of the program, the CCC had amassed over 460 million pounds of domestic wool. It could not dispose of the wool

31. Letter to Senator Barkley on the Attempt to Override the Taft-Hartley Veto, June 23, 1947, *Public Papers: Truman, 1947*, 305; U.S. *Congressional Record*, 80th Cong., 1st sess., 1947, XCIII, Part 6, p. 7538.

because the law prevented the CCC from selling below parity, and the market price had not risen to parity levels. The Senate bill extended the support program but provided that the CCC could sell wool below parity.[32]

Because of heavy importation of foreign wool, the government would suffer considerable loss in selling wool at the market price. Thus, Secretary of Agriculture Clinton Anderson had suggested early in 1947 that Congress place an import fee on foreign wool providing that it not run counter to any existing or future reciprocal-trade agreements. The House added an import-fee provision to the Senate bill, but it did not add Anderson's protective stipulation. The result was dismay in the State Department and immediate repercussions at Geneva, where the success of tariff negotiations depended on U.S. willingness to make concessions on wool.[33]

The conference committee kept the import-fee provision but provided that the President could impose import quotas. It also exempted wool already covered in international agreements; however, it permitted no future exemptions. Over the strong objections of Secretary of State Marshall, the House approved the bill, 191 to 166, as did the Senate, 48 to 38. The division represented old patterns in that consideration of the bill provided an opportunity for attacking the reciprocal-trade program and for suggesting a way to reduce government expenditures. Additionally, such supporters of the Administration's foreign and domestic policies as Senators Tom Connally of Texas, Sheridan Downey of California, and Joseph C. O'Mahoney of Wyoming reflected the wool-producing interests of their states by supporting the bill. Conversely, senators from states with large textile industries (and thus wool buyers) and with substantial wool trade voted against the bill.[34]

32. Allen J. Matusow, *Farm Policies and Politics in the Truman Years*, 79–94; *The New York Times*, May 24, 1947, pp. 1, 21.

33. U.S. House of Representatives, Committee on Agriculture, *Providing Support for Wool*, House Report 257 to accompany S. 814, 80th Cong., 1st sess., 1947, 1, 4; Matusow, *Farm Policies and Politics*, 95.

34. *The New York Times*, June 12, 1947, p. 1, June 17, 1947, p. 1, June 20, 1947, pp. 1, 14; Clifford R. Hope to Herb W. Hoover, June 30, 1947, Hope Papers.

Under Secretary of State Will Clayton, chairman of the U.S. delegation at Geneva, had already rushed back to Washington to oppose the bill. He had been too ill to appear before Congress, but he recovered in time to plead with Truman for a veto, arguing that the bill would "wreck the Trade Conference." The President concurred, and in his veto message, he emphasized the bill's threat to reciprocal-trade policy in general and the Geneva negotiations in particular. However, he did express approval of the original Senate measure, and the Senate promptly passed a bill free of provisions for import fees or quotas. The House leaders were furious; Majority Leader Halleck attacked Truman for refusing to "cooperate with the Congress in its program to save the taxpayer's money." While the Geneva negotiations remained at a standstill, the House delayed until July 27, when it finally approved the Senate bill.[35]

Still smarting from the President's rebuff on the wool bill, Congress sent to the White House a measure to extend rent control. This bill sparked a legislative-executive battle over the critical housing shortage and the rising cost of living. The battle was to intensify, and in 1948, the issue would rank close to the Taft-Hartley act in importance. The controversy about rent control also reflected poor coordination within the Administration and lack of firm presidential leadership.

In January, 1947, rent control was one of the few remaining emergency powers, and the President recommended that Congress extend such authorization past its expiration date of June 30, 1947, since housing was still in very short supply. In a subsequent news conference, however, Truman refused to explain specifically what he desired and tossed the responsibility for the details to Congress to work out. Meanwhile, sentiment in Congress for a 10 to 20 per cent rise in rent prices drew support from Maj. Gen. Philip B. Fleming, an Administration official. His Office of Temporary Controls was on the verge of issuing an order providing for

35. William L. Clayton, "GATT, the Marshall Plan, and OECD," *Political Science Quarterly*, 78 (December, 1963), 494, 499; William L. Clayton, interview, 1947, Ellen Clayton Garwood Papers; Veto of the Wool Act, June 26, 1947, *Public Papers: Truman*, 1947, 309–10; *The New York Times*, June 27, 1947, p. 7, July 25, 1947, p. 7, July 27, 1947, p. 40.

a 10 per cent rent increase when the White House learned of the plan and squelched it. Fleming submitted the President's views before the Senate Banking and Currency Committee but said that he personally still favored the increase in order to correct "existing hardships." The President, however, continued to oppose any general increase, and on April 1, he sent a message to Congress formally requesting the extension of effective rent control.[36]

The House Banking and Currency Committee reported a bill to extend rent control, but it had significant modifications. The most important change was a provision to allow a 15 per cent increase where tenant and landlord signed a lease extending through December, 1948. Other objectionable provisions excluded new rental and transient housing from control and ended executive authority to control all building materials except those used for amusement or recreational construction. Committee Democrats Mike Monroney of Oklahoma, J. Caleb Boggs of Delaware, Albert Rains of Alabama, and Donald L. O'Toole of New York opposed decontrol on building materials, and O'Toole and Frank Buchanan of Pennsylvania opposed the 15 per cent voluntary increase because tenants would be forced to agree to it under threat of eviction. Republican Frederick C. Smith of Ohio dissented on the grounds that all rent controls should be eliminated. After amending the bill to provide for local governing bodies to end control where they deemed it no longer necessary, the House approved the measure, 205 to 182. The bill received the votes of 63 Democrats and 142 Republicans; 71 Republicans and 110 Democrats voted against it. The opposition consisted of those liberal Democrats who believed that tenants would not be protected by the bill and those congressmen of both parties who wanted to end all control.[37]

36. Annual Budget Message to the Congress: Fiscal Year 1948, January 10, 1947, *Public Papers: Truman*, 1947, 86; Special Message to the Congress: The President's First Economic Report, January 8, 1947, *ibid.*, 29; The President's News Conference of January 23, 1947, *ibid.*, 105; *The New York Times*, January 28, 1947, p. 10, February 1, 1947, pp. 1, 8; The President's News Conference of February 1, 1947, *Public Papers: Truman*, 1947, 115; Special Message to the Congress Recommending Extension of Rent Controls, April 1, 1947, *ibid.*, 189–90.

37. U.S. House of Representatives, Committee on Banking and Currency, *Housing and Rent Controls*, House Report 317 to accompany H.R. 3203, 80th

In the Senate, the record vote on rent control came with the adoption, 48 to 26, of an amendment similar to the House provision to allow a voluntary increase of 15 per cent. There were 40 Republicans and 8 Southern Democrats who supported the measure, while Republicans Aiken and Tobey and 24 Democrats voted No. The measure then passed by voice vote. The conference committee eliminated the provision for permitting decontrol by local agencies, and the bill was sent to the President just as the existing legislation was about to expire.[38]

Although Administration officials concerned with housing expressed dissatisfaction with H.R. 3203, they felt that the kind of control it provided was better than none at all and recommended approval. The President was critical of parts of the bill, but he approved it and urged action on other legislation dealing with the housing shortage. Truman was especially displeased about the 15 per cent increase, which he believed would be voluntary only on the part of the landlord, and also about the elimination of federal authority to prevent diversion of construction materials from housing to nonessential and deferable building. In addition, he lambasted Congress for not taking action on the Taft-Ellender-Wagner bill, which provided for federal support for middle-income and low-income housing, slum clearance, and urban redevelopment; urged the Senate to approve his reorganization plan for government housing functions; asked it to restore cuts made by the House in the National Housing Agency's budget; and requested a congressional investigation of the "selfish and short-sighted" real-estate lobby.[39]

This message led to another outburst from House Majority Leader Halleck. He called the message "shameful," denounced

Cong., 1st sess., 1947, 9, 12–13, 37–40. For examples of the variety of the opposition, see remarks by Rankin, Hoffman, Douglas, Holifield, and Buchanan in U.S. *Congressional Record*, 80th Cong., 1st sess., 1947, XCIII, Part 4, pp. 4302–3, 4319, 4392, 4394, 4413. Helen Gahagan Douglas to F. G. Pellett, July 7, 1947, Helen Gahagan Douglas Papers.

38. *The New York Times*, May 30, 1947, p. 1, June 3, 1947, pp. 1, 28, June 12, 1947, pp. 1, 16.

39. James E. Webb to M. C. Latta, June 28, 1947, Bureau of the Budget, Reports to the President on Pending Legislation; Special Message to the Congress Upon Signing the Housing and Rent Act, June 30, 1947, *Public Papers: Truman*, 1947, 313–17.

Truman for attempting to usurp legislative prerogatives, and charged that Truman's "reckless and unfair accusation will be resented by every member of Congress." A more positive response, however, was Senate approval of the creation of the Housing and Home Finance Agency, which was to give permanent direction to federal housing policy. Also, the Senate Banking and Currency Committee reported out the Taft-Ellender-Wagner comprehensive housing bill, but Taft abandoned it because he believed that it had no chance of passing the House. The House Republican leaders, charged with indifference to housing, promoted a resolution for a joint congressional committee to study all aspects of the housing problem and to report back in March, 1948. The resolution was a face-saving and delaying tactic, for an exhaustive examination had already been made by Taft's subcommittee in the Senate. Although forced to accept an unsatisfactory rent-control bill and inaction on a comprehensive housing program, Truman had outlined a firm position on two of the most pressing domestic problems—housing and inflation—and had cast his opponents as reactionary Republicans catering to the selfish demands of the real-estate lobby.[40]

Meanwhile, the Republican leaders decided to make another attempt to reduce taxes after Democratic Senators Byrd, George, and Edwin C. Johnson of Colorado offered to support a bill that would go into effect in January, 1948, and thereby reduce the revenue loss for fiscal 1948 to about $2 billion. On July 3, the House Ways and Means Committee reported a bill identical to H.R. 1, but with its effective date changed from July, 1947, to January, 1948. In the House, Democratic support for tax reduction almost doubled, the most significant convert being Robert Doughton, who influenced many other Democrats to switch. This time, 233 Republicans and 69 Democrats voted for the tax cut, and 109 Democrats, 1 American Laborite, and Republicans Hull and Andersen opposed it.[41]

40. *The New York Times,* July 1, 1947, p.1; Richard O. Davies, *Housing Reform During the Truman Administration,* 63–65, 67.

41. *The New York Times,* June 26, 1947, pp. 1, 12; U.S. House of Representatives, Committee on Ways and Means, *Individual Income Tax Reduction Act of 1947,* House Report 795 to accompany H.R. 3950, 80th Cong., 1st sess., 1947,

Two days after the House had passed H.R. 3950, but before the Senate had acted, President Truman announced he would veto it. Taft called the President's statement an attempt to "dictate to Congress," Millikin called it "obnoxious and outrageous," and Democrats George, Byrd, Johnson, McCarran, and Tom Stewart of Tennessee announced that they would vote to override. All amendments from the Senate floor were defeated, but this time McClellan's community-property amendment drew 40 votes. The bill passed, 60 to 32, with 12 Democrats supporting, and Republicans Morse and Langer opposed.[42]

As he had promised, Truman vetoed the bill, and he repeated the objections he had made to the first measure. The House immediately overrode, 299 to 108, but the Senate was 5 votes short of a two-thirds majority. The vote was 57 to 36, with Aiken and Democrats Millard E. Tydings of Maryland and Umstead of North Carolina reversing their original votes for the measure. Once more the Administration had thwarted tax reduction. It had kept the Democratic coalition fairly well intact—15 Southern senators supported the Administration—and it had been helped by 3 liberal Republicans. At the same time, as Doughton pointed out, the veto could have been overridden if the Republicans had "made some slight concessions by adopting the community property provision."[43]

The first session of the Eightieth Congress closed on a note of bitter conflict between the Republicans and the Administration and some congressional Democrats. Senate Republicans tried to obtain unanimous consent to vote on a resolution to investigate the Justice Department, which, they claimed, had not fully looked into charges of fraud in the Kansas City Democratic primary of 1946. This claim was a direct attack upon the President, for Tru-

---

1–15, Part II, "Minority Views," 4–17; U.S. *Congressional Record*, 80th Cong., 1st sess., 1947, XCIII, Part 7, p. 8468.

42. The President's News Conference of July 10, 1947, *Public Papers: Truman*, 1947, 329; *The New York Times*, July 11, 1947, p. 1; U.S. *Congressional Record*, 80th Cong., 1st sess., 1947, XCIII, Part 7, pp. 8835, 8839.

43. Veto of Second Bill to Reduce Income Taxes, July 18, 1947, *Public Papers: Truman*, 1947, 342–44; U.S. *Congressional Record*, 80th Cong., 1st sess., 1947, XCIII, Part 7, pp. 9282, 9304; Doughton to C. A. Cannon, July 28, 1947, Doughton Papers.

man had intervened in the primary to defeat incumbent Representative Roger Slaughter, who had consistently obstructed legislation sponsored by the Administration. To the extreme frustration and anger of the Republicans, the Democratic minority blocked a vote on the resolution, and the session ended with what *The New York Times* called "the bitterest partisan fight in many years." The battle over the proposed investigation foreshadowed the depths to which relations between the Republican majoriy and the President and his Democratic supporters in Congress would fall during the second session.[44]

A second incident during the last week of the first session marked the President's final effort toward conciliation. On July 23, the President walked into the Senate, took his old seat there, and "sat beaming like a schoolboy at the surprise of former colleagues." The spontaneous incident followed a luncheon with senators that Truman had just attended. A warm, friendly interchange took place between Truman and President Pro Tem Vandenberg, whereupon the President returned to the White House. Coming as it did after a month and a half of vetoes and criticism of bills, Truman's gesture was of little more than symbolic significance, but the incident received favorable publicity and perhaps soothed some ill feelings.[45]

The executive-legislative conflicts that began in June and intensified during the remainder of the session did not end with adjournment, for Truman found it necessary to pocket veto two additional bills and criticize a third. The first of these measures provided for the establishment of a National Science Foundation to further and coordinate scientific research and education. The President supported the idea, but the bill sent to him, despite objections from the Administration, placed the foundation almost completely outside presidential control. According to Budget Director Webb, the "enactment of this legislation would be injurious to the whole tradition of Presidential responsibility for the administration of the Executive branch and would also serve as a bad precedent for future enactments." The President vetoed the

---

44. *The New York Times*, July 18, 1947, pp. 1, 8, July 27, 1947, p. 2.
45. *Ibid.*, July 24, 1947, pp. 1, 24.

bill but called for the next session of Congress to enact it without the objectionable provisions.[46]

On the same day, August 8, the President vetoed a bill excluding newspaper vendors from social security coverage on the grounds that they were independent businessmen. The bill, which resulted from a court decision holding that such persons were subject to coverage, had passed both houses by voice vote and without debate. Both the Treasury Department and the Federal Security Agency, however, as well as various union spokesmen, advised veto. Truman justified his disapproval by pointing out that many news vendors were bona fide employees, that the bill would establish a precedent for future piecemeal attacks on the social security system, and that the program should be expanded and strengthened, rather than weakened. Once again, Truman aligned himself with the little man.[47]

Finally, the President dealt with a bill concerning consumer-credit controls in the same manner that he had the rent-control measure. The legislation extended authority for controls only until November, 1947. Truman signed the bill, but he argued that permanent controls were necessary and re-emphasized his disagreement with Congress about the necessity and means of controlling inflation.[48]

Although Republican voting behavior did not follow any rigidly consistent patterns, rough groupings appeared during the first session and continued throughout the Eightieth Congress. In the Senate, Aiken, Langer, and Morse represented the extreme liberal bloc and supported Administration policy on major tax, labor, and appropriations measures, although Aiken voted for the Taft-Hart-

46. James E. Webb to M. C. Latta, August 1, 1947, Bureau of the Budget, Reports to the President on Pending Legislation; Memorandum of Disapproval of the National Science Foundation Bill, August 6, 1947, *Public Papers: Truman, 1947,* 368–71.

47. U.S. *Congressional Record,* 80th Cong., 1st sess., 1947, XCIII, Part 7, pp. 9058–59, 9838; H.R. 3997, August 6, 1947, Bureau of the Budget, Reports to the President on Pending Legislation; Memorandum of Disapproval of Bill to Exclude Newspaper and Magazine Vendors from the Social Security System, August 6, 1947, *Public Papers: Truman, 1947,* 371–72.

48. Statement by the President Upon Approving Resolution Continuing Regulation of Consumer Credit, August 8, 1947, *ibid.,* 379–80.

ley act and Morse voted for the portal bill. Aiken and Morse consistently voted for the Administration's measures on foreign policy, while Langer represented an isolationist position. A second, larger, group of Republicans supported the Republicans' tax reduction but voted for Lilienthal's confirmation, smaller budget reductions, and a more temperate approach to restrictions on labor. This bloc, which included Knowland of California, Lodge and Saltonstall of Massachusetts, Ives of New York, and Young of North Dakota, also supported the Administration's foreign policy. They were frequently joined on domestic issues by Cooper of Kentucky, Raymond E. Baldwin of Connecticut, Vandenberg of Michigan, Edward J. Thye of Minnesota, Zales N. Ecton of Montana, Malone of Nevada, Tobey of New Hampshire, Arthur V. Watkins of Utah, and Flanders of Vermont. All of them, except Ecton and Malone, supported bipartisan foreign policy. Finally, there was a conservative bloc of Republicans who were primarily from the Midwest and who consistently opposed the Administration and, at times, their fellow Republicans. In this group were C. Douglass Buck and John J. Williams of Delaware, Henry C. Dworshak of Idaho, Brooks of Illinois, Wilson of Iowa, Kem of Missouri, Butler and Wherry of Nebraska, Albert W. Hawkes of New Jersey, Bricker of Ohio, Moore of Oklahoma, and Edward V. Robertson of Wyoming. The voting behavior of Republican leader Taft, as well as several other Republicans, fell between the latter two groups. The middle group held the balance of power and thus assured the success of the Administration's foreign policy and forced a more moderate approach to budget-cutting and labor legislation.

Because House leaders exerted stronger party control, and because there were infrequent roll-call votes, voting blocs were less discernible in the House. The group of from 5 to 25 Republicans who bolted their party on labor legislation were unable to influence the final outcome. Engel of Michigan, who had defected on labor legislation, and two other Republicans had also been unable to affect the vote on tax reduction. Their objections, however, contributed to the decision of the House leaders to accept Senate revisions in the tax and labor bills. A group of about seventy representatives, predominantly Midwesterners, consistently opposed the Administration's foreign policy, and at times, as many as ninety of their colleagues joined them.

While Senate Democratic defections from Administration policy were primarily Southern, only McKellar of Tennessee, W. Lee "Pappy" O'Daniel of Texas, and Byrd of Virginia always broke ranks on both foreign and domestic legislation. The remaining opposition to the Administration's foreign policy came from a tiny group of liberals, including Pepper of Florida, Taylor of Idaho, and Murray of Montana, who supported Truman's domestic program. Southern and border-state Democrats George of Georgia, O'Conor of Maryland, Clyde R. Hoey of North Carolina, Stewart of Tennessee, and A. Willis Robertson of Virginia voted with the Republicans on tax reduction. They and ten other Southerners voted for the Taft-Hartley bill—a group large enough to ensure passage. No Democrats except those from the South, Southwest, and border states defected on important domestic legislation.

Voting behavior of Democrats in the House was similar. Opposition to the Truman Doctrine came primarily from non-Southern liberals who supported the Administration's domestic policy. But most of those who attacked other parts of Administration foreign policy by attempting to cut funds for foreign aid were Southerners who also voted for Taft-Hartley and tax reduction. All but eleven of the Democratic votes in support of these Republican programs were from representatives of the South or border states.

The domestic legislation of the first session depended on the influence of moderate Republicans, the extent of unity the Democrats were able to muster, the ability of the President to control Administration officials, the degree to which he exercised the full powers of his office on behalf of Administration objectives, and the way in which Truman perceived political advantages.

The Republicans' successful and extensive revision of the Wagner act was based on the public's clamor for labor legislation, and that clamor fortified Southern Democrats in their willingness to desert the Administration. Also, Truman failed to use his full range of formal and informal powers. On the other hand, the threat of veto and the influence of Republican moderates, especially in the Senate, helped to dilute the attack on labor. Finally, the President's rousing denunciation of Taft-Hartley enhanced his image as champion of the New Deal and labor.

Truman's successful fight against tax reduction in 1947 owed much to the firm and consistent position of all Administration officials. Also, the issue did not cause the usual ideological split in the Democratic coalition, because many Southern Democrats, traditionally concerned about the fiscal integrity of the Federal Government, supported the Administration. Finally, the Republicans refused to make the number of concessions that they had made during consideration of the Taft-Hartley bill. In 1948, these conditions were absent, and tax reduction was enacted.

The anti-inflation legislation of the first session provided Truman another issue from which he could make political capital for the 1948 election. Failing to offer a specific proposal himself and unable to control his own officials, the President was forced to accept an inadequate rent-control bill. His rhetoric, however, identified Truman with the average citizen suffering from inflation and placed the responsibility for rising prices outside the Administration.

CHAPTER 5

THE SPECIAL SESSION OF 1947

ADJOURNMENT of the first session did not mark a hiatus in legislative-executive relationships. During the remainder of 1947, trends that had begun earlier intensified and foreshadowed major developments of 1948, both in domestic politics and foreign policy. Administration Democrats, as well as congressional Republicans, took the results of the first session before the public and, in interpreting legislative action, sought votes for 1948. Simultaneously the Administration began action that would culminate in bipartisan passage of the Marshall Plan in 1948. Finally, Truman took a spirited position on inflation, contrasting the Administration's proposals for comprehensive controls with Republican inaction on rising prices, which would become a significant issue in the 1948 elections. The President drew public attention to these issues in October when he called a special session to deal with interim aid for Europe and an anti-inflation program.

During the regular session, the President had emphasized the Administration's position toward Congress through his veto messages and statements issued to accompany bills that he had signed reluctantly. After adjournment, Truman relied primarily on his record, but he also commented caustically on the record of the Republican Congress. In reviewing the budget on August 20, he gave the executive branch sole credit for the surplus of $700 million for fiscal 1947. As for fiscal 1948, Truman pointed out that Congress had saved only $528 million, despite Republican assertions to the contrary. He also noted specific cuts in national defense, veterans' services, international affairs, agriculture, natural resources, transportation, communications, and the budgets of the Labor and Treasury departments. However, he expressed no opinions on the reductions, except for noting that Labor would be limited in its functions and the Treasury would encounter difficulties in enforcing tax laws. In his Labor Day statement Truman

102

pointed up Republican shortcomings by emphasizing the need to raise the minimum wage, extend social security, and establish a program of national health insurance and suggesting that the next session of Congress give immediate attention to these programs.[1]

Other Democrats were more critical of the record of the first session. Senate Minority Leader Barkley contrasted the results of the first session with the President's program and scored the Republicans for both what they did and what they did not enact. They had passed the "punitive" Taft-Hartley act, made "piecemeal disorganized cuts" in the budget, loosened rent and housing controls, and wasted time trying to effect tax reductions that favored the wealthy. They had neglected a housing program, antimonopoly legislation, medical care, universal military training, extension of social security, revision of the minimum wage, and development of other river systems on the TVA pattern. Barkley concluded that the "80th Congress has painted a sorry picture of partisanship, of subservience to special interests, ignoring the needs of the mass of people." The Democratic National Committee also sought to arouse the public to the failures of the Republican Congress. In a national radio program, Democratic party leaders emphasized Taft-Hartley, inflation, agriculture, and housing and predicted "a sweeping popular repudiation of the Republican-controlled 80th Congress." Labor leaders William Green of the AFL and Philip Murray of the CIO also attacked the Eightieth Congress.[2]

Republican leaders responded in kind. Taft and Halleck pointed to Republican accomplishments in labor legislation, budget reduction, wartime controls, foreign policy and defense, and the near success of tax reduction, which they said was obstructed only by the President's abuse of the veto power. They praised Republi-

1. The President's News Conference on the Review of the Budget, August 20, 1947, *Public Papers of the Presidents of the United States: Harry S. Truman, 1947*, 386; Statement by the President on the Review of the 1948 Budget, August 20, 1947, *ibid.*, 401–2; Statement by the President: Labor Day, August 30, 1947, *ibid.*, 428.

2. U.S. *Congressional Record*, 80th Cong., 1st sess., 1947, XCIII, Part 13, pp. A4058–60; Democratic National Committee, news release of Democratic Radio Rally, September 2, 1947, Harry S. Truman Papers, OF 299–A (1947); *The New York Times*, September 2, 1947, pp. 1, 14, 16.

can efforts to get along with the President but charged Truman with insincerity in his pledge of cooperation. Both Republicans continued to assume that wide popular support could be formed behind rhetorical opposition to the New Deal, but they did not attack specific New Deal programs, preferring to equate the New Deal with radicalism, bureaucracy, and excessive spending. Halleck ignored Republican inaction on social legislation, except to blame the housing shortage on "bureaucratic controls and red tape." The shortage would be solved, he asserted, when "the newly-released building industry gets fully underway and shows what American initiative can do." Taft acknowledged the need for federal aid to the states in health, education, and housing, but he asked for time to "crystallize opinion" among Republicans, who hesitated to initiate such programs while New Dealers would be responsible for setting up the programs. When the last statement aroused a small storm of protest from George Aiken and other Republicans, Taft reversed himself and called for passage of his education, housing, and health bills, as well as for extension of social security to domestic and agricultural labor, an increase in unemployment benefits, and establishment of a plan for federal aid to the states for emergency public works projects. This reversal not only acknowledged that Republicans were sensitive to charges of inaction, but also reopened issues that were to divide the party in 1948.[3]

Attention soon shifted from the first session to the reconvening of Congress. As early as May, 1947, the press began to speculate about the possibility of a special session later in the year. Reporters based their calculations on the Administration's plans for a substantial aid program for Europe. While formulating the program of Greek-Turkish aid, Under Secretary of State Dean Acheson had become concerned about the failure of the European economy to recover from the war. On March 11, he instructed a special interdepartmental committee to investigate and report

3. Taft, text of speech at Republican Leaders' Dinner, Columbus, Ohio, July 31, 1947, in *The New York Times*, August 1, 1947, p. 8; Halleck, speech in U.S. *Congressional Record*, 80th Cong., 1st sess., 1947, XCIII, Part 13, pp. A4068–75; *The New York Times*, September 17, 1947, p. 19, September 18, 1947, p. 20, September 27, 1947, p. 10.

on all countries that might be in need of both long-range and emergency aid from the United States. On May 8, armed with the committe's figures and the approval of the President, Acheson made public the magnitude of the economic problems confronting Europe and stressed U.S. responsibility for economic reconstruction.[4]

At the Foreign Ministers Council in March and April, 1947, Secretary of State Marshall became increasingly alarmed about European economic disintegration and Russian hopes to exploit the situation. Consequently, the day after his return, he asked George Kennan and his Policy Planning Staff to analyze the problem of European reconstruction and make recommendations for action. While Kennan's staff was completing its report, Will Clayton, Under Secretary of State for Economic Affairs, returned from six weeks in Europe and added further alarming evidence of the deteriorating situation. Identifying the roots of Europe's economic crisis and linking it with her political stability, Clayton insisted that the United States would have to undertake an aid program of $6 billion to $7 billion a year for three years.[5]

Assuming that large-scale aid was essential, people within the Administration confined their discussion to the nature of the proposal. Kennan's Policy Planning Staff made several important recommendations in an effort to reorient the Administration from the approach taken on the Greek-Turkish issue. They sought to soften the emphasis on communism by maintaining that the root of Europe's difficulties was not communist activities but economic dislocation. U.S. aid, they argued, should be a positive program for economic reconstruction, not a negative weapon against communism. They also insisted that the initiative should come from

4. *Ibid.*, May 25, 1947, p. 13; Joseph M. Jones, *The Fifteen Weeks (February 21–June 5, 1947)*, 199–213.

5. Charles E. Bohlen, *The Transformation of American Foreign Policy*, 88; Jones, *The Fifteen Weeks*, 223–24, 246–49; Harry S. Truman, *Memoirs*, Vol. II, *Years of Trial and Hope*, 112–13; Robert H. Ferrell, *George C. Marshall*, Volume XV of *The American Secretaries of State and Their Diplomacy*, Ferrell and Samuel F. Bemis, eds., 70–71, 99; William L. Clayton, "GATT, the Marshall Plan, and OECD," *Political Science Quarterly*, 78 (December, 1963), 495–98; Clayton, memorandum, March 5, 1947, Clayton, memorandum, "The European Crisis," May 31, 1947, William L. Clayton Papers, Speech File.

Europe as a joint undertaking by all the countries in need of U.S. help. Specifically, they urged the correction of two important misconceptions about the Truman Doctrine: (1) that U.S. aid was only a by-product of opposition to communism, rather than a program to be undertaken on its own merits and (2) that the Truman Doctrine was a blank check to be cashed by any country in which communist gains appeared likely. Thus, the new emphasis was to be upon European economic realities rather than upon ideological conflict. The Administration would then concentrate on a positive effort to rehabilitate the economy of a specific area. Whereas the Truman Doctrine, in theory but not in application, overextended U.S. interest and power, the new program was limited and in harmony with the interests and resources of the United States.[6]

The Administration refrained from anti-Russian rhetoric, but it clearly viewed European aid as a means of implementing containment. Clayton, as well as Kennan's staff, believed that economic recovery was essential if Europe was to have stable, non-communist governments. Moreover, the Administration was not prepared to include the Soviet Union and her satellites among aid recipients except on terms unpalatable to Russia. The inclusion of Eastern Europe would substantially increase the difficulty of getting congressional authorization because the project would be much costlier and conservatives probably would not support a program involving aid to the Soviet Union. To Marshall, the involvement of Russia would kill the program. An open-ended offer of aid was made, however, because Acheson, Kennan, Bohlen, and others did not want the United States to be blamed for the division of Europe by limiting the proposal to the Western-oriented nations. In any case, most officials believed that the Soviet Union would reject the offer because any country participating had to provide full information about its internal financial and economic conditions. Thus, the Administration took a calculated risk of tendering the proposal to all countries that were willing to accept U.S. terms.[7]

6. Harry Bayard Price, *The Marshall Plan and Its Meaning*, 22–25.

7. Jones, *The Fifteen Weeks*, 252–54; Bohlen, *Transformation of American Foreign Policy*, 91.

Marshall formally made the offer in a speech at Harvard's commencement exercises on June 5. He described the physical destruction of Europe's economy, as well as the less visible dislocation of normal production and trade relationships. "The truth of the matter," he said, "is that Europe's requirements for the next three or four years of foreign food and other essential products—principally from America—are so much greater than her present ability to pay that she must have substantial additional help or face economic, social, and political deterioration of a very grave character." The Secretary of State also noted the effects on the United States should Europe fail to recover. An economic breakdown in Europe would ultimately jeopardize the U.S. economy, contribute to political instability in Europe, and lessen the chances for world peace. He maintained that U.S. policy was directed not against "any country or doctrine, but against hunger, poverty, desperation and chaos." The situation demanded a comprehensive approach rather than one carried out on a piecemeal basis from crisis to crisis. Finally, Marshall insisted that before the United States could proceed with its plans for aid, the countries of Europe must agree on the requirements and define their own responsibilities to the program: "The initiative, I think, must come from Europe."[8]

The prompt and comprehensive response from Europe was unexpected. Less than two weeks after Marshall's speech, the British and French foreign ministers had begun talks in Paris, and on June 27, Soviet representative Vyacheslav Molotov joined them. The Soviet Union, however, was unwilling to agree to full disclosure of economic information and U.S. control over parts of Russia's budget. On August 2, Molotov abruptly left the conference, and the Soviet Union subsequently discouraged the participation of Poland, Czechoslovakia, and Yugoslavia, which had displayed initial eagerness. The sixteen-nation Committee on European Economic Cooperation, which included all the nonsatellite European countries except Spain, began on August 12. On September 22, the conference transmitted a report detailing what the countries could do on their own or jointly and what contributions would be necessary from the United States. At this point, the responsibility shift-

8. Text of Marshall's speech in Jones, *The Fifteen Weeks*, 281–84.

ed once more to the United States—particularly to Congress for its authorization of the program.[9]

The Soviet Union's withdrawal had removed the greatest obstacle to legislative action, but the Administration had still to convince the public and Congress that massive aid to Europe was vital to U.S. interests and within U.S. capabilities. The first step was to enlist the support of Vandenberg. The Senator was immediately concerned about the domestic economic impact of large-scale aid and requested "a sound over-all inventory of our own resources to determine the latitudes within which we may consider these foreign needs." Responding quickly to Vandenberg's demand, Truman appointed three special study groups on June 22. The first and most important was the President's Committee on Foreign Aid. Called the Harriman Committee after its chairman, Secretary of Commerce Averell Harriman, it consisted of nineteen eminent citizens from business, labor, agriculture, education, and public service, and its task was to investigate all questions relating to European aid. Truman also appointed an intergovernmental committee headed by Secretary of the Interior Julius A. Krug to examine the relationship between the aid program and U.S. resources and capabilities, and he instructed the Council of Economic Advisers to estimate the effects of such a program on domestic production, consumption, and prices. While these committees gathered information, Marshall and other State Department officials met weekly with Vandenberg to discuss the European situation. The State Department courted other congressional leaders by briefing them on major developments in the Committee of European Economic Cooperation before making public releases.[10]

Congress itself began to appreciate the need to authorize the Marshall Plan. Traveling with various committees and subcommittees, more than two-hundred congressmen witnessed at first

9. Price, *The Marshall Plan and Its Meaning*, 26–29, 36–39; Ferrell, *Marshall*, 112–20.

10. Arthur H. Vandenberg, Jr., ed., *The Private Papers of Senator Vandenberg*, 376; Price, *The Marshall Plan and Its Meaning*, 39–40, 50; Vandenberg to Marshall, June 24, 1947, Arthur H. Vandenberg Papers, William L. Clements Library, University of Michigan; Robert A. Lovett to John Taber, September 21, 1947, John Taber Papers.

hand the conditions in Europe that had prompted the massive aid proposal. Some of these groups were in Europe primarily for other purposes but were inevitably confronted by the destruction of the European economy. The main objective of a subcommittee of the House Armed Services Committee was to inspect U.S. occupation forces in Germany and Austria, but its report emphasized "the ever-present threat of Communism" in Germany, France, and Italy and called for long-term economic aid to counter the "chaos, misery and discontent" upon which "Communism thrives." In addition, special committees were appointed in the House and Senate to study European conditions in light of Marshall's proposal.[11]

Truman's public attitude toward the Marshall Plan from June to September was restrained. In speeches on June 11 and 17, he supported European aid in general terms and endorsed the Marshall Plan in his news conference of June 26. Further than this he would not go. Aware of congressional irritation at his recent vetoes and criticisms of domestic measures and conscious, too, of strong reservations about large-scale aid among isolationist congressmen and those determined to cut government spending, he preferred to sit back and watch the situation develop. After the press had published speculations in July and August, the President told reporters that he foresaw no need for calling a special session in the fall. But while the President publicly dragged his feet, pressure was building for reconvening Congress. Under Secretary of State Clayton and the three principal United States ambassadors in Europe met in Paris and agreed that European financial problems called for immediate emergency aid. On September 9, Marshall told reporters at his press conference that assurance of emergency aid in the form of fuel and food was necessary before the year ended and that Congress alone could give such assurance.[12]

Finally, on September 25, the President took two steps toward

11. Joseph Alsop, "Congressmen Heading Home from Europe," St. Louis *Post-Dispatch*, October 24, 1947, p. 1D; U.S. House of Representatives, Subcommittee of the Armed Services Committee, report, undated, transmitted by Walter G. Andrews to Arthur Capper, October 31, 1947, Arthur Capper Papers; Price, *The Marshall Plan and Its Meaning*, 51–55.

12. Address Before the Canadian Parliament in Ottawa, June 11, 1947, *Public Papers: Truman, 1947*, 275–76; Commencement Address at Princeton University, June 17, 1947, *ibid.*, 284; The President's News Conference of June 26, 1947, *ibid.*,

action on European aid. He appointed a Citizens' Food Committee to plan a program of voluntary food conservation by the public that would enable the United States to increase food exports to Europe. He then released the report of the sixteen-nation conference at Paris and called a meeting with congressional leaders "to discuss plans for determining the action to be taken by the United States" on aid to Europe. Still he would not commit himself to a special session, preferring to let Congress take the initiative.[13]

Meanwhile, the President received additional reports that resources for aiding Europe through the winter were exhausted. On September 28, the chairman of the Export-Import Bank wrote Truman that he could find no way under existing laws to expand credits to France and Italy. The next day, Truman held an inconclusive meeting with congressional leaders. Truman said afterward that as a first step toward emergency aid, he would request the House and Senate Appropriations committees, the Senate Foreign Relations Committee, and the House Foreign Affairs Committee to consider "the urgent need for aid to Western Europe." There was no suggestion of a special session, but the President for the first time made it clear that the Administration had examined all possible means of aid not requiring congressional authorization but had found that France, Italy, and Austria needed an additional $580 million to get through the winter. Although emergency aid was separate from the long-range Marshall Plan, the latter could not succeed unless means were found "for aiding France and Italy to survive this critical winter as free and independent nations." Congress had the responsibility, specifically the committees that Truman was asking to convene. As he put it, "If they were not in favor of doing anything, there would be no necessity for the special session."[14]

307; The President's News Conference of July 10, 1947, *ibid.*, 330–31; The President's News Conference of August 21, 1947, *ibid.*, 421; *The New York Times*, August 7, 1947, p. 7, September 11, 1947, p. 1.

13. The President's News Conference of September 25, 1947, *Public Papers: Truman, 1947*, 437–41.

14. Herbert Gaston to Truman, September 28, 1947, Clark M. Clifford Papers,

The chances for favorable action by Congress improved when the Soviet Union began to appear more hostile in October. It revived the Comintern in an effort to obstruct the Marshall Plan, particularly in France and Italy. At the same time, congressmen returning from Europe, many of whom had begun their investigations with strong reservations about European aid, called for immediate action to save Europe from communism, and a private group of prominent citizens—the Committee for the Marshall Plan—solicited public support for the aid program. Still, important Republicans refused to admit the necessity of a special session. On October 8, Vandenberg reminded Taft of "our strong desires" against a special session. Vandenberg preferred to "let the foreign situation jell a bit" and wait for the conclusion of all the investigations before calling a meeting of the Republican Steering Committee. On the House side, Christian Herter, chairman of the Select Committee on Foreign Aid, returned from Europe with the impression that no special session was required.[15]

Administration advisers and Democratic legislators increased the pressure on Truman to call the session. Clark Clifford stressed the importance of congressional action on emergency aid by Christmas and urged Truman to "utilize the full power of his office" toward this end. Mike Mansfield, Democratic Representative from Montana, went to Truman immediately upon his return from traveling in Europe with a joint committee. He emphasized commodity shortages, disease, fear, and discontent and urged the President to call a special session. Another Democrat, Carl A. Hatch of New Mexico, similarly recounted his impression of European conditions, appealed for a special session, and also speculated about the political implications. He suggested that Republicans did not want a special session:

Subject File; The President's News Conference Following a Meeting with Congressional Leaders, September 29, 1947, *Public Papers: Truman, 1947*, 445–48; Truman to Bridges, Taber, Vandenberg, and Eaton, September 30, 1947, Truman Papers, OF 426.

15. *The New York Times*, October 10, 1947, p. 3, October 12, 1947, p. E1, October 19, 1947, pp. 1, 7, E3; Price, *The Marshall Plan and Its Meaning*, 55–56; Vandenberg to Taft, October 8, 1947, Vandenberg Papers; Herter to Vorys, October 14, 1947, John M. Vorys Papers.

They do very much want to be in a position of saying that if the emergency relief is not granted soon enough, the responsibility rests upon the Executive branch of the Government. I can hear them now publicizing all over the country the fact that they were ready to assume their legislative duties had the President not failed in his duty and responsibility—Had he called the special session, they would have met him more than halfway.[16]

On October 23, Truman called congressional leaders to the White House and told them he would ask Congress to reconvene on November 17. His long delay worked to his advantage in the end. Republicans had not liked the Administration's handling of the proposal for Greek-Turkish aid. In contrast, the months that elapsed between Marshall's speech and the call for legislative action offered opportunity for discussion, investigation, and the cultivation of congressional leaders. Also, by the end of October, Truman's special committees were completing their studies, and the Administration was able to present definite plans and information. Finally, public pressure had been allowed to build before a concrete proposal was made. As one observer described the situation, "Truman's delay was agonizing. He didn't cry 'Fire,' till the flames were almost singeing the hairs of the Congressmen's heads and till the exasperated public was yelling at him almost as much as at Congress. Now it is all yelling at Congress."[17]

In calling for the special session, the President not only assumed the initiative that he had unsuccessfully tried to pass to Congress, but also expanded the scope of the session. He told the public that immediate congressional action was necessary for controlling inflation, as well as for providing $642 million in stopgap aid to Europe. Indeed, in his radio address explaining his decision, he placed the problem of rising prices ahead of interim aid and devoted more time to the former than the latter. By interjecting the inflation issue, the President made himself vulnerable to charges of playing politics and risked obliterating the distinction between

16. Clifford, "Memorandum for the President," draft of October 3, 1947, Mike Mansfield, memorandum, undated, Clifford Papers, Subject File; The President's Appointment Calendar, October 17, 1947, Matthew Connelly Files; Hatch to Truman, October 16, 1947, Clifford Papers, Subject File.

17. "Washington Wire," New Republic, 117 (November 3, 1947), 3.

foreign and domestic policy that the Administration had sought to maintain. He justified his call for action against rising prices on the grounds that prosperity was endangered by the threat of inflation. The need was "too pressing—the results of delay too grave" for congressional action to wait until the next regular session in January.[18]

Although inflationary dangers were real and although the President did not attack Republicans for killing OPA as he had done on previous occasions, political considerations dictated his decision to request anti-inflation measures. Since early 1947, the rising cost of living had been causing concern. As early as March, Democratic congressmen noted high prices and blamed Republicans for defeating OPA. In April the press reported a Cabinet discussion of the first quarter review of the Council of Economic Advisers, in which the council had expressed concern about inflationary trends and the relative decline of purchasing power among large groups of consumers. In response to questions about the price situation, the President said that the Administration had very little authority and that it was up to business to work out a solution. He repeated this viewpoint on April 21, citing examples of rising prices and the dangers resulting therefrom, but he maintained that private enterprise—including this time workers and farmers as well as business—"had the responsibility for prices," since the Seventy-ninth Congress had withdrawn the government's authority in that area.[19]

While the President called only for voluntary price reductions, the cries for action continued, and other Democrats seized upon the political potential of the inflation issue. In May, Chester Bowles suggested to Truman that he could gain advantage by

18. The President's News Conference Announcing the Calling of a Special Session of Congress, October 23, 1947, *Public Papers: Truman, 1947*, 475–76; Radio Address to the American People on the Special Session of Congress, October 24, 1947, *ibid.*, 476–79; Richard E. Neustadt, *Presidential Power, The Politics of Leadership*, 53–54.

19. U.S. *Congressional Record*, 80th Cong., 1st sess., 1947, XCIII, Part 2, pp. 1859, 2038–39, 2160–62; Council of Economic Advisers to the President, April 4, 1947, John D. Clark Papers; *The New York Times*, April 10, 1947, p. 15, April 13, 1947, p. 1; The President's News Conference of April 10, 1947, *Public Papers: Truman, 1947*, 198–200; Address in New York City at the Annual Luncheon of the Associated Press, April 21, 1947, *ibid.*, 213–15.

"dumping a series of [anti-inflation] proposals in the lap of Congress." To John W. McCormack of Massachusetts, high-ranking Democrat in the House, Bowles urged that Democrats make speeches emphasizing the "theme of Republican responsibility." In June, McCormack asked his colleague Helen Gahagan Douglas of California to organize a group of Democrats to speak out on the rising cost of living. "I consider this," wrote McCormack, "constructive and important politically." Gael Sullivan of the Democratic National Committee seconded the suggestion and urged, "Keep needling them."[20]

In August, the CIO urged the President to call a special conference of labor and industry to discuss rolling back prices. By September, floods and droughts had severely curtailed the domestic corn crop, but foreign demand for food and grain rose. Food prices soared as much as 30 per cent, and demands for inflation curbs increased. Both the Republican leaders and the President began to respond.[21]

Before adjourning, Congress had passed a resolution establishing a joint committee to make field investigations into consumer prices. The resolution was sponsored by Raymond E. Baldwin, Republican Senator from Connecticut, in response to petitions expressing concern about rising costs from such groups as the American Veterans Committee, the NAACP, the CIO, and the Americans for Democratic Action. On September 15, the Joint Committee to Investigate High Prices of Consumer Goods began investigations in Eastern cities, and after almost a month of hearings, its chairman, Ralph Flanders of Vermont, indicated that allocations and rationing controls might be necessary. Senate leaders, however, were not willing to go that far. Taft blamed the price spiral on the Administration and proposed his own five-point program. He suggested that the government cut spending, reduce taxes, reduce exports, control purchases in the United

20. Bowles to Truman, May 12, 1947, Truman Papers, OF 426–D; McCormack to Douglas, May 23, June 29, 1947, Sullivan to Douglas, July 2, 1947, Helen Gahagan Douglas Papers.

21. The President's News Conference of August 14, 1947, *Public Papers: Truman, 1947*, 382; *The New York Times*, September 12, 1947, p. 1, September 14, 1947, p. E1; Mail to Truman requesting a special session, Truman Papers, OF 419–A.

114

States for export, and persuade labor to stop demanding wage increases.[22]

The President, in turn, placed the responsibility for rising prices upon Congress. Responding to the urging of CIO President Philip Murray, Truman wrote, "I can't bring myself to believe that this backward looking Congress will do anything to alleviate it [inflation]." To George H. Fallon, Democratic Congressman from Maryland, he wrote, "The 79th and 80th Congress [sic] were extremely anxious to turn the control situation over to 'free enterprise.'" To the National Chairman of the League of Women Shoppers he said, "The 80th Congress has not been very friendly toward controls. . . . [But] perhaps, we can convince Congress of the necessity that exists to do something about prices." But in response to Congresswoman Douglas' appeal for a special session to act on inflation, Truman expressed pessimism.[23]

By demanding inflation-control legislation that he did not expect to get, Truman publicly linked the Republican party with the high cost of living, but he was not merely creating an issue. The Administration's concern over rising prices was real, and the prospect of increased foreign aid would intensify inflationary pressures. In their third quarter Economic Report to the President, the Council of Economic Advisers called rising prices "the focal point of our economic problem." Noting that "disturbing price advances" had resumed, the council urged the President to continue to emphasize education and voluntary cooperation but suggested that the Administration begin immediately to study and plan for a full range of anti-inflation measures, including direct price and allocation controls over selected commodities.[24]

Truman, however, went beyond the council's recommendations

22. U.S. *Congressional Record*, 80th Cong., 1st sess., 1947, XCIII, Part 6, pp. 7268–69, Part 8, pp. 10188, 10311–12, 10478; *The New York Times*, October 11, 1947, pp. 1, 2, October 29, 1947, p. 1.

23. Truman to Murray, September 26, 1947, Truman to Fallon, September 25, 1947, Truman to Mrs. Julie C. Algase, October 4, 1947, Truman Papers, OF 327; Douglas to Truman, September 26, 1947, Truman to Douglas, September 29, 1947, Douglas Papers, General File.

24. Council of Economic Advisers to the President, "The Impact of Foreign Aid Upon the Domestic Economy," October, 1947, Council of Economic Advisers, Third Quarter Economic Report, October 1, 1947, Edwin G. Nourse Papers, Daily Diary.

in scheduling anti-inflation legislation for the special session. The council's report, while urging that preparations begin, asserted, "We do not at this time certify our belief in the desirability of all these proposals, or any number of them in combination. We do certify our belief that some of these proposals will become essential in the unfolding situation, and that their further development should not be delayed." Truman instructed the council members to treat their report as a confidential document, perhaps to conceal the fact that the report made no immediate call for comprehensive legislation. In fact, Truman expanded the scope of the special session to deal with inflation independently of the CEA. Chairman Edwin G. Nourse recalled that the council "had not suggested the need of a special session or participated in any discussion that led up to it."[25]

When the special session convened on November 17, Congress first considered interim aid as the President had requested; indeed, congressional committees had begun work on the bill even before Truman's formal message. In hearings held from November 10 through 12, Secretaries Marshall and Harriman; Robert A. Lovett, Under Secretary of State and Acheson's successor as the department's liaison man with Congress; and Lewis Douglas, ambassador to Great Britain and special liaison officer for the Marshall Plan, presented the case for the specific request of $597 million to aid France, Italy, and Austria through March, 1948. Although the Administration continued to distinguish interim aid from the Marshall Plan, Marshall told the Senate Foreign Relations Committee that the three countries could not survive economically beyond January without U.S. aid and that if such assistance were not available, the Marshall Plan would be doomed before Congress had a chance to consider it. His argument also stressed Cold War considerations more than those of humanitarianism or international economic stability as the rationale for European aid. Interim aid, he told the senators, was necessary to prevent the iron curtain from moving west.[26]

25. *Ibid.*; Nourse to Woodlief Thomas, October 3, 1947, Nourse Papers, Daily Diary; Edwin G. Nourse, *Economics in the Public Service: Administrative Aspects of the Employment Act,* 211.

26. James W. Pratt, "Leadership Relations in United States Foreign Policy

Minor objections to parts of the proposal were handled through amendments acceptable to senators and State Department officials. The only serious difference appeared when Republicans used the interim-aid hearings to press the Administration about the civil war in China. Early in 1947, Vandenberg had expressed relief that the Administration was abandoning efforts to get Chiang Kai-shek to establish a coalition government with the communists. At the same time, he pressed for more vigorous support of the Nationalist government: "It seems to me that we might just as well begin to face the Communist challenge on *every* front." Other Republicans also took up the cry for more attention to Asia. Members of the House Appropriations and House Armed Services committees who visited China in the fall of 1947 urgently requested more military equipment and training for Nationalist troops. Their report discounted the corruption in Chiang's government and argued that a "free though unmoral government" in China was preferable to a "hostile government no matter how pure and moral but dominated by communist influence." The committee members concluded, "It is a tragic error for our country in its efforts to stem the spread of communism in the world to concentrate its programs exclusively in the European theater." By October, Vandenberg was determined that whatever form the Marshall Plan took, it must include aid to China. When he pressed Marshall on this matter, the Secretary promised to submit later a program of assistance to China. Satisfied for the time being, the Senate Foreign Relations Committee unanimously approved the bill for interim aid on November 19.[27]

On November 24, Vandenberg opened debate on the interim-aid bill, justifying it on the basis of humanitarian concern, the

---

Making: Case Studies, 1947–1950" (Ph.D. dissertation, Columbia University, 1963), 120; State Department press release, Secretary of State Addressing the joint session of the Senate Foreign Relations Committee and the House Foreign Affairs Committee, November 10, 1947, George M. Elsey Papers, Speech File.

27. Vandenberg to J. B. Montgomery, January 27, 1947, Vandenberg to William Loeb, February 10, 1947, Vandenberg Papers; W. Sterling Cole, mimeographed report to W. G. Andrews, November 19, 1947, Clarence Cannon Papers; Vandenberg to C. Redi Webber, October 14, 1947, Vandenberg Papers; H. Bradford Westerfield, *Foreign Policy and Party Politics: Pearl Harbor to Korea*, 262; *The New York Times*, November 20, 1947, pp. 1, 4.

maintenance of freedom in Western Europe, and U.S. self-interest. He presented the measure as indispensable to the success of the long-range European Recovery Program, but he absolved those senators who supported interim aid from commitment to the long-range program. The Senator documented the need for aid, demonstrated how the figures had been cut to the bone, and pointed out the conditions under which the aid would be administered. In addition, he attempted to correct what he termed the President's mistake in tying interim aid to anti-inflation legislation by showing that nothing in the bill necessitated domestic controls. Finally, he acknowledged with regret that China was not included in the program but noted that the State Department was working on a plan for China.[28]

Although a few Democratic senators, led by Claude Pepper of Florida and Glen H. Taylor of Idaho, objected to the bill as "a weapon in an ideological war" and preferred to see the aid administered by the United Nations, the greatest opposition came from conservative, primarily Midwestern Republicans and a handful of Southern Democrats. This opposition worked primarily through two kinds of amendments. The first group of revisions was designed to provide fuel and food directly to individual recipients. The United States Government was not, according to George W. Malone of Nevada, to be "in the business of setting up a WPA in Europe," nor should it support "socialist-inclined governments" by giving them credits to purchase supplies and resell goods. These senators were willing to provide direct relief to European people but rejected the ideas of joint expenditures for recovery projects and gearing the aid to balance-of-payments deficits. Vandenberg denounced the amendments as destructive of the very nature of the program, and the Senate defeated them by voice vote.[29]

The second attack on the interim-aid bill came as an amendment to reduce the authorization to $400 million. Supporters of

28. U.S. *Congressional Record*, 80th Cong., 1st sess., 1947, XCIII, Part 9, pp. 10701–5.

29. *Ibid.*, pp. 10899–10900, 10903–6. Sponsors of the amendments included George W. Malone (Nevada), John W. Bricker (Ohio), James P. Kem (Missouri), Zales N. Ecton (Montana), Henry C. Dworshak (Idaho), and William E. Jenner (Indiana).

118

this change reflected general opposition to the program, as well as a desire to reduce government spending, and included Republican leader Taft and Democrats Byrd and George. To advocates of interim aid, the proposed reduction was utterly objectionable: Vandenberg compared it to "throwing a 15-foot rope to a man who is drowning 20 feet from shore." Support for the amendment represented the maximum resistance to the program and paralleled opposition to the Administration's other major foreign-policy proposals, but it was defeated, 56 to 30. Supporters of the amendment included 20 Republicans, most of whom had voted against Greek-Turkish aid and post-UNRRA relief, and 10 Democrats, 8 from the South and Southwest. Unable to modify it, most of the dissidents voted for the bill, which passed, 83 to 6, on December 1.[30]

On the following day, the House Foreign Affairs Committee reported its bill. Marshall's promise of a future aid program did not deter House Republicans, and on its own initiative the committee amended the measure to provide $60 million for China. The total authorization was $590 million, thus reducing European aid by about 12 per cent. Opposition to the bill was similar to that in the Senate, but in addition, farm-state Republicans and Southern Democrats attempted to limit or prohibit shipment of goods in short domestic supply, such as grain fertilizer, fuel, and farm machinery. These amendments, which were sponsored by Democrats John Bell Williams of Mississippi, W. M. Wheeler of Georgia, Thomas G. Abernethy of Mississippi, and Republican H. Carl Andersen of Minnesota, would have destroyed the interim-aid program, since Europeans were in desperate need of exactly these materials and goods. The amendments were defeated by division votes of 109 to 136 and 107 to 135. An amendment sponsored by Foreign Affairs Committee member Bartel J. Jonkman of Michigan to cut the amount of aid by $300 million was likewise defeated, 78 to 171, and the House passed the bill by voice vote on December 11.[31]

---

30. *Ibid.*, pp. 10907–10, 10980.
31. Pratt, "Leadership Relations in Foreign Policy Making," 136–38; U.S. *Congressional Record*, 80th Cong., 1st sess., 1947, XCIII, Part 9, pp. 11180, 11210, 11271, 11307.

The conference committee resolved the disagreement over Chinese aid in favor of the House, but it accepted the Senate and Administration figure of $597 million and provided that if funds for China could be found elsewhere, China's share of the interim-aid appropriation could be transferred to Europe. The Senate passed the amended bill by voice vote, and the House, in the only roll call taken on interim aid, approved it, 313 to 82. A group of 70 Republicans, predominantly Midwestern conservatives, 11 Democrats—10 of them Southerners—and American Laborite Vito Marcantonio voted No. Later, Congress whittled the funds to carry out the authorization down to $540 million ($522 million for Europe and $18 million for China), and the appropriations bill pinned some restrictions on the purchase of goods in short domestic supply. The Administration, however, obtained an adequate program to sustain the economies of France, Italy, and Austria through the winter and thereby gained time in which to perfect and seek support for the large-scale Marshall Plan.[32]

The favorable outcome resulted not only from the energetic labors of the Administration but also from the activities of legislators themselves. Administration officials painstakingly cultivated Republican leaders and carefully separated interim aid from the domestic political controversy over inflation controls. In addition, the reports of the three special committees appointed to study the ramifications of foreign aid lent strength to the proposal. Of extreme importance on the congressional side were the many committees that had studied conditions in Europe firsthand. Many of these legislators, originally skeptical or hostile, returned from abroad converted to active support or at least passive acceptance of aid to Europe. While impressed with the suffering of people in need of food and shelter, most congressmen, reinforced by the nature of the Administration's argument, supported European assistance, not as a humanitarian gesture, but as a Cold War measure.[33]

32. Pratt, "Leadership Relations in Foreign Policy Making," 147; U.S. *Congressional Record*, 80th Cong., 1st sess., 1947, XCIII, Part 9, pp. 11412–13; *The New York Times*, December 20, 1947, pp. 1, 5, 7.

33. Pratt, "Leadership Relations in Foreign Policy Making," 133; Vandenberg, ed., *Private Papers of Senator Vandenberg*, 380; Minutes of the Executive Com-

During the special session, the Senate acted upon an additional foreign-policy measure related to the containment policy. The Inter-American Treaty of Reciprocal Assistance established the Organization of American States and provided for collective action among the Western Hemisphere countries against any aggressor. The groundwork for this pact had been laid during the war years of cooperation and collaboration among the American nations. By including Senators Vandenberg and Connally, Representative Bloom, and UN Representative and former Republican Senator Warren Austin among the U.S. negotiators of the treaty, the Administration won bipartisan congressional support in advance. The treaty was completed only in September, but Vandenberg wanted quick consideration by the Senate not only as a means to facilitate the Pan American Economic Conference scheduled for January, 1948, but also "as a further and highly significant and impressive notification to potential Communist aggressors." With little debate, the Senate ratified the treaty, 72 to 1.[34]

In contrast to the legislative-executive cooperation on foreign policy, the rift between President and Congress on domestic issues intensified as Congress began to work on Truman's anti-inflation proposals. Less than a month elapsed between Truman's announcement of the special session and its convening, so the Administration had time to prepare only a broad outline of requests. On the advice of the Budget Bureau, the President decided to ask for an extensive range of measures that, if Congress complied, would give the Administration adequate powers to deal with inflation. If the President asked for and received an inadequate program and prices continued to rise, the responsibility would be his. At least one Administration adviser was concerned

---

mittee Meeting, November 26, December 18, 1947, Committee for the Marshall Plan, Records; Holbert N. Carroll, *The House of Representatives and Foreign Affairs*, 215–17; Price, *The Marshall Plan and Its Meaning*, 51–55; Jacob K. Javits, *Order of Battle: A Republican's Call to Reason*, 239; George B. Schwabe to Benjamin C. Conner, December 11, 1947, George B. Schwabe Papers, Legislative File.

34. U.S. *Congressional Record*, 80th Cong., 1st sess., 1947, XCIII, Part 9, pp. 11122, 11137; Vandenberg to Taft, December 2, 1947, Vandenberg Papers; Dexter Perkins, *A History of the Monroe Doctrine*, 362–65.

because Republicans seemed to be more receptive to the need for controls than they had been, which might cost the Democrats a campaign issue. Therefore, he urged that Truman propose such an extensive program "as to be absolutely unpalatable to the Republican majority." Having obtained the reluctant endorsement of price controls from the Council of Economic Advisers, Truman embraced every measure that the council had suggested for study in its October report. On November 17, the President recommended to Congress a ten-point anti-inflation program: (1) restoration of consumer credit controls and action to curb inflationary bank credit, (2) regulation of commodity speculation, (3) extension of export controls, (4) extension of authority to allocate transportation facilities, (5) measures to induce the marketing of poultry and livestock at weights and grades that represented the most effective utilization of grain, (6) measures enabling the Department of Agriculture to encourage domestic conservation, and action to increase foreign production of food, (7) allocation and inventory controls over scarce commodities basically affecting the cost of living or industrial production, (8) extension and strengthening of rent control, (9) rationing of scarce consumer products basically affecting the cost of living, and (10) price controls over scarce products basically affecting the cost of living or industrial production and wage controls where they were necessary to maintain price controls.[35]

Truman's message put the Republicans on the spot. It not only shoved the responsibility for controlling rising prices on the opposition but also revealed discord among Republicans. Joe Martin attempted to throw doubt on the President's sincerity by demanding draft bills. Taft and Halleck cried "Politics!" They sought to place the blame for inflation back on the Administration and equated Truman's program with totalitarianism. Taft's response, however, was criticized by Senators Raymond E. Bald-

35. James E. Webb to Clark Clifford, "Suggestions for the Anti-Inflation Section of the President's Message to Congress," November 13, 1947, James E. Webb Papers; Council of Economic Advisers to the President, November 5, 1947, unsigned memo to Clifford, undated, Clifford Papers, Prices; Special Message to the Congress on the First Day of the Special Session, November 17, 1947, *Public Papers: Truman*, 1947, 495–98.

win and Ralph Flanders, who as members of a subcommittee investigating high prices, participated in hearings in the East. Their subcommittee had suggested congressional consideration of a long list of proposals, including rationing scarce foods, allocating grains, controlling consumer credit and exports, and raising the minimum wage. Republicans split among those completely opposed to inflation controls, those favoring acceptance of minor portions of Truman's program, and a small, highly vocal group who supported most of the ten points.[36]

The Republicans had no monopoly on internal disharmony. The Administration's failure to present a consistent united front before congressional committees lent credence to the Republicans' charge that the President's program represented a hasty attempt to gain political advantage with no expectation of legislative results. Three weeks elapsed before draft bills for Truman's program reached the Hill, and in the meantime, officials could not specify where controls would apply and what administrative standards would be established. With the Commerce Department favoring a piecemeal approach, Secretary Averell Harriman made a weak case for the President's program before the Joint Economic Committee. When Secretary of Agriculture Clinton Anderson first appeared before the committee, he said he could not implement Truman's request for authority to induce efficient marketing of livestock and indicated his distaste for price controls. Only later did he speak strongly and without reservation for the entire ten-point program.[37]

But the most spectacular example of disharmony in the Ad-

36. Marion T. Bennett to B. Carroll Reece, November 18, 1947, Bennett to Taft, November 22, 1947, Taft to Bennett, November 29, 1947, Marion T. Bennett Papers; John M. Vorys to Frances J. Wright, December 22, 1947, Vorys Papers; *The New York Times*, November 15, 1947, p. 1, November 18, 1947, pp. 1, 6, 8, November 19, 1947, p. 4, November 22, 1947, p. 4; Unsigned memorandum, November 20, 1947, Harley M. Kilgore Papers, Political File, Franklin D. Roosevelt Library.

37. T. J. Lynch to Snyder, December 10, 1947, John W. Snyder Papers; James E. Webb to Clifford, November 13, 1947, Webb Papers; "The Week," *New Republic*, 117 (December 8, 1947), 5; *The New York Times*, November 27, 1947, pp. 1, 28, December 2, 1947, pp. 1, 6; Allen J. Matusow, *Farm Policies and Politics in the Truman Years*, 163–64.

ministration involved the means of establishing bank credit controls. During the drafting of Truman's program, Clark Clifford asked Marriner Eccles, chairman of the Federal Reserve Board, to draw up a proposal for restraining inflationary consumer and bank credit. Eccles favored a special reserve requirement for member banks, but his proposal was scuttled by Secretary of the Treasury John Snyder, who reflected bankers' views. Eccles, nonetheless, took his case before Congress. Arguing that the bulk of Truman's program—direct controls—dealt with the effects rather than the causes of rising prices, he explained that monetary and fiscal policies were more viable weapons against inflation and urged enactment of the special reserve requirement. Snyder, on the other hand, insisted that Eccles' plan was unworkable but, when asked to present an alternative, had no response.[38]

Although the Council of Economic Advisers frantically pleaded with Truman to push for the special reserve clause—"an essential element in any anti-inflation plan"—the President refused to intervene in the Eccles-Snyder controversy. His inaction reflected the strong influence of the conservative Snyder, as well as Truman's ambivalent approach to inflation controls. No doubt he hesitated to sanction monetary controls that might apply the brakes too sharply to currency expansion. Direct controls, which Truman emphasized, would have no such effect on the money supply; at the same time, they had much greater appeal to a general public unschooled in economic complexities. When it came to definite programs to deal with inflation, Truman wavered, but his public rhetoric evoked the image of a vigorous President determined to check the high cost of living and blocked only by a reactionary Congress. Thus, in his press conference of December 11, he blithely ignored the confusion of his administrative subordinates, refused comment on the Snyder-Eccles controversy, and reasserted his demand for his entire ten-point program. "I

38. Marriner S. Eccles, *Beckoning Frontiers: Public and Personal Recollections,* 429–32; James L. Knipe, *The Federal Reserve and the American Dollar: Problems and Policies, 1946–1964,* 50–52, 59–60; U.S. Congress, Joint Committee on the Economic Report, *Hearings on the Anti-Inflation Program as Recommended in the President's Message of November 17, 1947,* 80th Cong., 1st sess., 1948, 137–42, 245, 250–51.

want it carried out to the letter," he said, "I think anything short of that will be inadequate to do the job."[39]

As expected, congressional response fell far short of the President's program. On December 11, the House Banking and Currency Committee reported a bill embodying two of the Administration's requests—extension of export and transportation controls. With regard to allocation and inventory controls over scarce commodities, regulation of commodity speculation, and marketing of livestock and poultry at weights and grades representing the most efficient use of grain, the bill provided for voluntary agreements between the government and producers with immunity from antitrust laws. In addition, the House bill raised the gold requirements for Federal Reserve banks. The committee's report defended its limited response to the President's requests by stating that if these "less controversial" and voluntary measures proved inadequate, Congress could consider granting additional authority when it had more time.[40]

Because the resolution was introduced under suspension of the rules, it required a two-thirds majority. This procedure, which allowed no amendments, drew attacks from Democrats Brent Spence of Kentucky, Sam Rayburn of Texas, and Mike Monroney of Oklahoma, all of whom found the measure inadequate and demanded an opportunity to strengthen the bill. Some Republicans, including Frederick C. Smith of Ohio, Albert M. Cole, and Edward H. Rees of Kansas, objected that the bill went too far. With opposition from both sides, the bill failed to obtain two-thirds majority, 202 to 188. Every Democrat, 26 Republicans, and Marcantonio voted against the resolution. Just before the vote, Majority Leader Halleck predicted that if the resolution were defeated, there would be no action that session and the minority would be responsible. It thus appeared that the strategy of House leaders was to make a gesture toward inflation control, put it in

39. Council of Economic Advisers to the President, November 25, 1947, Nourse Papers, Daily Diary; The President's News Conference of December 11, 1947, *Public Papers: Truman, 1947*, 508–9.

40. U.S. House of Representatives, Committee on Banking and Currency, *Aiding in the Stabilization of Commodity Prices and to Aid in Further Stabilizing the Economy of the United States*, House Report 1160 to accompany H.J. Res. 273, 80th Cong., 1st sess., 1947, 1–4.

a form that would be rejected, and then blame the Democrats for inaction.[41]

Despite the failure of control legislation in the House, the Senate continued to consider measures to curb prices. On December 17, it passed by voice vote a bill reinstating consumer credit controls and the following day turned its attention to a broader anti-inflation bill. The measure included most of the substance of the unsuccessful House resolution, plus authorization for the President to limit the use of grain by distillers and the use of price criteria in licensing exports. The Senate bill omitted the House provisions for poultry and livestock marketing agreements and for increasing the gold requirements for Federal Reserve banks. Democratic strategy on the floor consisted of attempts to make the bill conform more closely to Truman's requests. With Taft's approval, the minority won an amendment authorizing the Commodity Credit Corporation to engage in programs, subject to congressional veto, that would conserve food at home and stimulate production abroad. The Senate voted down Alben Barkley's amendment to grant the President, subject to congressional veto, powers to allocate and give priority to scarce commodities. The division, 48 to 35, generally followed party lines, but Byrd and Robertson of Virginia and O'Daniel of Texas joined the Republicans, and Morse and Langer voted with the minority. Barkley then introduced an amendment to eliminate completely the section providing for voluntary agreements among producers to control scarce commodities, arguing that they would be inadequate without compulsory controls in reserve and therefore did not warrant the relaxation of antitrust laws. The amendment won the support of all Democrats and Republicans Langer and Morse, but it lost, 44 to 42. Failing in these attempts to alter the measure substantially, most Democrats supported the bill as better than nothing, and it passed, 77 to 10.[42]

After the Senate's action, the House reconsidered its earlier

41. U.S. *Congressional Record*, 80th Cong., 1st sess., 1947, XCIII, Part 9, pp. 11388–92, 11395–96; *The New York Times*, December 18, 1947, p. 28.

42. U.S. *Congressional Record*, 80th Cong., 1st sess., 1947, XCIII, Part 9, pp. 11512, 11580, 11601–2, 11610; U.S. Senate, Committee on Banking and Currency, *Stabilization of Commodity Prices and the National Economy*, Senate Report 780 to accompany S.J. Res. 167, 80th Cong., 1st sess., 1947, 1–3.

decision on inflation. Its Banking and Currency Committee reported the Senate resolution without change and secured a closed rule, which limited debate and allowed no amendments. A Democratic attempt to open the bill to amendment failed, 203 to 143, by a vote paralleling the close party lines that had been drawn in the Senate. Democrats Alfred D. Elliott and Clarence F. Lea of California and E. C. Gathings of Arkansas broke ranks, and Republicans William Lemke of North Dakota, Alvin E. O'Konski of Wisconsin, Smith of Ohio, and Stockman of Oregon voted with the Democrats. The resolution passed, 281 to 73, with the opposition composed of such Democrats as Mike Mansfield and Mike Monroney, who considered the bill utterly inadequate, and such Republicans as Buffett of Nebraska and Smith of Ohio, who believed that it went too far. The House adjourned without taking action on the Senate bill to restore consumer credit controls.[43]

When he signed the bill, Truman took full advantage of the opportunity to strike a political blow at Congress. He compared his own proposals with the "pitifully inadequate" bill enacted by Congress and expressed "deep disappointment" at the "feeble" legislative action. Despite his expressions of dismay, the special session of 1947 resulted in a twofold triumph for Truman. He did not receive authorization for an adequate inflation-control program, but there is little reason to believe he expected or wanted it. What he wanted was to identify himself with popular frustrations over rising prices and to place the blame on the Republican-controlled Congress. In this he succeeded. The unity within Democratic ranks, unparalleled on any other important domestic legislation, was testimony to the potential political advantage of the inflation issue. Finally, these political maneuvers were accomplished without obstructing bipartisan support for the interim-aid measure. By late 1947, it was clear that a majority of Republicans would vote for containment of the supposed threat of communism, no matter how bitter the hostilities over domestic issues.[44]

43. U.S. *Congressional Record*, 80th Cong., 1st sess., 1947, XCIII, Part 9, pp. 11727–28, 11738.
44. Statement on the Resolution Enacted in Response to the President's Message of November 17, December 28, 1947, *Public Papers: Truman, 1947*, 532.

CHAPTER 6

BUILDING THE RECORD

BY THE BEGINNING OF 1948, the President's approach to domestic affairs for the remainder of the Eightieth Congress had been established. Truman continued and intensified his strategy of unequivocal demands for action on a variety of social and economic questions and sharp resistance to even the most limited congressional attacks on Administration programs. His primary objective was not legislative results, but the building of a record against the Eightieth Congress for the 1948 campaign. On the eve of the second session, the President recorded privately, "Congress meets —too bad, too. They will do nothing but wrangle."[1] His lack of hope for favorable action on domestic affairs was further indicated by his failure to work hard on behalf of his proposals and, in the early months of the second session, to cooperate closely with Democratic legislators. Truman made several important legislative requests without consulting the Democratic leaders and frequently vetoed bills that both liberal and conservative Democratic legislators had supported.

His strategy for 1948 was outlined in a memorandum drafted by Clark Clifford in November, 1947. Assuming that a politically advantageous approach would also be in the public interest, Clifford predicted the political developments of 1948 and suggested a winning strategy. He assumed that Thomas E. Dewey would be the Republican candidate but that Truman could win if he could hold the West and South. Clifford predicted—wrongly, as it turned out—that the South was "safely Democratic" and could be "safely ignored." Southern Democrats were extremely powerful in Congress, but it was not necessary to conciliate the South because there was no chance of getting a domestic program through Congress anyway. Instead, Clifford argued, it was neces-

1. William Hillman, *Mr. President; The First Publication from the Personal Diaries, Private Letters, Papers, and Revealing Interviews of Harry S. Truman,* 124.

sary to concentrate on Western progressives, farmers, labor, liberals, and urban minorities.

According to Clifford's memorandum, there were two principal threats to Truman's renomination and election. One was the probability of a third-party ticket headed by Henry A. Wallace—a prediction borne out when Wallace announced his candidacy on December 29 and began a campaign based on peace and radical reform. Clifford urged strong efforts to dissuade Wallace, to isolate him, and to undercut his appeal by moving to the left. He also believed that the Republicans would seek votes by embracing reform legislation in the second session. For this reason, too, Truman should adopt a strong liberal stance to the left of the Republicans.

After demonstrating the necessity for creating an image of progressive reform, Clifford detailed the correct legislative strategy. Since the Administration could not get legislative approval for its major domestic programs, he stated, "Its tactics must . . . be entirely different than if there were any real point to bargaining and compromise. Its recommendations . . . must be tailored for the voters, not the Congressmen; they must display a label which reads 'no compromise.' " The President should emphasize issues upon which there would be conflict between the Administration and Congress. Clifford dealt specifically with six controversial issues—high prices, housing, tax revision, natural resources, civil rights, and the Marshall Plan. His urging the President to take positions on the five domestic issues that would provoke domestic political controversy indicates Clifford's apparent belief in the strength of bipartisan support for the Marshall Plan. The need for European aid was so obvious and U.S. fear of communism so great that Congress would go along with the President on this crucial foreign-policy measure.[2]

Truman's State of the Union message reflected the influence of Clifford and the other Administration liberals, who had been working since early 1947 to commit the President to a strong and consistent liberal position. In their informal meetings, these men paid close attention to the drafting of the address and operated

2. Clifford, "Memorandum for the President," November 19, 1947, Clark M. Clifford Papers, Political File.

on Charles Murphy's assumption that the message should be the basis of the Democratic platform of 1948, "a comprehensive statement of the economic and social issues upon which the November election will be won or lost." Although the more blatantly partisan rhetoric in early drafts was toned down at the suggestions of Nourse and others, the State of the Union address clearly sounded the bell for the opening round of the 1948 campaign and showed the record of the Eightieth Congress to be the principal target of the Democrats.[3]

In sharp contrast to his address of the previous year, Truman's recommendations were comprehensive and boldly stated. He outlined four major domestic goals. His first was "to secure fully the essential human rights of our citizens," and he promised Congress a special message on this subject. The second objective was the development of human resources, for which Truman demanded the expansion of social security and increases in benefit payments, a program of national health insurance, federal aid to education, department status for the Federal Security Agency, and enactment of the long-range housing program. Third, the President dealt with the protection and development of natural resources, pressing for the expansion of soil conservation and reclamation programs, construction of more multipurpose dams with government transmission facilities to deliver power directly to consumers, and extension of the TVA idea to other river systems. His fourth goal was to strengthen the economy and facilitate a more equitable distribution of its rewards. To this end, Truman asked Congress to lessen the disparity between farm and nonfarm incomes through extension and revision of the price-support program, extension of crop insurance and rural electrification, and encouragement of soil conservation and marketing cooperatives. Competition should be strengthened through the tightening of the antitrust laws. As for labor, Truman recalled his position on Taft-Hartley but promised to enforce the law. In

3. Clark Clifford, interview, August 23, 1965, Washington, D.C.; David A. Morse to Clifford, January 2, 1948, Murphy to Clifford, September 19, 1947, Clifford Papers, Political File; Nourse to Clifford, January 3, 1948, Edwin G. Nourse Papers, Daily Diary.

addition, he called for an increase in the minimum wage, recommending for the first time that it be raised to seventy-five cents.[4]

The President insisted that all of these goals, as well as U.S. foreign-policy objectives, were threatened by inflation, and he called again for enactment of his entire anti-inflation program of November, 1947. Further, he asserted that since a government surplus was a potent weapon against inflation, revenues must not be reduced. However, since many people were suffering unduly from rising prices, individuals should be granted tax relief in the form of a $40 credit for each person and dependent, the revenue deficit to be compensated for by a corresponding tax increase in corporate profits.[5]

From Senator Taft came the official Republican response to the message. In a radio speech following the President's address, Taft correctly viewed the message as an affirmation of the President's commitment to the defense and expansion of the New Deal. Accordingly, he selected this theme as his major line of attack: "He has raised all the ghosts of the old New Deal with new trappings that Tugwell and Harry Hopkins never thought of." Taft expressed agreement with Truman's objectives but attacked the New Deal methods as economically unsound, something-for-nothing schemes that ignored the principles of freedom. He specifically attacked the President's anti-inflation program as unnecessary and tending toward totalitarianism, called the tax-cut plan discriminatory and inflationary, and equated the national health-insurance proposal to a demand for the "power to socialize and nationalize medicine." The Republicans, according to Taft, would go ahead with their own program to reduce expenditures, cut taxes, and where necessary, simultaneously provide federal assistance for, but maintain local control over, programs of health, education, housing, and social security.[6]

Taft's statement reflected the dilemma of the Republicans and

---

4. Annual Message to the Congress on the State of the Union, January 7, 1948, *Public Papers of the Presidents of the United States: Harry S. Truman, 1948*, 1–10.
5. *Ibid.*
6. U.S. *Congressional Record*, 80th Cong., 2d sess., 1948, XCIV, Part 1, pp. 65–66.

their inability to formulate a simple philosophy that adequately expressed the dominant ideas of the party. While attacking the New Deal in general terms and the expense of its programs in particular, many Republicans were reluctant to destroy specific programs, and Taft himself acknowledged the need to expand federal assistance for social welfare. Yet Republicans failed to recognize the popular appeal of the phrase itself and appeared to oppose all the reforms of the past fifteen years by indiscriminately denouncing the New Deal. Their dilemma was intensified by the ability of their more conservative members, especially in the House, to obstruct programs sponsored by many Republicans. The entire situation played into the hands of the President, who repeatedly equated the Eightieth Congress with the Republican party, and the Republican party with its most reactionary members.

The congressional majority made tax reduction its first business of the second session, and it displayed remarkable unanimity. Truman had opened the door to tax reduction with his proposal for the $40 cost-of-living tax adjustment. This proposal was a response to his advisers' prediction that the Republicans could obtain enough votes to override a veto of the tax cut in the second session. Thus Truman had asked the Council of Economic Advisers to formulate a plan that would offer relief to low-income groups, who were most seriously affected by rising prices, yet not contribute to inflationary pressures by reducing the federal surplus. The resulting plan had three parts: (1) a $20 tax abatement to each taxpayer and dependent, (2) opposition to the income-splitting provision for married couples, and (3) an excess-profits tax to compensate for revenue lost through the cost-of-living credit. Treasury Secretary Snyder opposed the excess-profits tax on the grounds that its anti-inflationary effects would be insubstantial, but Truman accepted all of the council's recommendations and boosted the cost-of-living tax credit to $40. Administration officials argued that this plan would minimize the inflationary effect of tax reduction by reducing corporations' inflationary investment spending and by curbing workers' demands for wage increases. Moreover, both the government surplus and the amount of money in circulation would remain constant. Finally, they maintained that the corporate-tax increase would neither reduce necessary and desirable expansion of production nor result in higher prices.[7]

Political considerations were equally potent. Predicting that a tax cut would be enacted despite the President's opposition, Clifford argued in his November memorandum that "the Administration might as well get the credit for it and save what it can of its taxation principles." Truman did not consult Democratic leaders in Congress about his tax proposal, and after hearing the President's recommendation in the State of the Union message, Minority Leader Barkley reportedly told Clifford, "This is like playing a night ball game. I'm supposed to be the catcher and I should get signals. I not only am not getting the signals but someone actually turns out the lights when the ball is tossed." Robert Doughton, ranking Democrat on the House Ways and Means Committee, described the proposal as a political move, and he too complained, "We Democrats were not called into consultation when the bill was being prepared." That the President did not try to secure prior Democratic support for his recommendation indicates that it was primarily an attempt to dissociate himself from opposition to a popular demand, rather than a bona fide proposal. In fact, the nature of his plan coincided well with the strategy of juxtaposing "the image of a reactionary 'rich man's' Congress with that of a more liberal Administration."[8]

The tax-abatement plan was of course anathema to Republicans. Their main line of attack was that it was inflationary because almost all of the relief would go to those who spent practically all of their current incomes, because the budget surplus for fiscal 1948

7. John D. Clark, "The President's Economic Council" (undated MS, John D. Clark Papers), Chapter V; Council of Economic Advisers to the President, December 13, 1947, Snyder to the President, December 24, 1947, Clifford Papers, Political File; unsigned "Memorandum on General Economic Merits of the President's Tax Plan," undated, Charles S. Murphy Papers, State of the Union Message.

8. Clifford, "Memorandum for the President," 36–38; *The New York Times,* March 10, 1948, p. 24; Doughton to Arthur W. Thomas, Jr., January 29, 1948, Robert L. Doughton Papers; A. E. Holmans, *United States Fiscal Policy, 1945–1959: Its Contributions to Economic Stability,* 89.

and 1949 would be reduced by the lag in collecting corporate taxes, and because the tax on corporation profits would discourage production. In an effort to win additional Democratic support, the Republicans did revise their own program. Besides reductions on individual income taxes ranging from 30 to 10 per cent, the bill they introduced in the House raised the general exemption from $500 to $600 and provided an additional $600 exemption for persons over sixty-five and for the blind. Moreover, it incorporated the income-splitting provision that so many Democrats had supported in the first session. Sensitive to the issue of inflation, the Republicans argued that the committee bill was anti-inflationary because it would increase incentive and thus increase production.[9]

While the House debated the committee bill, Democratic leaders attempted to work out a compromise measure around which the minority could unite. Their proposal differed from the President's, which emphasized Truman's lack of close cooperation with Democratic congressmen. Their plan was incorporated in a motion sponsored by Rayburn to recommit the committee bill with instructions to report back a measure providing for a general increase in exemptions from $500 to $700, which Rayburn professed would approximate Truman's $40 tax credit for the low-income groups and be slightly more for those in higher brackets; a 75 per cent corporate excess-profits tax; and an allowance for married couples in all states to split incomes, as well as gifts and inheritances for federal tax purposes. Doughton and 21 other Democrats, mostly Southerners, voted against Rayburn's motion, but the Republican lines were solid, and they defeated the substitute, 258 to 159. The Republican bill then passed, 297 to 120, with the support of 63 Democrats, 47 of whom had voted for the Rayburn motion. Only one Republican, Andersen of Minnesota, voted against the bill. Although Democratic defections had not increased since the last vote on tax reduction, they were enough to override a presidential veto. The crucial test for tax reduction would be in the Senate. Republican Clifford Hope of Kansas predicted that because the House bill would not win enough converts

9. U.S. House of Representatives, Committee on Ways and Means, *Revenue Act of 1948*, House Report 1274 to accompany H.R. 4790, 80th Cong., 2d sess., 1948, 1–20.

134

among Democratic senators, it would have to be modified to meet their objections.[10]

The bill reported by the Senate Finance Committee was designed to do just that. The total revenue loss was reduced about $2 billion by limiting the percentage reductions to a range from 12.6 per cent in the lowest brackets to 5 per cent for the upper income groups. In all other respects the Senate bill was identical to the House measure, including the income-splitting provision favored by substantial numbers of Democrats in the first session. GOP strategy proved effective, as one by one Democrats who had opposed tax reduction in 1947 rose to explain that they would now support the bill because it included the income-splitting provision and the general increase in exemptions which made the bill more equitable. The bill passed, 78 to 11, with solid Republican support and the votes of 30 Democrats. Of the 30 minority supporters, 11 had supported the two 1947 bills, and 16 had opposed the tax-cut measures of the first session but had voted for either the McClellan income-splitting amendment or the Lucas amendment to raise exemptions or both. Southerners gave the Republicans most of their minority support, but as A. E. Holmans has pointed out, the tax bill was not simply the work of a conservative Republican-Southern Democratic coalition—it drew support from Northern and Southern liberals as well as from Southern conservatives. According to Holmans, "What happened was that nearly all Senators were in favor of tax reduction of some sort, and that H.R. 4790 included something of all the widely canvassed forms of tax reduction, whereas its predecessors did not."[11]

The President accused Congress of "reckless disregard for the soundness of our economy and the finances of our Government" and outlined two major objections to the bill: It would cut revenues by $5 billion at a time when a large surplus was necessary to reduce the debt and to serve as a cushion for unforeseen expendi-

10. U.S. *Congressional Record*, 80th Cong., 2d sess., 1948, XCIV, Part 1, pp. 916, 925–26; Hope to John McKenna, March 1, 1948, Clifford R. Hope Papers.
11. U.S. Senate, Committee on Finance, *Revenue Act of 1948*, Senate Report 1013 to accompany H.R. 4790, 80th Cong., 2d sess., 1948, 2–5. For Democratic support, see remarks by McClellan, O'Conor, Lucas, Holland, and Murray in U.S. *Congressional Record*, 80th Cong., 2d sess., 1948, XCIV, Part 3, pp. 3061, 3167, 3207–10, 3213, 3233; Holmans, *United States Fiscal Policy*, 95.

tures; moreover, the tax bill would contribute to inflation by substantially increasing purchasing power, thus creating a demand
that could not be filled because employment and production were
already at record levels. While emphasizing the economic un-
soundness of the measure, he also took a crack at Congress for leg-
islating in the interests of the wealthy. He pointed out the in-
equity of a measure that would permit almost 40 per cent of the
relief to go to persons with net incomes of more than $5,000, a
group that constituted less than 5 per cent of the tax-paying population. Truman's veto had little effect. Fulbright was the only senator who switched to support the Administration, and the veto
was overridden, 78 to 10. Only 3 Democrats who had supported
the bill in the House—Richard F. Harless of Arizona, James W.
Trimble of Arkansas, and W. J. Bryan Dorn of South Carolina—
voted to sustain the veto. Their votes were more than cancelled
by the 27 Democrats who jumped on the bandwagon going in the
opposite direction. Republicans Andersen and Thruston Morton
of Kentucky voted to sustain.[12]

The Republicans had fulfilled the second major objective that
they had expressed upon capturing control of Congress. The Administration had weakened its case by admitting that some form
of tax relief was desirable, yet the threat of a presidential veto
enabled the Democrats to demand major revisions—greater relief
for low-income groups, extension of the income-splitting provision, and reduction in the total revenue loss—as their price for
supporting tax reduction. Thus, the Republicans made only a
limited assault on the Administration's tax program: They had
not undermined the principle of progressive taxation, and un-
expectedly, the dangers of inflation abated by the end of 1948.
Although he suffered the immediate embarrassment of large
Democratic desertions, the President did not lose the political
advantage, for he had strongly put himself on record in favor of
tax relief to the more populous low-income groups through a plan
that would have minimized the inflationary effects of tax
reduction.

12. Veto of the Income Tax Reduction Bill, April 2, 1948, *Public Papers:
Truman, 1948*, 200–203; U.S. *Congressional Record*, 80th Cong., 2d sess., 1948,
XCIV, Part 3, pp. 4026, 4053.

Finally, Truman's tax-cut veto marked a departure from traditional relationships between the White House and the Democratic leaders in Congress. George Elsey called the cooperation with party leaders "unprecedented." The date of the veto message was set at the request of Rayburn and Senator J. Howard McGrath, new chairman of the Democratic National Committee. Barkley's suggestions on the content of the message were incorporated, and draft copies were sent to Rayburn and Barkley before the message was delivered. While this cooperation did not forestall passage of the motion to override, Elsey felt that it was the kind of strategy essential for effective presidential leadership. Lack of such cooperation in the past, he believed, had made many congressional Democrats bitter. "If this type of liaison had been carried out continuously during the last couple of years, White House-Congressional relations would . . . have been much better than they are now."[13]

The President also made political capital out of congressional revision of the social security system. As with the tax legislation, however, the Republicans took a moderate approach, and the support of a majority of Democrats led to the Republicans' success. The first attack on social security consisted of an attempt to enact a measure identical to the one pocket-vetoed at the close of the first session. The bill, which excluded newspaper and magazine vendors from coverage, was explained and defended by Congressman Bertrand W. Gearhart, Republican of California. He agreed that these individuals should be included in the social security system and predicted that Congress would do so, but he thought they should be brought in as independent contractors, not as employees as the federal district court had ruled. That decision, Gearhart charged, was a usurpation of legislative authority and would result in endless confusion because vendors had many employers. His description of the court decision revealed his real attitude. The court had used "fantastic" reasoning "in order to scoop them [the vendors] into the voracious maw of Social Security against their will and over their violent objection." Most congressmen were friendlier to the idea of social security, but the House passed

13. Elsey, "Memorandum for the File; Subject: Veto of Tax Bill, H.R. 4970," George M. Elsey Papers, Subject File.

the bill without debate by voice vote, and the Senate followed its example on March 23.[14]

Truman sent a vigorous message of disapproval three days after his tax-cut veto. He based his objections on the fundamental issue of whether social security coverage should be diminished or expanded. The administrative difficulties of protecting news vendors as employees, he asserted, and the possibility of future coverage under a different category did not destroy their right to immediate coverage or reduce the necessity to defend the entire program against piecemeal attack. Truman found little support even among staunch Administration Democrats. In the brief debate, only Congressman Herman P. Eberharter of Pennsylvania defended the President's position, while other Democrats argued that vendors should be protected in the category of independent contractors through special legislation and emphasized the administrative problems of covering vendors as employees. The House overrode, 308 to 28, and the Senate, 77 to 7.[15]

Meanwhile, the House had already sought to undercut a different set of court rulings affecting social security coverage. In 1947, the Supreme Court had held that economic realities as well as common-law definitions should be used to determine which groups were entitled to protection as employees. It had ruled that various groups, including door-to-door salesmen, home workers, and taxi and truck drivers—totaling from 500,000 to 750,000 persons—rightfully belonged in the social security system as employees. On the basis of this ruling, the Treasury Department had amended existing regulations to bring these groups under coverage. The House bill negated the Court's rulings and Treasury regulations by providing that persons who did not fall under the usual common-law definitions of employees were to be excluded from coverage. The basic issue, sponsors of the bill maintained, was the authority of Congress, not another branch of government, to determine the scope of social security coverage. Although Ad-

14. U.S. *Congressional Record*, 80th Cong., 2d sess., 1948, XCIV, Part 2, p. 2143, Part 3, p. 3268.
15. Veto of Bill to Exclude Vendors of Newspapers and Magazines from Social Security Coverage, April 5, 1948, *Public Papers: Truman, 1948*, 205–6; U.S. *Congressional Record*, 80th Cong., 2d sess., 1948, XCIV, Part 4, pp. 4430–33, 4594.

ministration Democrats opposed this exclusion in larger numbers than they had the news-vendors bill, it passed by a large majority, 275 to 52.[16]

The Senate took a more restrained approach by the addition of two amendments. The first, written in the Finance Committee, provided that those persons in the excluded group who were already contributing to the fund would retain their coverage. Thus, the bill would exclude only those who had never been under the system. The second amendment, sponsored by a large number of Republicans and Democrats, provided for increasing benefits for the blind, the aged, and dependent children. The bill passed, 74 to 6, with Democrats Barkley, Brien McMahon of Connecticut, Pepper, and Taylor, and Republicans Ives and Morse voting No.[17]

The second Senate amendment put the President in a dilemma. From one point of view, consistency demanded another veto, but the measure also increased public-assistance benefits, a step the President had recommended in his special message of May 24 on social security. Administration officials, with the exception of Federal Security Administrator Oscar R. Ewing, believed that preventing the exclusion of up to 750,000 persons outweighed the desirability of increasing federal aid to the states for public-assistance payments, which in any case fell short of the President's recommendations. The President finally vetoed the bill, pointing out that Congress had ample time to enact separate legislation to increase federal public-assistance payments, as well as time to comply with his other recommendations for extending social security.[18]

16. Snyder to James E. Webb, June 9, 1948, John W. Snyder Papers; U.S. House of Representatives, Committee on Ways and Means, *Maintaining the Status Quo in Respect of Certain Employment Taxes and Social Security Benefits Pending Action by Congress on Extended Social Security Coverage*, House Report 1319 to accompany H.J. Res. 296, 80th Cong., 2d sess., 1948, 1–4; U.S. *Congressional Record*, 80th Cong., 2d sess., 1948, XCIV, Part 2, p. 1908. See remarks by Eberharter, Lynch, Price, and Douglas opposing the bill, *ibid.*, pp. 1896–98, 1905, 1906–7.

17. *Ibid.*, Part 6, pp. 7033, 7133–34.

18. Special Message to the Congress on Social Security, May 24, 1948, *Public Papers: Truman, 1948*, 274–75; Ewing to Truman, June 10, 1948, Webb to Hopkins, June 9, 1948, Nourse to Staats, June 8, 1948, U.S. Bureau of the Budget Files, Reports to the President on Pending Legislation; Veto of Resolution Ex-

Truman's veto gained some support for the Administration's position, but both houses voted to override by large majorities. In the Senate, 28 Democratic senators, mostly Southerners but including liberals Francis J. Myers of Pennsylvania, Harley Kilgore of West Virginia, and Sheridan Downey of California, deserted the Administration, and Langer and Morse were the only Republicans to support the veto. The voting in the House was similar: 89 Democrats, primarily Southerners but with a few such Administration stalwarts as John R. Murdock of Arizona, Clarence Cannon of Missouri, and John F. Kennedy of Massachusetts, voted to override, and only 4 Republicans—Welch of California, Keating and Javits of New York, and James G. Fulton of Pennsylvania—voted to sustain.[19]

Just before overriding the President's veto of House Joint Resolution 296, the House acted on one more revision of the social security system. This bill incorporated the restrictive features of House Joint Resolution 296, but it also provided for extending coverage to include about 3,500,000 persons, primarily employees of municipal and state governments and workers in nonprofit organizations. The catch was that the coverage was conditional upon the approval of their employers. The House passed the bill unanimously, but Administration Democrats pointed out its restrictive features. They criticized the Republican leaders for preventing the introduction of amendments or recommittal motions, and contrasting the bill with the comprehensive recommendations of the President, they derided the measure as "a feeble, futile effort of the Republican Eightieth Congress to leave the false impression that it is interested in social legislation." When the Senate took no action on the measure during the remaining five days of the session, Democrats insisted that the Finance Committee bottled it up when Republicans realized that the minority would attempt to amend the bill to make it meaningful.[20]

---

cluding Certain Groups from Social Security Coverage, June 14, 1948, *Public Papers: Truman, 1948*, 344–46.

19. U.S. *Congressional Record*, 80th Cong., 2d sess., 1948, XCIV, Part 6, pp. 8093, 8191.

20. *Ibid.*, pp. 8142–43, 8144, 8146, 8166; Democratic National Committee,

Such was the record of the Eightieth Congress on social security. The attack on this New Deal program was limited in the sense that the groups excluded had never been protected even though federal courts had declared their eligibility under existing legislation. Moreover, legislators consistently asserted that coverage should be extended, although by special legislation, and Congress did provide for some increase in public-assistance payments. Republican defections on social security were few—Ives, Langer, and Morse in the Senate, and Javits, Keating, Welch, and Fulton in the House—and largely paralleled Republican support for the Administration on other domestic issues. Democratic votes made the presidential vetoes ineffective, and the bloc of Southerners who often deserted the Administration on domestic issues drew at this time additional support from non-Southerners.

The legislative-executive conflict over functions of the Labor Department resulted in another congressional victory, but the margin was smaller and revealed fewer Democratic and more Republican defections from party voting. The issue involved an attempt by the President to strengthen the department by giving it permanent authority over the United States Employment Service, which handled unemployment compensation as a part of the Federal Security Agency. USES had been under the Labor Department during the war, but it was due to revert back to the FSA six months after the official proclamation terminating the war. In 1947, Truman had submitted a reorganization plan transferring USES permanently to the Labor Department, but Congress had rejected it on the grounds that USES and the Bureau of Employment Security, which was then in the FSA, belonged in the same agency. Trying a new approach, in January, 1948, the President submitted a reorganization plan placing both offices in the Labor Department. This plan was not simply an attempt to forge another weapon for the campaign attack on Congress. Since the Senate had rejected the 1947 proposal by only two votes, Truman asked Charles Murphy to approach Republican Senator Joseph H. Ball of Minnesota, who had led the support for the plan. Ball

"Files of the Facts, I. Human Resources," Democratic National Committee Records.

predicted that the Senate would approve a reorganization to place both USES and BES in the Labor Department, and the Administration made substantial efforts to get the 1948 plan approved.[21]

By this time, however, the argument of the congressional opposition had shifted. Republican John Vorys of Ohio reported privately that it was not a question of where USES and BES belonged functionally. Instead, he wrote, "The Department of Labor, under New Deal management, had such a bad record that Congress has been cutting down its jurisdiction, as in the Taft-Hartley bill, rather than giving it new powers, as the President now requests." Publicly, opponents of reorganization objected to giving the Labor Department authority over unemployment compensation, arguing that the department was designed to foster the interests of labor and thus could not be impartial in supervising unemployment compensation in which employers, as well as labor, had a stake. They also asserted that no reorganization should take place until the Hoover Commission on organization of the executive branch submitted its report. Despite protests from Democrats that the Eightieth Congress was further crippling the Labor Department, the House rejected the plan by a voice vote.[22] The reorganization proposal received strong support in the Senate Committee on Labor, which approved it, 9 to 4. When the bill came to the floor, however, only 5 Republicans broke ranks, while 19 Southern, Southwestern, and border-state Democrats defected, and it was defeated, 58 to 25.[23]

Not content with thwarting the reorganization plan, Congress next tried to achieve immediate transfer of USES back to the FSA

21. U.S. *Congressional Record*, 8oth Cong., 2d sess., 1948, XCIV, Part 2, p. 1716; Murphy to Truman, August 15, 1947, Murphy Papers; David A. Morse to Schwellenbach, February 5, 1948, U.S. Department of Labor Files, Secretary's File; Gibson to Gael Sullivan, February 5, 1948, John W. Gibson Papers.

22. Vorys to C. I. Weaver, February 16, 1948, John M. Vorys Papers; U.S. House of Representatives, Committee on Expenditures in the Executive Department, *Reorganization Plan Number 1 of 1948*, House Report 1368 to accompany H. Con. Res. 131, 8oth Cong., 2d sess., 1948, 5–7; U.S. *Congressional Record*, 8oth Cong., 2d sess., 1948, XCIV, Part 2, pp. 1708–9, 1712, 1716–18, 1721.

23. *The New York Times*, March 5, 1948, p. 13. In committee, four Democrats and Republicans Aiken, Ball, Cooper, Smith, and Morse supported the plan; Taft, Donnell, Jenner, and Ives opposed it. U.S. *Congressional Record*, 8oth Cong., 2d sess., 1948, XCIV, Part 3, pp. 2907, 2909–14, 2921.

through a rider attached to a supplemental appropriations bill for the Federal Security Agency. Although Truman took the highly unusual action of vetoing an appropriations bill, he defended his position by saying that such legislation did not belong in an appropriation bill, that Congress itself had earlier opposed any Administration changes pending the report of the Hoover Commission, and that USES properly belonged in the Labor Department.[24]

Faced with a vast amount of unfinished business in the remaining four days of the session, neither house paid close attention to the President's veto message. The Senate overrode, 72 to 17, and the House, 288 to 115, with 55 Southerners providing the necessary margin.[25]

The issue of public power provided another opportunity for the Eightieth Congress to attack in a minor way an Administration program. Congress cut only about 12 per cent from budget estimates for the Interior Department, but it curtailed federal transmission facilities and barred the construction of a supplementary steam plant for the Tennessee Valley Authority. While approving record funds for reclamation and power development, the House Appropriations Committee argued that it was "unsound and against the principles of our form of government to appropriate Government funds for the construction of transmission lines, switchyards, substations, and incidental facilities where private capital is prepared to provide them." By prohibiting the government from engaging in such projects, Congress enabled private companies to benefit from the transmission and sale of government-produced electricity.[26]

Legislative action on TVA appropriations followed voting behavior in general on matters of public power. The Administration

24. Veto of Bill Making Supplemental Appropriations for the Federal Security Agency, June 15, 1948, *Public Papers: Truman, 1948,* 354–55.
25. U.S. *Congressional Record,* 80th Cong., 2d sess., 1948, XCIV, Part 7, pp. 8437, 8473–74.
26. John R. Waltrip, "Public Power During the Truman Administration" (Ph.D. dissertation, University of Missouri—Columbia, 1965), 73; U.S. House of Representatives, Committee on Appropriations, *Interior Department Appropriation Bill, 1949,* House Report 2038 to accompany H.R. 6705, 80th Cong., 2d sess., 1948, 7–9, 20.

requested $4 million to begin construction of a new steam plant with which the TVA could supplement water power during dry periods. In order to operate efficiently by assuring a constant supply of electricity, private utilities routinely combined hydro power with steam power, and the TVA had steam capacity in its system from its beginning. The new request was necessary to meet an increasing demand for power in the area, and the Administration insisted that more power was essential to national defense since TVA supplied the Oak Ridge atomic energy installation, as well as aluminum and chemical industries. Reflecting not only Republican efforts to cut federal expenditures but also hostility to expanding government involvement in business, the House Appropriations Committee turned down the request. A House attempt to restore the funds failed, 192 to 152. Few legislators crossed party lines: Democrats James Domengeaux of Louisiana, Alfred J. Elliott of California, W. F. Norrell of Arkansas, and Francis E. Walter of Pennsylvania opposed the amendment, and 16 Republicans voted for it. GOP supporters of the steam plant included some liberals who often supported Truman, like Javits and Hull, but predominantly consisted of Western Republicans whose interest in public power overcame their usual opposition to the Administration on domestic issues.[27]

After the defeat in the House, Truman intervened and urged the Senate Appropriations Committee to restore the steam-plant funds. The Senate acceded to the President's plea and passed a committee amendment to restore the funds, 45 to 37. Only 3 Democrats—Byrd of Virginia, O'Daniel of Texas, and Umstead of North Carolina—deserted the Administration, while 10 Republicans voted with the minority. As in the House, power-state Republicans supported the Democrats, while Republican opponents of the steam plant included those consistently adamant on the issue of public power and federal spending, as well as moderates from New England who objected to subsidizing cheap public

27. U.S. House of Representatives, Committee on Appropriations, *Government Corporations Appropriation Bill*, 1949, House Report 1880 to accompany H.R. 6481, 80th Cong., 2d sess., 1948, 74–76; U.S. *Congressional Record*, 80th Cong., 2d sess., 1948, XCIV, Part 4, pp. 5623–24.

power in areas that might attract industry from their states. After considerable haggling, the conference committee struck out the amendment, and in the last hours of the session, the Senate conceded without debate.[28]

The President took full advantage of the political opportunity presented in the Interior and TVA appropriations bills. His position was strengthened by overwhelming Democratic support for the Administration's policy. Upon signing the bills on June 20, he lashed out at Congress with two statements. The rejection of the steam plant, he said, was inconsistent with previous congressional policy, and he called the decision bad, foolish, reckless, and irresponsible. The refusal to appropriate funds for federal transmission facilities, Truman asserted, was congressional "capitulation to special interest groups" and nullification "by indirect action [of] the purposes of permanent legislation which the Congress has refused to change by direct action."[29]

The Eightieth Congress, over Truman's objections, also struck at the antitrust program in a limited way. Since 1945, various bills had been introduced to exempt carrier associations and rate-setting bureaus from antitrust legislation. In the Reed-Bulwinkle measure under consideration by the Eightieth Congress, the Interstate Commerce Commission retained its power to approve rates and related matters, but it would be possible for carriers to agree among themselves which rates proposed by individual carriers would be submitted or withheld from the ICC. Operating within these associations, carriers could exercise an initial veto over rates proposed by individual carriers and thus hinder the filing of pro-

28. Letter to the Chairman, Senate Appropriations Committee, Urging Restoration of Funds for a TVA Steamplant, May 26, 1948, *Public Papers: Truman, 1948*, 278; U.S. *Congressional Record*, 80th Cong., 2d sess., 1948, XCIV, Part 7, p. 8282. For opposition by Republican moderates, see remarks by Baldwin (Connecticut) and Flanders (Vermont), *ibid.*, Part 6, p. 8116, Part 7, p. 8278. Similar sentiment probably accounted for opposition from Lodge and Saltonstall of Massachusetts, who on other issues were more disposed to support the Administration. *Ibid.*, pp. 9090–91.

29. Statement by the President Upon Signing the Government Corporation Appropriation Act, June 30, 1948, *Public Papers: Truman, 1948*, 389; Statement by the President on the Interior Department Appropriation Act, June 30, 1948, *ibid.*, 390–91.

posed rates that might be in the public interest. The bill, moreover, would kill two antitrust suits then pending in the courts. Opponents of the measure felt that Congress should delay action pending judicial clarification of the antitrust laws. They maintained that necessary cooperation in the public interest could proceed without violation of existing law. The bill's real purpose, they argued, was to permit objectionable practices by carriers. Its supporters professed that efficient transportation required cooperation among carriers and that the ICC would retain full authority to protect the public against monopolistic practices.[30]

The Senate passed the bill, 60 to 27, at the close of the first session, and the House followed suit in 1948, 273 to 53. Although the ICC recommended approval, Truman heeded the advice of the Justice Department and his Council of Economic Advisers and vetoed the measure on the grounds that it was inconsistent with the Administration's antimonopoly program. Both houses voted to override within three days of similar action on the FSA appropriations and social security bills. In the Senate, 16 Democrats deserted the Administration, and the veto was overridden, 63 to 25, with four votes to spare. Half of the Democrats voting with the majority were those who usually opposed the Preisdent, but some Democrats who routinely supported the Administration responded to the pressure of shipper interests and voted to override. On the other hand, a group of anti-Administration Southerners supported the veto in order to keep alive pending suits against railroads for alleged discrimination against the South. Republicans Aiken, Langer, and Tobey voted to sustain. The House divided similarly, overriding the veto 297 to 102. In all, 69 Democrats opposed Truman, and 4 Republicans supported him.[31]

30. Webb to Hopkins, June 8, 1948, Bureau of the Budget, Reports to the President on Pending Legislation; Charles Murphy to Truman, March 25, 1948, Murphy Papers.

31. Robert L. Branyan, "Antimonopoly Activities during the Truman Administration" (Ph.D. dissertation, University of Oklahoma, 1961), 176; Veto of Bill to Exempt Certain Carriers in Interstate Commerce from the Antitrust Laws, June 12, 1948, *Public Papers: Truman, 1948*, 330–32; *The New York Times*, June 17, 1948, p. 1; U.S. *Congressional Record*, 80th Cong., 2d sess., 1948, XCIV, Part 7, pp. 8435, 8633–34.

The vetoes of legislation that would alter the Administration's policies for taxes, social security, labor, public power, and antitrust revealed the extent to which Truman had moved away from the conciliatory position he had taken when he approved the portal bill in early 1947. His steadfast opposition did not prevent these assaults, but it did enable him to build a case against the Republican-controlled Congress on issues that had widespread appeal among voters. During the second session, the President also built a case against Congress for what it did not do. He followed his State of the Union address with a series of special messages demanding action on housing, civil rights, social security, federal aid to education, and an increase of the minimum wage. In bombarding Congress with requests that were certain to be denied, Truman cast himself as the Galahad of reform pluckily fighting the dragon of privilege.

The legislative-executive battle over the President's demands for new legislation split the Republicans more sharply than the assault on existing programs and frequently found Taft, the oft-termed conservative marching with the Administration. Legislation for federal aid to education had been introduced in Congress several times but had received little presidential support. Speaking with Truman in 1947, Elbert Thomas found him hesitant because it was a "pretty hot issue and full of controversy." Although he ignored the issue in his 1947 State of the Union message, in 1948 Truman spoke of the "financial crisis" in public education and insisted that the Federal Government must provide funds. There was substantial Republican support in the Senate, and under Taft's leadership, a bill providing federal grants to the states for public education was passed, 58 to 22. Only 5 Democrats (4 Southerners and 1 from Maryland) voted against the bill, objecting primarily because the program would involve too much federal spending—about $300 million for the first year—and unnecessary federal interference in state affairs. The 17 Republican opponents included conservatives, such as Kem of Missouri and Hawkes of New Jersey, who used the States'-rights argument, senators who objected to the fact that poorer states would receive the lion's share of federal aid, and those with large Catholic constituencies who disliked the bill's failure to provide for parochial schools. Despite these objections, a majority of senators from both parties supported the bill.[32]

Nonetheless, the measure lay inert in the House Labor and Education Committee. Finally late in the session, the President decided to strike hard for congressional action. On May 25, he met with Democratic leaders and asked them to press for passage of the education bill, as well as minimum-wage revision, and the next day he sent a letter to House Speaker Martin urging support of the education measure. Martin, however, as soon as he had learned of the May 25 meeting, had indicated that the House would not act. He told the press that the Democrats were not united behind the measure and that Truman, by making his plea less than a month before adjournment, had "clearly placed these bills in the realm of politics." A petition sponsored by Democrat W. M. Wheeler of Georgia to pry the bill from the committee failed to obtain the necessary signatures before Congress adjourned. This failure saved the House minority from embarrassment, since Rayburn himself opposed federal aid to education because he feared federal interference with segregated schools.[33]

Truman's request for increasing the minimum wage failed to pass even one house, but it reflected his move to the left as dramatically as his action on the education issue. Early in 1947, an informal committee composed of Labor Department officials and union representatives had begun to plan a strategy that focused on efforts to raise the minimum wage to at least 65 cents an hour. When approached by representatives of the committee, Taft approved of raising the minimum wage to 65 or 70 cents but refused to sponsor the bill. Late in the first session, a House subcommittee held hearings on amendments to the Fair Labor Standards Act but reported no bills. During the first session, Truman had asked for a minimum figure of 65 cents. Labor officials privately ex-

32. Thomas to Glenn E. Snow, November 6, 1947, Elbert D. Thomas Papers; U.S. *Congressional Record*, 80th Cong., 2d sess., 1948, XCIV, Part 3, pp. 3911–58.
33. *The New York Times*, May 26, 1948, pp. 1, 20; Letter to the Speaker on Federal Aid to Education, May 26, 1948, *Public Papers: Truman, 1948*, 276–77; Rayburn to Sherry Arrington, February 23, 1948, Rayburn to Belle Dent, August 9, 1948, Sam Rayburn Papers, Miscellaneous File.

pressed satisfaction with this increase, and a bill introduced by Barkley provided for 65 cents, as did one introduced by Republicans Aiken, Tobey, Ives, and Cooper. Yet in 1948, the President upped his request to 75 cents, thereby distinguishing his proposal from that of the Republicans and making it even more favorable to labor.[34]

By May, 1948, Labor Department officials concluded that Congress probably would not raise the minimum wage before adjournment. The Senate Labor Committee had heard testimony on two bills, but the department considered the measure sponsored by Republicans so complex and controversial that there was no chance for action, and it believed that the majority would not approve the Democrats' bill, which embodied Truman's request. Many officials felt, however, that the President should "attempt to make a further record." The meeting with Democratic leaders on May 25 contributed to the building of Truman's record, but little except Martin's recriminations came of it.[35]

The most notable failure of the Eightieth Congress was the Republicans' inability to enact the comprehensive housing legislation sponsored by Taft. Throughout the early months of 1948, Truman prodded Congress to act on the measure, which had been under consideration since 1945. The Senate passed the Taft-Ellender-Wagner bill by acclamation on April 22, but the key vote came on an amendment sponsored by Republican Harry P. Cain of Washington to eliminate the controversial provisions for low-rent public housing and slum clearance. It was rejected, 49 to 35, with 24 Republicans and 25 Democrats voting against the amendment. With one exception, Democratic opposition to public housing came from a group of 14 Southerners and 2 border-

34. Robertson to Schwellenbach, May 22, 1947, U.S. Department of Labor Files, Secretary's File; Robertson to Schwellenbach, February 27, 1947, U.S. Department of Labor Files, Record Group 174, John W. Gibson File; *The New York Times*, June 28, 1947, p. 6; William Tyson to the Secretary's Staff Committee, February 3, 1947, Department of Labor, Gibson File; Schwellenbach to Truman, June 10, 1947, Department of Labor, Secretary's File; George Johannes to Elmer Staats, December 1, 1947, U.S. Bureau of the Budget Files, Files Retained by the Bureau in the Executive Office Building.

35. Robertson to Morse, May 21, 1948, U.S. Department of Labor Files, David A. Morse File.

state senators, a group that usually opposed the Administration. The 18 Republican votes against public housing likewise followed established patterns of opposition to welfare-state proposals.[36]

For a short time, it seemed that the House would have an opportunity to vote on the bill that a majority of both parties in the Senate had supported. The prospect for House action brightened when 3 Republicans voted with 11 Democrats in the Banking and Currency Committee to report the bill. But Chairman Jesse P. Wolcott of Michigan, an inveterate opponent of public housing, devised another means of killing the bill; he went before the Rules Committee and testified against his own committee's bill. The Rules Committee supported him and refused a rule. Despite Taft's pleas for action, the House leaders stood behind Wolcott and the Rules Committee. A petition sponsored by Javits to pry the bill loose failed to get the necessary 218 signatures, and the measure died.[37]

House action on the housing bill came while Truman was touring the West on what he delighted in calling a nonpolitical tour. At every opportunity, he lashed out at the Republican-controlled Congress and with obvious relish explained to his audiences why the House was not permitted to vote on the housing issue. Constructing his theme of the special-interest Congress, he declared, "They have emasculated the housing bill in the interest of the real estate lobby."[38]

The pattern of strong presidential demands and congressional inaction, followed by presidential castigation of Congress, which operated on issues of inflation control, federal aid to education, minimum-wage amendments, housing, and national health insurance was not followed in the area of civil-rights legislation. First

36. U.S. *Congressional Record*, 80th Cong., 2d sess., 1948, XCIV, Part 4, p. 4683.

37. Signing the petition were 45 Republicans and 125 Democrats. If every Democrat had signed, there would have been enough names to release the bill.

38. Rear Platform and Other Informal Remarks in Washington, June 9, 1948, *Public Papers: Truman, 1948*, 305–6; Address in Seattle Before the Washington State Press Club, June 10, 1948, *ibid.*, 314; Address Before the Greater Los Angeles Press Club, June 14, 1948, *ibid.*, 350; Rear Platform Remarks in Missouri, Illinois, Indiana, and Ohio, June 17, 1948, *ibid.*, 372–74; Rear Platform Remarks in Pennsylvania and Maryland, June 18, 1948, *ibid.*, 374–75.

of all, Truman displayed caution on this issue. Although he went much further than had any previous President, his advocacy was hesitant and restrained, and to an even greater extent than on most proposals, he failed to match rhetoric with concrete efforts. Also, congressional Democrats were less committed to action on civil rights than on other Administration programs, and finally, Truman refused to emphasize civil rights in his crusade against the Eightieth Congress. This refusal can be ascribed to his less-than-total commitment, as well as to the political dangers in the Administration's civil-rights proposals.

The initial impetus for the President's civil-rights program had come from personal conviction and political necessity. Truman was disturbed by discrimination and particularly outraged at the violence against Negroes, some still in military uniform, in the postwar years. He was also acutely sensitive to the importance of the black vote and the liberals' lack of enthusiasm for him. Civil-rights leaders applied increasing pressure on the President to use his office on behalf of the Negro. With such motivations, he created the Committee on Civil Rights in December, 1946, and appointed to it prominent leaders sympathetic to the cause of minorities. Thus, Truman had set in motion influences that he could not later ignore. The committee's report of October, 1947, documented the obvious fact that blacks were unjustly treated and called for a wide range of measures attacking segregation and discrimination. Although it was perhaps more far reaching than Truman had expected, the report obliged him to act.[39]

Political necessities made presidential action even more essential. In his November memorandum, Clifford identified liberals and Negroes as two groups to whom the Administration needed to make special appeal. Liberals were "not overly enthusiastic about the Administration," and black leaders were disillusioned

39. William C. Berman, "The Politics of Civil Rights in the Truman Administration" (Ph.D. dissertation, Ohio State University, 1963), 45, 67–68; Harry S. Truman, Memoirs, Vol. II, Years of Trial and Hope, 180; Barton J. Bernstein, "The Ambiguous Legacy: The Truman Administration and Civil Rights" (MS, Truman Library, 1966), 8–13; Barton J. Bernstein, "America in War and Peace: The Test of Liberalism," in Barton J. Bernstein, ed., Towards a New Past: Dissenting Essays in American History, 304–5; Richard M. Dalfiume, Desegregation of the U.S. Armed Forces: Fighting on Two Fronts, 1939–1953, 134–45.

about the possibility of gains through the Democratic party. Specifying civil rights as one of the six big issues, he acknowledged the vulnerability of the Democratic party and advised Truman to "go as far as he feels he possibly could go in recommending measures to protect the rights of minority groups." The impact of Clifford's advice was heightened when Wallace announced his candidacy in December, 1947.[40]

On February 2, 1948, the President, as he had promised in his State of the Union address, delivered a special message on civil rights. He set forth a ten-point program, including legislation outlawing the poll tax and providing federal protection against lynching, establishment of a permanent Fair Employment Practices Commission, statehood for Hawaii and Alaska, home rule for the District of Columbia, and equalization of naturalization laws. He also requested that existing laws be strengthened and discrimination in interstate transportation be prohibited. He advocated establishing a permanent Commission on Civil Rights, a civil-rights division in the Department of Justice, and a joint congressional committee on civil rights. In addition, Truman promised to end discrimination in federal employment and in the armed services, a pledge that he did not fulfill until the heat of the campaign.[41]

The reaction of Congress to the President's message was not surprising. Truman himself had predicted, "They no doubt will receive it as coldly as they did the State of the Union message. But it needs to be said." Southern Democrats more than met his expectations. Senator Tom Connally of Texas put it mildly when he wrote a constituent, "We are deeply distressed in the utterances of the President and the position in which he has placed our party." An angry delegation of Southern governors called on Senator J. Howard McGrath, chairman of the National Democratic Committee, but were told that the Administration would not modify its proposals. While a movement began immediately in the South to deny the national party its usual place on the ballot,

40. Clifford, "Memorandum for the President," Clifford Papers; Bernstein, "The Ambiguous Legacy," 13.
41. Special Message to the Congress on Civil Rights, February 2, 1948, *Public Papers: Truman, 1948*, 121–26; Dalfiume, *Desegregation of the Armed Forces*, 156–71.

the response of most congressional Democrats was restrained. Answering a call from E. H. Crump to organize a fourth party, Senator Kenneth McKellar advised caution and delay. Rayburn condemned the legislative proposals but insisted, "I am not going to vote against the Democratic ticket just because I don't agree with President Truman on these matters," a note echoed by Senators Maybank of South Carolina and Sparkman of Alabama. These Democrats reminded their constituents of the benefits to the South of Democratic rule and argued that the Republican party was no better on the issue of civil rights. Congressman John Kerr of North Carolina summed up the predominant mood: Truman's message was a "foolish piece of politics," but many civil-rights measures had long been advocated by the Republican party, and that party had "never been sympathetic in respect to some of the grave problems of the South."[42]

While refusing to abandon Truman and the national party, Southern Democrats were determined to obstruct all civil-rights legislation. With the lone exception of Claude Pepper, all the Southern senators planned a filibuster if any part of the President's program reached the floor. Minority Leader Barkley, after gauging the Southern reaction to the message and discovering that no congressman had been consulted on the proposals, refused to sponsor an Administration omnibus bill, whereupon the bill was shelved. Nor did the Republicans demonstrate vigorous support for the President's program. Over the objections of Taft, the Senate Labor Committee reported a bill for a permanent FEPC, but the leaders refused to allow it to reach the floor, and Fred Hartley, chairman of the House committee, would not even hold hearings. The Senate Judiciary Committee reported an antilynching bill, but a small group of Republicans holding the balance of power

42. Hillman, *Mr. President*, 134; Connally to J. K. West, March 30, 1948, Thomas C. Connally Papers, Political File; Jack Redding, *Inside the Democratic Party*, 133–39; Crump to McKellar, February 3, 1948, McKellar to Crump, February 7, 1948, Kenneth D. McKellar Papers; Rayburn to E. L. Covey, February 10, 1948, Rayburn to R. H. Cochran, February 10, 1948, Rayburn Papers, Miscellaneous File; Maybank to Sam C. Augustine, February 9, 1948, Burnet R. Maybank Papers; Mimeographed press release, Address of John Sparkman to Young Democrats of North Carolina, February 7, 1948, Kerr to W. S. Pritchard, February 25, 1948, Kerr, news release, February 23, 1948, John H. Kerr Papers.

had combined with Southern Democrats to remove its teeth. The measure was reported only five days before the end of the session and did not reach the floor, where it would have met with a filibuster in any case.[43]

The one important part of the President's domestic program that met with substantial congressional approval was in agriculture. With the 1948 elections close at hand, Republicans were much less anxious to cut budget estimates for the farm programs. They supported figures for the school-lunch program and farm-tenant loans, increased the REA authorization by $100 million, and appropriated $262.5 million for the AAA soil-conservation program, only $37 million less than had been in effect before the 1947 cuts.[44]

The major agricultural legislation of the Eightieth Congress dealt with the government's price-support program. The existing program, due to expire at the end of 1948, supported basic commodities at 90 per cent of parity and maintained the New Deal emphasis on limiting production. Reflecting the views of liberal economists who wanted to attack the problem of low farm income by increasing consumption rather than reducing production, the Administration presented a program in 1948 based on abundance instead of scarcity. Continuing to respond to the political pressure of the farm bloc, the Department of Agriculture asked for the extension of price supports, production control, and the concept of parity. However, it wanted to revise the parity formula; price supports were to be flexible and considerably below the level deemed to be desirable in the long run. Production controls would be used selectively to deal with chronic surpluses of particular crops rather than to limit agricultural production in general. The Administration thought these devices would encourage farmers to adjust production to the market, but it also proposed measures

43. *The New York Times*, March 7, 1948, pp. 1, 31, March 10, 1948, pp. 1, 24; Berman, "The Politics of Civil Rights," 77, 86; Elmer W. Henderson to the Board of Directors of the National Council for a Permanent FEPC, June 8, 1948, Philleo Nash Papers; *The New York Times*, May 19, 1948, pp. 1, 23, June, 15, 1948, p. 1.
44. *Congressional Quarterly*, 4 (1948), 76–78.

to expand consumption, including a food-allotment program for low-income families.[45]

In spite of a few Republicans who decried "picking up where the New Deal left off," it was clear that Congress would extend the farm program in some form. Whether it would follow the new directions charted by the Department of Agriculture was another question. Ignoring the proposals for expanding consumption, Congress spent most of its time debating the form of price supports. Although spokesmen for the Farm Bureau and the Farmers Union—the latter somewhat reluctantly—came out in favor of a flexible support schedule, cotton and wheat farmers wanted to retain the high, fixed supports. Reflecting these pressures and unwilling to abandon rigidly guaranteed prosperity for larger farmers, the House Committee on Agriculture reported a bill sponsored by Representative Clifford Hope of Kansas extending the existing price-support program, which provided for 90 per cent of parity. The committee maintained that because demand had not yet dropped to normal levels, it was impossible "to formulate a long-range agricultural price-support policy which will be effective under conditions which may be expected to exist under normal peacetime situations and at the same time meet conditions as they exist at present." The Administration opposed the Hope bill, but it received strong support from most Democrats and a substantial number of Republicans and passed by voice vote.[46]

The Senate bill, sponsored by George Aiken of Vermont, provided for immediate adoption of a flexible system of supports that would range from 90 to 72 per cent of parity, depending upon supply and demand. Floor debate centered on attempts by a group of about twenty-five Democrats, mostly Southerners and includ-

45. Allen J. Matusow, *Farm Policies and Politics in the Truman Years*, 115–24, 132–35; Special Message to the Congress on Agriculture, May 14, 1948, *Public Papers: Truman, 1948*, 256–58.

46. U.S. *Congressional Record*, 80th Cong., 2d sess., 1948, XCIV, Part 6, pp. 7983–8014; Matusow, *Farm Policies and Politics*, 136–42; U.S. House of Representatives, Committee on Agriculture, *Stabilization of Agricultural Prices*, House Report 1776 to accompany H.R. 6248, 80th Cong., 2d sess., 1948, 1–3; Reo M. Christenson, *The Brannan Plan: Farm Politics and Policy*, 17.

ing Minority Leader Barkley, to extend the existing program. The Senate approved an amendment sponsored by Kentucky Senators Cooper and Barkley to retain the 90 per cent support for tobacco, but efforts by Democrats to substitute the House bill for the committee bill failed, and the latter passed, 79 to 3. While conferees of both houses stood firm for their respective bills, the time approached for adjournment. Finally, to prevent expiration of the program, they reached a compromise whereby the provisions of the House bill would apply until 1950, at which time the flexible formula of the Senate bill would go into effect. Thus, Congress postponed a decision on a long-range farm program.[47]

Although most Republicans favored the sliding scale and Democrats were responsible for the Administration's defeat, Truman castigated Congress, when he signed the bill, for failing to establish a long-range agricultural policy. He also noted that because a bill extending the Commodity Credit Corporation prohibited it from acquiring more storage space, the CCC would be unable to store commodities close to the farms and would encounter increased costs. The "special interests who will make money by unnecessary handling of grain will profit from this provision," the President charged, and the farmers and consumers would pay. Finally, Truman attacked Congress for failing to comply with other presidential requests, including expansion of consumption, adequate funds for soil conservation, improvement of rural housing, health, and education. "In the field of agriculture, as in so many others," he concluded, "most of the business of the 80th Congress was left unfinished."[48]

Congressional attacks on the Administration's labor, social security, tax, and antimonopoly programs in the Eightieth Congress were supported almost unanimously by Republicans and a large, primarily Southern, group of Democrats. In the House, GOP defections never surpassed eleven and shifted from issue to issue, with the exceptions of Merlin Hull of Wisconsin, Jacob Javits of

47. *Ibid.*, 16–17; Matusow, *Farm Policies and Politics*, 139–44; U.S. *Congressional Record*, 80th Cong., 2d sess., 1948, XCIV, Part 7, pp. 8537–44, 8557, 8573, 8598, 8612.

48. Statement by the President Upon Signing the Agricultural Act, July 3, 1948, *Public Papers: Truman*, 1948, 399–400.

New York, and Richard Welch of California, who usually supported the Administration. A group of about fifty legislators, predominantly from Southern and border states, gave fairly consistent Democratic support to the successful Republican position. In the Senate, Langer, Morse, and Aiken were the only Republicans who consistently supported Truman's attempts to defend New Deal programs, and Cooper sometimes joined them, but they were outnumbered by the ten to fifteen Southerners who formed the nucleus of Democratic opposition to the Administration.

The divisions over public power and agriculture were somewhat different. Democratic defections on the TVA steam-plant votes were few, and although a good many power-state Republicans voted with the Democrats, there were not enough votes to defeat the Republican leaders. Both parties overwhelmingly supported extension of the price-support system, but members of the President's own party defeated the flexible program.

Again, slightly different patterns emerged on the Administration's proposals for aid to education, housing, and civil rights. In the latter case, Southern Democrats were adamantly opposed, but Republican leaders displayed no great interest. The housing and education bills did not come to a vote in the House. If the 45 Republicans, primarily from urban areas, who signed the release petition for the housing bill had been joined by all the Democrats, the bill would have been released. The petition lacked 44 names, and 58 Democrats, mostly Southerners, did not sign. The nucleus of the 30 Senate Republicans who supported the education bill and the 26 who favored federal assistance for slum clearance and low-rent housing consisted of about 15 Republicans who had taken a moderate approach on Taft-Hartley and budget reduction in the first session. Senate Democratic opponents of the federal education and housing programs were generally opposed to other Administration domestic programs: 5 of the 6 Democrats opposed to federal aid to education, and 14 of the 17 against federal slum clearance and public housing were among the Administration's consistent antagonists.

Truman ignored the complex voting patterns and credited Republicans in general with all the iniquities of the conservative members of both parties. Throughout the second session, he had

157

been building his case against the Eightieth Congress. At times he was defensive, responding to legislation attacking Administration policies with resounding vetoes. At other times, and increasingly as the session progressed, Truman took the offensive with a series of demands for extension of social and economic reform. Congress had not delivered, and Truman was fully armed to take his case to the people.

CHAPTER 7

ENDURANCE OF THE
COLD WAR CONSENSUS

RANCOROUS legislative-executive relations in domestic matters did not hinder the Administration in pursuing its Cold War foreign policy. During the second session, Congress authorized the European Recovery Program, laid the groundwork for the North Atlantic Treaty Organization—the first peacetime alliance for the United States—and expanded the military with increased defense appropriations and a temporary draft. In areas of foreign policy that had less anticommunist appeal and much domestic importance, Congress was more reluctant to support Administration proposals. Yet, despite its lack of enthusiasm, the Republican Congress extended the program for reciprocal-trade agreements and relaxed immigration policy to admit displaced persons from Central Europe. More importantly, in agreement with the executive, it launched U.S.-Soviet relations on the course that they would follow for the next twenty years.

Although the Administration had laid intricate groundwork for the Marshall Plan in the preceding six months, there was no certainty that Congress would approve when it began consideration early in 1948. Impressions he received during the debate over interim aid troubled Vandenberg. As he wrote his wife in December, 1947, "If the resistance which is showing up to the little short-range European relief bill . . . is any criterion, our friend Marshall is going to have a helluva time down here when he gets to his long-range plan." When Truman officially requested a $17 billion, four-year program, some Republican leaders were cool. Taft spoke in favor of a "reasonable" amount of relief on a year-to-year basis but opposed a large, long-term recovery program and called Truman's proposal "a kind of five-year plan, like Stalin's or a European TVA." The election-year political climate and the inevitable battles over domestic policy further complicated prospects for the European Recovery Program. Potential obstacles lay all over the political landscape: Southern uneasiness about Truman's domestic program, farm-state concern about shortages and commodity controls, distrust of containment on the left and right, and conservative unwillingness to support "socialism" in Europe with large U.S. expenditures.[1]

Samplings of public opinion showed support increasing for the Marshall Plan, and Vandenberg and the Administration worked harder to sell the program to reluctant congressmen. Their efforts were fortified by the work of the Committee for the Marshall Plan and the favorable reports of the committees Truman had appointed. In December, Vandenberg told Under Secretary of State Lovett that it was "*vitally* important" for the Administration to enlist "four or five top-level business executives as . . . aggressive witnesses" before congressional committees. Truman recalled from London Ambassador Lewis Douglas, a former congressman with business and government experience, to serve as special liaison between the State Department and the Senate Foreign Relations Committee. Vandenberg also convinced the Administration that it was wise to delete the specific figure of $17 billion from its draft bill and to provide for the administrator of the program to be independent of the State Department.[2]

Before presenting the bill to the Senate, Vandenberg pushed for one other revision, one that he had not discussed with the Administration. During the committee hearings, considerable attention focused on the $6.8 billion requested for the first fifteen months. Taft spearheaded the opposition to this figure, citing former President Herbert Hoover's statement that $4 billion was adequate. The issue was further complicated because only $4.5 billion of the $6.8 billion requested was to be spent during fiscal

1. Arthur H. Vandenberg, Jr., ed., *The Private Papers of Senator Vandenberg*, 378–80; *The New York Times*, December 31, 1947, p. 1; Bennett to O. J. Bingman, February 13, 1948, Marion T. Bennett Papers.

2. Harold L. Hitchens, "Influences on the Congressional Decision to Pass the Marshall Plan," *Western Political Quarterly*, 21 (March, 1968), 52–53; Vandenberg to Lovett, December 10, 1947, Vandenberg to Marshall, December 31, 1947, Lovett to Vandenberg, January 2, 1948, Arthur H. Vandenberg Papers, William L. Clements Library, University of Michigan; Vandenberg, ed., *Private Papers of Senator Vandenberg*, 386; The President's News Conference of January 29, 1948, *Public Papers of the Presidents of the United States: Harry S. Truman, 1948*, 115, 117.

1949. While Marshall refused to budge from the Administration's figure, which he considered the absolute minimum, State Department representatives explained to the committee that the extra $2.3 billion represented goods to be contracted for at that time but not to be paid for until later. To ward off attacks on the floor, the committee, under Vandenberg's leadership, reduced the authorization to $5.3 billion and limited its duration to twelve months. This change represented no real decrease, but one committee member predicted that the maneuver would convert ten or twelve doubtful senators. The committee also proposed to use $3 billion of the surplus for fiscal 1948 for ERP, thus minimizing opposition from advocates of tax reduction. Two developments abroad strengthened Vandenberg's case before he took the bill to the floor. On February 27 a Communist *coup d'état* overthrew the Czech government, and two days later the press reported Soviet pressures on Finland for military bases and economic agreements.[3]

The largest threat to ERP was the possibility of major revision of the committee bill on the floor. Since January, a group of from 20 to 30 Republicans, including some senators who completely opposed ERP, as well as those who wanted substantial alterations, had been planning strategy. This bloc objected especially to the large amount to be spent, to the possibility that Russia and her satellites would benefit through the revival of East-West trade, and to support of what they called socialist governments in Western Europe. Opponents and revisionists attained their fullest strength in the amendment sponsored by Taft to cut the first year authorization to $4 billion. This amendment, which was rejected, 56 to 31, brought out the maximum Senate Republican opposition to foreign aid in the Eightieth Congress. In all, 23 Republicans—18 from inland and 5 from the East Coast—supported the amendment; 13 coastal Republicans and 11 from the interior voted No. Of the Democrats, 4 Southerners, 2 Southwesterners, and 1 each from Colorado and Idaho supported the

3. *The New York Times*, January 19, 1948, p. 1, January 22, 1948, p. 1, January 29, 1948, p. 1, February 1, 1948, pp. 1, 20, February 15, 1948, pp. 1, 29, February 18, 1948, pp. 1, 3; Lynch to Snyder, January 29, 1948, John W. Snyder Papers; Vandenberg, ed., *Private Papers of Senator Vandenberg*, 386. Hearings on tax reduction were being held simultaneously with hearings on ERP.

attempt to cut foreign-aid spending. The other objectives of the revisionist bloc were to separate relief from recovery, eliminate calculations of need on the basis of balance-of-payments deficits, and strengthen private enterprise by supporting specific industrial and agricultural projects rather than a program based on government planning. Homer Capehart's substitute amendment embodying these ideas was rejected, 68 to 22.[4]

Opposition from the left was slight. It was led by Glen H. Taylor of Idaho, who two weeks earlier had announced his candidacy for the Vice-Presidency on the third-party ticket sponsored by the Progressive Citizens of America. Expressing the views of Wallace supporters, who assumed that Soviet-U.S. cooperation was possible and necessary, Taylor charged that ERP would "bypass the United Nations, permanently divide the world, and lead to war." The Senator's substitute bill provided for a program of European recovery administered by the United Nations and supported by contributions from all countries, with the United States providing $5 billion for the first year. Senators William Langer and Claude Pepper alone supported Taylor's proposal as the Senate voted it down, 74 to 3.[5]

Having failed to modify the bill in any important respect, many of the revisionists ultimately swung over. Pepper, 9 Republicans, and 7 Democrats who had backed the Taft or Capehart amendments voted or were paired in favor of the final measure. Including pairs, only 16 Republicans and 4 Democrats opposed ERP, which passed the Senate, 69 to 17.[6]

The Marshall Plan had a rougher time in the House Foreign Affairs Committee, where the question of aid to China reap-

4. Clyde M. Reed to Kenneth S. Wherry, January 27, 1948, Reed to George Ball, Kenneth S. Wherry, C. Wayland Brooks, and William F. Knowland, January 13, 1948, Kenneth S. Wherry Papers. Senators Wherry, Dworshak, Kem, Jenner, Malone, Reed, Watkins, Brooks, Ecton, Moore, Cordon, Knowland, Brewster, Capehart, McCarthy, Revercomb, Cain, and Ball were reported in attendance at a strategy meeting on January 30. *The New York Times*, January 31, 1948, pp. 1, 6; U.S. *Congressional Record*, 80th Cong., 2d sess., 1948, XCIV, Part 2, pp. 2116–19, 2190–92, 2206, 2211, 2518–20, 2708, 2775.

5. Karl M. Schmidt, *Henry A. Wallace: Quixotic Crusade, 1948*, 43–44, 61; U.S. *Congressional Record*, 80th Cong., 2d sess., 1948, XCIV, Part 2, pp. 2458–60.

6. *Ibid.*, p. 2793.

peared. Republicans had demanded a program of Chinese aid during consideration of the interim-aid bill. At that time, Administration spokesmen promised to submit a plan later, and Truman renewed the pledge in his State of the Union message. On January 23, Senator Styles Bridges published a letter he had written to Marshall pressing for a program for China. In it, he had stated, "Only the immediate submission . . . of a proposal for the protection of the vital interest of the American people in Chinese independence can create confidence in the good faith of the Administration's Far Eastern policy." Reluctant to increase its military commitment and doubtful that the Nationalist government would pursue policies essential to ease social and economic unrest, the Administration nonetheless sent to Congress a plan for $570 million of economic aid.[7]

Important Republicans immediately criticized the absence of military assistance and received support from former Ambassador to Russia William C. Bullitt, Lieutenant General A. C. Wedemeyer, who had been a commander in the Far East, and General Douglas MacArthur. Declining to leave his duties in Japan to testify before the House Foreign Affairs Committee, MacArthur disqualified himself as an expert adviser on China or the European Recovery Program. He did send a lengthy telegram to the committee, in which he rated the goal of an independent, friendly China as one of highest priority for U.S. foreign policy:

> The Chinese problem is part of a global situation which should be considered in its entirety in the orientation of American policy. Fragmentary decisions in disconnected sectors of the world will not bring an integrated solution. . . . It would be utterly fallacious to underrate either China's needs or her importance.

As the Republican critics did, MacArthur emphasized the need for a military solution and relegated internal reforms to a position of secondary importance. But Marshall would give no more ground to Asia-Firsters. He continued to insist that Chinese aid should be separate from ERP and that the shortcomings of Na-

7. *The New York Times*, January 22, 1948, p. 1; Special Message to the Congress on the Need for Assistance to China, February 18, 1948, *Public Papers: Truman*, 1948, 144–46.

tionalist military leaders would make military aid a waste. Vandenberg's and Eaton's efforts to give priority to European aid were overruled by party leaders Martin, Halleck, Taft, and Wherry, who insisted on an omnibus approach despite the fact that the Senate was ready to pass its bill providing for only European economic aid. The Foreign Affairs Committee, after defeating along party lines a Democratic attempt to report the bill approved by the Senate, reported an omnibus measure of $5.3 billion of aid to Europe, $275 million of military aid to Greece and Turkey, $420 million of economic and $150 million of military aid for China, and $60 million for the International Children's Fund. It also limited the authorization for any appropriation to one year and tightened U.S. control over exports from participating countries to Eastern Europe.[8]

The House ratified the committee bill with only one significant change, the inclusion of Spain among the recipients of European aid. The amendment passed on a division vote, 149 to 52, after Congressman Vorys announced that the committee would not object because joint action by the participating countries to include Spain would still be necessary. An attempt to reduce the amount for European aid was defeated by a division vote, 112 to 61. On the only roll call taken on the measure, the House approved the final version, 329 to 74. Of the 11 Democrats opposed, 7 were from the South; the largest bloc of Republican opposition came from Midwesterners. Of the 61 Republicans who voted No, only 3 represented coastal states, while 12 were from Illinois, 5 from Indiana, 2 from Iowa, 2 from Kansas, 4 from Nebraska, 7 from Ohio, and 2 from Wisconsin.[9]

The Senate conferees capitulated to the House omnibus approach, as well as the stipulation for yearly authorization, but the upper house insisted upon excluding Spain and pared down aid to China to $338 million in economic assistance, plus an addi-

8. *The New York Times,* February 19, 1948, p. 2, February 24, 1948, p. 12, March 3, 1948, p. 1, March 5, 1948, p. 1, March 20, 1948, p. 1; MacArthur to Charles A. Eaton, March 3, 1948, John M. Vorys Papers; James W. Pratt, "Leadership Relations in United States Foreign Policy Making: Case Studies, 1947–1950" (Ph.D. dissertation, Columbia University, 1963), 175, 180–81.

9. U.S. *Congressional Record,* 80th Cong., 2d sess., 1948, XCIV, Part 3, pp. 3706, 3828, 3874–75.

tional $125 million to be used at the President's discretion, which eliminated military aid. The House also agreed to the special "watch-dog" committee on European aid that the Senate had authorized. Both houses accepted the conference report without change. Although riddled with Republican changes, the Administration's program emerged from the legislative process substantially intact.

Final enactment came even as executive-legislative relationships were sadly deteriorating in the domestic area. However irate Southern congressmen were over the President's civil-rights message, Southern opposition to ERP was slight, and it came from legislators who had opposed Administration foreign policy before Truman took a stand on civil rights. The President contributed to the separation of domestic and foreign policy by delaying his veto of tax reduction until the Marshall Plan was passed. Moreover, although Congress had just overridden his tax veto, Truman praised the legislature when he signed the ERP bill "for the cooperation it has evidenced in the prompt passage of this measure." Again, the overriding consideration of most supporters was the potential of ERP for containing the presumed threat of communism. Acheson maintained that the paramount objective of the Administration was to combat "hunger, poverty, desperation, and chaos," but he readily acknowledged that Congress and the public were most interested in how the Marshall Plan would operate to check the expansion of Soviet power. To Republican Clifford Hope, economic recovery was essential to Europe's ability to "resist the march of Communism." Democratic Senator Elmer Thomas of Oklahoma put it much the same way when he said he had supported the Marshall Plan because it would "enable the free countries of Europe to prepare themselves to resist the aggression of Russia over their territories."[10]

The foreign-aid program still had to pass the hurdle of the ap-

10. *The New York Times*, April 2, 1948, pp. 1, 19; Statement by the President Upon Signing the Foreign Assistance Act, April 3, 1948, *Public Papers: Truman, 1948*, 203; Dean Acheson, *Present at the Creation: My Years in the State Department*, 233; Hope to David C. White, February 14, 1948, Hope to Mrs. Fred F. Freeman, February 5, 1948, Hope to Dr. Joseph F. Burket, January 24, 1948, Clifford R. Hope Papers; Thomas to Mrs. A. D. Bace, March 12, 1948, Elmer Thomas Papers.

propriations process. There, Republican revisionists in the House made one final attempt to curtail it. On June 5, the House Appropriations Committee reported a bill providing only $5 billion for ERP and extending its duration to fifteen months, thus cutting funds by almost 25 per cent. Maintaining that much of the postwar aid had been wasted and that the Administration could not justify the amount requested, the committee declared that the Congress must "safeguard the dwindling assets and domestic economy of this nation." The House leaders supported the committee, and although Dirksen, Vorys, and Javits attacked a cut, Dirksen's amendment to cut the time period to twelve months failed by teller vote, 148 to 113, and the House accepted the bill by voice vote.[11]

The House attempt to dilute the original intention of Congress dismayed Republican leaders in and out of Congress. Thomas E. Dewey, governor of New York and candidate for the presidential nomination, appealed to House Appropriations Chairman Taber personally to restore the cut, but without success. Vandenberg could think of nothing "more shocking or more subversive of every Republican pretense toward international cooperation" and in an unprecedented move went before the Senate Appropriations Committee to plead for restoration of the funds. He called the House cut a "meat-axe approach" that would "subvert the principles and purposes of the original Congressional commitment." Even as Vandenberg testified, Taber pledged himself to "fight to the end to retain this reduction . . . and resist all the special pressures which are being mustered to make a treacherous raid on the American taxpayer." The Senate accepted the House figure but reduced the duration of the appropriation to twelve months and thereby eliminated most of the cut. The House held firm, and the bill went to conference. As the time approached for adjournment, neither House nor Senate conferees would budge, and the whole program appeared to be in jeopardy. Finally, after Taft announced that he would hold Congress in session until the appropriations were passed and Taber's colleagues on the House committee be-

11. U.S. House of Representatives, Committee on Appropriations, *Foreign Aid Appropriation Bill,* 1949, House Report 2173 to accompany H.R. 6801, 80th Cong., 2d sess., 1948, 1–3.

gan to desert him, Taber capitulated. At the last minute, the conferees reached a face-saving compromise that retained the $5 billion but gave the President authority to spend the entire amount in twelve months if he saw fit. The skirmish over ERP appropriations revealed once again the reluctance of conservative Republicans to support fully the bipartisan foreign policy. Even more notably, it demonstrated Vandenberg's tremendous influence in the Senate and, indirectly, in the House.[12]

Before ERP had initially passed Congress, the President had escalated both his Cold War rhetoric and his requests for Cold War measures. By March, 1948, Administration officials were increasingly uneasy about the United States' prospects for maintaining its own interests and containing Soviet influence in Europe, the Middle East and Far East. In addition to the Czech *coup* in February and Soviet pressures on Finland, the Greek uprising had not been quelled, the U.S. commander in Germany reported growing tension in Berlin, and the U.S. ambassador at Nanking predicted that communist gains in China pointed to the defeat of Chiang Kai-shek or at least a negotiated peace with the communists. At home, these developments produced agitated demands for a tougher foreign policy.[13]

Election-year politics also contributed to a more vigorous Cold War policy. Both Clifford and Elsey felt that to escape defeat in November, Truman needed to act decisively to renew public confidence in his leadership on foreign-policy matters. Credit for the positive aspects of foreign policy, especially the Marshall Plan, was bypassing the President and going to Marshall and Vandenberg. Clifford and Elsey suggested that Truman devote his address before a Saint Patrick's Day dinner in New York to the topic of foreign relations, insisting that "a very strong speech" was essen-

12. Dewey to Taber, June 7, 1948, John Taber Papers; Vandenberg to John Foster Dulles, June 4, 1948, Vandenberg Papers; Pratt, "Leadership Relations in Foreign Policy Making," 217–19; Vandenberg, ed., *Private Papers of Senator Vandenberg*, 396–97; *The New York Times*, June 10, 1948, p. 5, June 16, 1948, p. 1, June 17, 1948, pp. 1, 12, June 19, 1948, p. 2, June 20, 1948, pp. 1, 40.

13. W. W. Rostow, *The United States in the World Arena*, 217; James Forrestal, *The Forrestal Diaries*, Walter Millis and E. S. Duffield, eds., 390–95; Warner R. Schilling, Paul Y. Hammond, and Glenn H. Snyder, *Strategy, Politics, and Defense Budgets*, 40; *The New York Times*, March 10, 1948, pp. 1, 5.

tial for "his own prestige and the prestige of the United States." The departments of Defense and State endorsed the idea of a foreign-policy statement by the President, but Marshall, with the backing of Snyder and Harriman, insisted that Truman go before Congress first. Marshall also pleaded for a simple, businesslike statement and no inflammatory or belligerent language. Clifford and Elsey argued that the phrasing had to be blunt in order to justify the message, as well as the requests for legislation. Moreover, they preferred a single speech in New York that would serve as a trial balloon for a later speech to Congress. Pointing out that details of a legislative program had not yet been worked out, they felt that groundwork should be laid with legislative leaders before Truman addressed the Congress. Marshall won out. Taking congressional leaders by surprise, the White House announced on March 15 that the President would make a foreign-policy statement to Congress two days later.[14]

The tone of the subsequent speeches, however, revealed that the advice of the White House aides had prevailed over Marshall's. Truman for the first time charged the Soviet Union with sole responsibility for obstructing world peace. The critical world situation, he maintained, existed because "one nation has not only refused to cooperate in the establishment of a just and honorable peace, but—even worse—has actively sought to prevent it." Truman accused Russia of violating international agreements, obstructing the work of the United Nations, and, in a "ruthless course of action," destroying "the independence and democratic character of a whole series of nations in Eastern and Central Europe." Because of this situation, Congress must act quickly on the European Recovery Program and enact universal military training and a temporary draft. Repeating these themes at the dinner that evening, Truman's rhetoric was even more hawkish. One by one he ticked off the countries brought under Soviet domination since the war and charged Russian agents with working to undermine freedom in Greece and Italy. Departing from his pre-

14. Elsey to Clifford, March 5, 1948, Clark M. Clifford Papers, Speech File; Elsey, handwritten notes, March 8, March 15, March 16, 1948, George M. Elsey Papers, Speech File.

pared text, Truman also berated his political challenger Henry Wallace and his "insidious propaganda" for peace:

> I do not want and I will not accept the political support of Henry Wallace and his Communists. If joining them or permitting them to join me is the price of victory, I recommend defeat. . . . Any price for Wallace and his Communists is too much for me to pay. I'm not buying.

Presenting the world situation in ideological and emotional terms, Truman equated communism with "tyranny" and "reaction," and called it "a false philosophy," that "even worse, denies the very existence of God."[15]

While Truman's language about the Soviets received widespread approval and support, Congress was less enthusiastic about his concrete requests. Two weeks after calling for prompt passage of the Marshall Plan, universal training, and temporary selective service, the Administration requested a supplemental budget appropriation of $3.375 billion to strengthen the military establishment. Congress responded with a watered-down version of the draft, rejected universal training, and appropriated extra defense money, but in a manner that added to the existing imbalance among U.S.military forces.[16]

Truman had unsuccessfully urged universal military training since October, 1945. Renewing his efforts in December, 1946, he appointed a special committee to investigate its feasibility and simultaneously deleted the word "military" from its title. The committee reported favorably in June, 1947, recommending universal training as an essential ingredient to national security. Upon releasing the report, Truman urged early consideration by Congress and called congressional leaders to a special meeting at the White House. While Vandenberg expressed approval of universal training, Taft denounced the proposal as "un-American, wasteful, and obsolete." The House Armed Services Committee

15. Special Message to the Congress on the Threat to the Freedom of Europe, March 17, 1948, *Public Papers: Truman, 1948*, 182–86; Saint Patrick's Day Address in New York City, *ibid.*, 186–90.

16. Letter to the Speaker Regarding Additional Appropriations for the National Security Program, April 1, 1948, *ibid.*, 198.

reported a bill that the Republican leaders refused to support, and the first session ended without action.[17]

Truman repeated his request in his 1948 State of the Union address, and in January and February, the National Security Committee—a private organization headed by former Supreme Court Justice Owen J. Roberts—began to urge House leaders to release the bill and Senate Republicans to begin hearings. In March, Secretary Marshall met with members of the Senate Armed Services Committee to impress upon them the relationship of universal training to the Administration's over-all foreign policy. After additional urging from military officials, the Senate committee voted on March 8 to begin hearings.[18]

Yet even after the President's militant message of March 17, the outlook for universal training was not promising. In the first place, congressmen were unwilling to support an expensive, unpopular program in an election year. Even more important, many legislators believed that a less costly, more popular, and more effective alternative existed. In January, a special committee headed by Thomas K. Finletter to study air policy had recommended expansion of the Air Force to seventy groups, asserting that national security depended primarily on air power. Taft and other congressmen immediately seized upon the Finletter Commission's report as a means of supporting the containment policy in a politically advantageous way. The notion of creating "the best and biggest air force in the world" appealed even to Midwestern Republicans who had refused to support containment through economic-aid programs.[19]

Truman's request for supplemental appropriations provided for additional men and equipment for the Air Force, but only to fill out its existing fifty-five group organization. While Secretary of

17. *The New York Times,* June 2, 1947, p. 5, June 27, 1947, p. 5; Ross to Karl T. Compton, June 24, 1947, Charles G. Ross Papers.

18. Archibald G. Thatcher to Edward A. Sumner, January 16, 1948; Thatcher to Leo Allen, January 27, 1948, Worthington Thompson to Roberts, February 21, February 23, 1948, National Security Committee Records; Forrestal, *The Forrestal Diaries,* Millis and Duffield, eds., 384, 388–89.

19. *Ibid.,* 388; Walter Millis, *Arms and the State: Civil-Military Elements in National Policy,* 205; *The New York Times,* January 16, 1948, p. 1, January 23, 1948, p. 19; Marion T. Bennett to E. J. Evens, January 23, 1948, Bennett Papers.

Defense Forrestal had no objection to the seventy-group idea, he opposed a program that would only exaggerate the existing imbalance in the military establishment, which was reflected primarily in the shortage of ground forces. Secretary of the Air Force Stuart Symington, however, insisted on a seventy-group program and even gave priority to expanding the Air Force over selective service or universal training. Thus, the Administration program was sabotaged from within. Although Truman gave unqualified support to Forrestal and at one point sent special letters to the service secretaries instructing them to "subordinate personal and service preferences to broader interests of the national program," Air Force advocates won out. The House voted unanimously to add $822 million to the supplemental appropriation as an initial move toward a seventy-group Air Force. Before the Senate acted, the Administration made one final attempt to reduce the emphasis on air power. On April 21, Forrestal presented to the Senate Armed Services Committee a compromise that increased his original proposal for the supplemental military budget by $481 million which would be used to expand the Air Force to sixty-six groups, largely through renovating World War II planes. The effort was fruitless; the Senate, with only two dissenting votes, followed the House. Forrestal well understood the relationship in the minds of legislators between an expanded Air Force and universal military training: "There is not the slightest chance . . . for UMT to come up before the Armed Services Committee of the Senate if the Appropriations Committee passes the 822 millions additional Air Force procurement."[20]

The Secretary's prediction was accurate. The Administration's schedule for increasing ground forces called for a temporary draft of a minimum of 220,000 men and a universal-training program of 850,000. As opposition increased, Forrestal agreed to a modified universal-training plan that provided for eighteen-year-olds to be

20. Forrestal, *The Forrestal Diaries*, Millis and Duffield, eds., 400–402, 415, 418–20, 426; Arnold A. Rogow, *James Forrestal, A Study of Personality, Politics and Policy*, 294–95; Truman to Secretary of the Air Force, May 13, 1948, Clifford Papers; The President's News Conference of April 8, 1948, *Public Papers: Truman, 1948*, 211; The President's News Conference of April 15, 1948, *ibid.*, 216–17; *The New York Times*, May 7, 1948, p. 1.

included in the draft program, but only for six months of service. While the Administration's plan had called for separate training followed by obligated reserve status, Forrestal viewed the committee proposal as offering at least some hope of later acceptance of universal training. When the committee bill reached the Senate floor, the Administration's proposal was further emasculated. The provision for compulsory training for eighteen-year-olds was eliminated by unanimous vote, and the duration of the draft was cut from 5 to 2 years.[21]

The House Armed Services Committee completed a similar bill for a two-year draft and no universal training on May 3, but the Rules Committee refused to act. Concentrating on the House leaders and members of the Rules Committee, the National Security Committee urged important contributors to the Republican party to put pressure on reluctant legislators. Through its state organizations, the National Security Committee tried to influence Rules Committee Republicans J. Edgar Chenoweth of Colorado, Ross Rizley of Oklahoma, and Forest A. Harness of Indiana. Finally, although a majority of the Rules Committee opposed the bill, it voted, 6 to 4, to let the House discuss the measure. Rizley and Harness, who opposed the bill but supported the rule, provided the crucial votes. Before passing it, the House mutilated the bill by cutting the time of service to one year and delaying initial call-ups to January, 1949, and then only at the discretion of the President. At the midnight hour before adjournment, Congress approved a conference committee's compromise providing for inductions ninety days after enactment, a twenty-one-month period of service, and a voluntary program for one year of service for a maximum of 160,000 eighteen-year-olds—a meaningless bow to the universal-training program.[22]

Truman's defense program had virtually disintegrated since he had presented it on March 17. Reluctance to support the Presi-

21. Forrestal, *The Forrestal Diaries*, Millis and Duffield, eds., 427; *The New York Times*, June 5, 1948, p. 1, June 10, 1948, p. 1.
22. Archibald G. Thatcher to James W. Wadsworth, May 24, 1948, Worthington Thompson to Owen J. Roberts, May 28, 1948, National Security Committee Records; *The New York Times*, June 15, 1948, p. 1, June 18, 1948, p. 1, June 20, 1948, pp. 1, 34.

dent was powerful among Democrats, as well as Republicans who, as Hanson Baldwin put it, in an election year preferred "to buy defense with dollars and not with their constituents." Symington and other Air Force officials strengthened congressional recalcitrance by emphasizing air power and thus encouraging the desire to act "as a world power without getting too deeply enmeshed in the complex, dangerous, interior affairs of Eurasia."[23]

Truman's message of March 17 had dealt with an additional matter of foreign policy. At Brussels on the same day, Britain, France, Belgium, the Netherlands, and Luxembourg entered into a fifty-year agreement for economic cooperation and national defense. Prior to the negotiations, Secretary Marshall, with Truman's authorization, told British Foreign Secretary Ernest Bevin that the United States was entirely sympathetic to such an arrangement and would assist it in any way possible. In his speech, Truman had noted the significance of the Brussels Pact and expressed confidence that the United States would "extend to the free nations the support which the situation requires."[24]

The Administration now concentrated on getting Congress to declare U.S. willingness to consider a regional agreement with the European nations based upon Article 51 of the United Nations Charter. According to Forrestal, "The tactics would be to have this action initiated by the Republicans and to have the ball picked up immediately by the President." The Administration's idea was quietly presented to Vandenberg, who recognized that there was now an opportunity to channel congressional demands for major reform of the United Nations into directions more acceptable to the Administration and himself than the proposals upon which the House Foreign Affairs Committee was preparing to hold hearings, proposals that Marshall believed would undermine the United Nations. Working together, Vandenberg and Under Secretary of State Lovett drafted a resolution expressing the Senate's support for collective agreements in accordance with

---

23. *Ibid.*, April 25, 1948, p. 10E; Robert E. Osgood, *Limited War: The Challenge to American Strategy*, 151; Rostow, *United States in the World Arena*, 224.

24. Harry S. Truman, *Memoirs*, Vol. II, *Years of Trial and Hope*, 243; Special Message to the Congress on the Threat to the Freedom of Europe, March 17, 1948, *Public Papers: Truman*, 1948, 184.

Article 51 and its desire to eliminate the United Nations veto on questions involving peaceful settlement of disputes or admission of new members.[25]

After obtaining unanimous approval from the Foreign Relations Committee, Vandenberg presented the resolution to the Senate on June 11. Debate was brief, with major objections coming from two sources. Republican George W. Malone of Nevada feared that collective agreements would destroy the Senate's prerogative in treaty making and involve the United States in European wars. Claude Pepper, still seeking a more peaceful U.S. posture argued that Article 51 did not sanction regional agreements for collective security and that such agreements would undermine the United Nations. Vandenberg replied that the resolution did not mean commitment and that Senate consent would still be required for U.S. involvement in regional pacts. After only one day of debate, the Senate approved the resolution, 64 to 4. The ease with which the resolution passed testified to the influence of its sponsor and vindicated the Administration's decision to have the Republicans take the initiative. Although the resolution committed the Senate to nothing and while many senators may not have realized its significance, the Senate had taken the first step toward abandoning the United States' historic policy against peacetime alliances. Only three weeks later, the State Department began discussions with European representatives that would lead to the establishment of the North Atlantic Treaty Organization in August, 1949.[26]

Congress responded more slowly to the more immediate problem of Europe's displaced persons. The domestic implications of the issue and the still-potent nativist sentiment produced a bill that fell short of the Administration's standards. Congressional attitudes toward admittance of displaced persons followed a regional pattern, and party distinctions were blurred. Since the

25. Forrestal, *The Forrestal Diaries*, Millis and Duffield, eds., 423; Pratt, "Leadership Relations in Foreign Policy Making," 254–57; Vandenberg, ed., *Private Papers of Senator Vandenberg*, 404–8.

26. U.S. *Congressional Record*, 80th Cong., 2d sess., 1948, XCIV, Part 6, pp. 7808–13, 7828–35, 7846; Vandenberg, ed., *Private Papers of Senator Vandenberg*, 411; Truman, *Years of Trial and Hope*, 247–51.

bipartisan approach was not followed on this question, the Administration apparently considered it less important than other foreign-policy matters. The legislation was handled by the Judiciary committees, with which the State Department had no tradition of cooperation, and the Administration could not count on the solid bloc of Democratic votes that usually formed the foundation of bipartisan foreign policy.

By 1947, there were nearly one million displaced persons in Germany, Austria, and Italy, and 600,000 in U.S. camps. Most of the homeless people were forced laborers whom the Nazis had imported from conquered territories. In addition, there were those who had fled before the Soviet advance through Poland and into Germany, as well as Jews who had survived the Nazi concentration camps. Their numbers were augmented after the war by Jews fleeing Polish persecution and by various nationality groups from the newly established Soviet satellites. Truman had urged congressional consideration of this matter in his 1947 State of the Union message, and in June, 1947, a House subcommittee began hearings on a bill introduced by Republican William G. Stratton of Illinois to provide for the admission of up to 400,000 displaced persons over a four-year period. Despite a special message from the President and a meeting with congressional leaders, the Stratton bill remained in the subcommittee when Congress adjourned. Although a modified version of Stratton's bill was introduced in the Senate, that body postponed action by appointing a special committee to study and report back in 1948.[27]

In May, 1948, the Senate committee submitted to pressures from the Administration and the public to produce displaced-persons legislation. However, the subcommittee that wrote the bill was dominated by restrictionists. Its chairman, Chapman Revercomb of West Virginia, Republican Donnell of Missouri, and Democrat McCarran of Nevada outvoted the more liberal

---

27. Robert A. Divine, *American Immigration Policy, 1924–1952*, 110–11, 118; *The New York Times*, June 8, 1947, p. E8; Special Message to the Congress on the Admission of Displaced Persons, July 7, 1947, *Public Papers of the Presidents of the United States: Harry S. Truman, 1947*, 327–29; The President's News Conference of July 10, 1947, *ibid.*, 330.

Republican Cooper of Kentucky and McGrath, and the bill emerged with discriminatory provisions. It provided for admission of only 100,000 over a two-year period; limited eligibility to those who had entered Western occupation zones before December 22, 1945, which eliminated approximately 100,000 Jews who fled the postwar Polish pogroms; and provided that 50 per cent of those admitted be agricultural workers and persons from the Protestant Baltic states that had been annexed by the Soviet Union, thus discriminating against Catholics and Jews.

Senators Revercomb and Alexander Wiley of Wisconsin, chairman of the Judiciary Committee, defended the committee bill primarily on domestic grounds that reflected traditional anti-immigrant sentiment. They argued that the numbers admitted must not be so large that they would compete with native Americans for jobs and housing. The 50 per cent priority given to farmers was justified on the need for agricultural workers in the United States and the desirability of distributing immigrants throughout the country. In the past, Wiley noted, immigrants tended to concentrate in urban areas, where they "form a whirlpool of foreignisms and create many of our problems." Finally, they maintained that the cut-off date should be December, 1945, because those entering the camps later were not real displaced persons uprooted by Hitler. On the contrary, asserted Revercomb, many were communist infiltrees planted by the Russians. The Democrats were generally silent during the debate, but Russell of Georgia, Eastland of Mississippi, and McCarran supported the views of the sponsors, and Eastland spoke at length on his objection to any admission of displaced persons. He suggested that they be left to rebuild Europe and argued that the bill opened a wedge for destruction of U.S. immigration policy.[28]

Republican Senators Cooper, Homer Ferguson of Michigan, Smith, Saltonstall, and Morse led the opposition to the bill. Morse and McGrath concentrated on a series of amendments to liberalize the bill, but they succeeded only once. The Senate approved their amendment to increase the number admitted, 40 to 33. On

28. U.S. *Congressional Record*, 80th Cong., 2d sess., 1948, XCIV, Part 5, pp. 6402–3.

their amendment to eliminate the Balkan and agricultural priorities, 12 Republicans shifted to the opposition, and the amendment was defeated, 40 to 31. Fourteen Republicans who had favored increasing admissions opposed an amendment to delay the cut-off date for entrance into the occupation zone to April, 1947, and the amendment lost, 49 to 29. The final bill, providing for the admission of 200,000 displaced persons, passed by a vote of 63 to 13, with twelve Southern and border-state Democrats and Republican Hawkes voting No.[29]

Senate voting on this legislation revealed five major blocs. At one extreme were 13 Republicans (8 Northeasterners, 3 Midwesterners, and 1 each from Oregon and Kentucky) and 18 Democrats, who supported every attempt to liberalize the bill. At the other extreme were 14 Democrats from the South, Southwest, or border states and Republican Hawkes, who opposed admittance of any displaced persons. A third group of Democrats from similar areas voted against some or all of the liberalizing amendments but supported the final bill. Two-thirds of the 15 Republicans who voted against every liberalizing amendment were Midwesterners, while 16 other Republican senators favored one or two, but not all, of the amendments. Most of those who opposed the measure itself and the attempts to eliminate its discriminatory provisions were Southern Democrats and Midwestern Republicans.

Before the House acted, Truman announced his objections to the "crippling" and discriminatory provisions in the Senate bill and urged Congress to give him a measure "without any qualifications which depart from our established American principles." The House Judiciary Committee had already reported a bill without discriminatory provisions. It provided for the admission of 200,000 displaced persons over a two-year period, had a cut-off date of April, 1947, and set no minimum quotas for specific groups. The only objectionable feature, other than the 200,000 limit, was a requirement that those admitted be charged to future immigration quotas—up to 50 per cent a year—until all were accounted for. The bill attracted wide support from Republicans

29. *Ibid.*, pp. 6180, 6189, 6646–47, 6456, 6577, 6584, 6810, 6864, 6869, 6900–6905, 6916.

and Democrats alike. Such advocates of a liberal immigration policy as Democrat Emanuel Celler of New York supported the measure because it was much better than the Senate version and the best that could be achieved. Mild restrictionists, on the other hand, approved the quota-mortgaging feature.[30]

Only the most extreme restrictionists attacked the House bill. They stressed the impact of increased immigration on housing and employment and resorted to more vitriolic denunciation of the displaced persons themselves than had the senatorial fundamentalists. Republican Robert F. Rich of Pennsylvania objected to making the United States "a dumping place" for "Communists" and other "unacceptable" persons, and Texas Democrat Ed Gossett called the bill an attempt to "inject more poison into the national bloodstream." Displaced persons were "bums, criminals, subversives, revolutionists, crackpots, and human wreckage." Yet the extremists mustered only 91 on the final vote. Of the 56 Democrats against the bill, 54 were from the South; 27 of the 35 Republican nays came from Midwestern congressmen.[31]

The discriminatory provisions of the Senate version prevailed in the final bill. At first it appeared that the Senate might yield when Wiley appointed Revercomb, Ferguson, and Kilgore as Senate conferees, for the latter two favored the liberalizing amendments. When he realized the implications of his original appointments, however, Wiley added Senators Eastland and Donnell and thereby tipped the balance toward restriction. Two days before adjournment, a majority of the House conferees realized that if they did not agree to the Senate stipulations, they would get no bill at all. They were able only to reduce the priority for farmers to 30 per cent and for persons from Baltic states to 40 per cent. The Senate agreed to the conference report by voice vote after several members had expressed their disappointment and their intention to support the bill then and attempt to amend

30. Address in Chicago Before the Swedish Pioneer Centennial Association, June 4, 1948, *Public Papers: Truman, 1948*, 288–89; U.S. House of Representatives, Committee on the Judiciary, *Emergency Displaced Persons Admission Act*, House Report 1854 to accompany H.R. 6396, 80th Cong., 2d sess., 1948, 1–4, 21; Divine, *American Immigration Policy*, 125; U.S. *Congressional Record*, 80th Cong., 2d sess., 1948, XCIV, Part 6, pp. 7741–44.

31. *Ibid.*, pp. 7733, 7747, 7887.

it later. In the House, Celler maintained that his fellow conferees had capitulated too quickly, but his motion to recommit was defeated, 266 to 133, and the report passed by voice vote.[32]

Contrasting the displaced-persons bill with congressional refusal in the 1930's to aid refugees, one scholar of U.S. immigration policy has maintained that it was, despite its flaws and cautious approach, a "significant departure" from previous policy due primarily to the new position of the United States in world affairs. The President, however, was already well into his second month of denouncing the Eightieth Congress and, anticipating the use of the displaced-persons legislation as a campaign issue despite the significant number of Democratic restrictionists, preferred to emphasize the bill's shortcomings. Since Congress was no longer in session, he explained, he could not veto the bill and ask for a better one. Instead, he would sign it and hope that Congress would remedy its "injustices" when it reconvened. Truman attacked Congress' "delay" and its "hasty, last-minute" action, as well as the bill's "niggardly conditions" for admission and its "callous discrimination" against Catholics and Jews, and cited the selection of the December, 1945, cut-off date as an example of "abhorrent . . . intolerance."[33]

The Administration's foreign policy also foundered among congressional obstacles to reciprocal-trade legislation. In this case, the division followed party lines almost precisely, for many Republicans viewed the reciprocal-trade policy as another New Deal monstrosity that was designed to aggrandize the executive at the expense of Congress. As in all foreign-policy legislation except the displaced-persons measure, the House was more hostile to Truman's position, and the program was rescued from complete emasculation by Republican moderates in the Senate.

Thwarted in their efforts to obstruct the reciprocal-trade program in 1947 by the compromise between the Administration and Senators Vandenberg and Millikin, House protectionists found another opportunity when the act came up for extension in 1948.

---

32. *Ibid.*, Part 7, pp. 8856–57, 8861, 8863, 9009, 9012–23.
33. Divine, *American Immigration Policy*, 129; Statement by the President Upon Signing the Displaced Persons Act, June 25, 1948, *Public Papers: Truman, 1948*, 382–84.

The publication in November of tariff concessions made at Geneva had added fuel to the fire. Even Millikin said that the concessions looked "very drastic" and in times of normal foreign production "would be catastrophic." But pressure for a complete change in tariff-making procedures was stronger in the House. In reply to Truman's message requesting extension of the act in its present form for three years, House Speaker Martin warned, "It will be impossible to get any extension of the act unless the Senate, at minimum, is granted the power of confirmation or rejection."[34]

With the approval of the House Republican Steering Committee, the Ways and Means Committee reported a bill on May 24. The usual three-year authorization was reduced to a one-year extension. It further provided that the independent Tariff Commission would hold hearings preceding negotiation of agreements. Concerned only with the effects of tariff cuts on domestic industry, the commission would set points below which tariff concessions should not be made. If concessions were then made below the minimum, the agreements would be subject to congressional veto. The division in the committee followed straight party lines, and the nine Democrats filed minority views, in which they charged the majority with a "clear and deliberate effort to smash the reciprocal trade program."[35]

House debate was intensely partisan. The Democrats were united in the conviction expressed by Doughton that the Republican bill, sponsored by Gearhart of California, would sound the "death knell" to the program of reciprocity. In support of his contention, Doughton, the ranking minority member of the Ways and Means Committee, quoted a letter from Secretary of State Marshall that labeled the measure "unworkable" and concluded that expiration of the program was preferable to the committee bill. Republicans Knutson and Gearhart answered with a denunciation of Marshall, who had previously been immune to partisan

34. *The New York Times*, November 20, 1947, p. 3, March 2, 1948, p. 4.
35. U.S. House of Representatives, Committee on Ways and Means, *Extending the Authority of the President Under Section 350 of the Tariff Act of 1930, As Amended, and for Other Purposes*, House Report 2009 to accompany H.R. 6556, 80th Cong., 2d sess., 1948, 1–2, 18.

attack. Most Republicans supported the measure, asserting that the revisions were only "minor" and accusing the Democrats of fabricating a political issue. Yet some Republicans, while supporting the bill, revealed their underlying opposition to reciprocal trade. They argued that domestic industries had been "wrecked" and favored a return to full congressional control over tariffs. Roy O. Woodruff of Michigan berated the President for seeking "unlimited, unrestricted, autocratic power." Daniel A. Reed of New York added the State Department to the list of villains and asked if it were in the United States' interest to entrust its trade policies to a "handful of Communist-minded self-admitted internationalists." Thomas A. Jenkins of Ohio viewed the program as one more abominable New Deal policy designed to usurp congressional power. Javits was the lone Republican to oppose the bill in House debate. He wanted Congress to wait for a new Administration to suggest changes in the program and specifically objected to the procedural revisions that would emphasize protection of domestic industries and delay negotiation of agreements. He believed that approval of the bill might cause foreign countries to doubt the U.S. commitment to economic recovery.[36]

The key vote in the House came on a motion by Doughton to recommit with instructions to report a straight three-year extension of the existing act. Voting to support the measure were 17 Republicans and 149 Democrats, while 205 Republicans and 6 Democrats voted No. After defeat of the recommittal motion, 11 Democrats and the 17 Republicans switched to support the bill, believing that it was better than nothing. The House approved the bill, 234 to 149.[37]

Truman, in the midst of his cross-country trip, said that the reciprocal-trade program had been "amended to death." Vandenberg also believed that the Gearhart bill was too restrictive; the Senator preferred a three-year extension of the program. More important, he strongly objected to the congressional veto over tariff making, and he worked with Millikin, chairman of the

36. U.S. *Congressional Record*, 80th Cong., 2d sess., 1948, XCIV, Part 5, pp. 6502–35. See remarks by Herter, Michener, Vorys, Kean, and Keating.
37. *Ibid.*, pp. 6537–38.

Finance Committee, to draft a bill for a one-year extension providing for the Tariff Commission's recommendations before tariff negotiations but not compelling the executive to follow the recommendations. Moreover, under the provisions of the Millikin bill, the agreements would not be subject to congressional veto. The committee report justified the procedural change as a means of focusing presidential attention on the implications of tariff cutting for domestic producers, a consideration that many felt was "being subordinated to extraneous, and perhaps overvalued, diplomatic objectives."[38]

The State Department's efforts to remove the emphasis on domestic industry only irritated Vandenberg. Will Clayton believed the Millikin bill to be "no improvement on the Gearhart bill" and predicted to Vandenberg that no trade agreements would be negotiated under such legislation. Vandenberg replied testily that the Millikin bill was "a very *great* improvement" and warned the Administration not to jeopardize the program by asking too much. "Frankly," he said, "I think it would be most unfortunate if an issue were made against the Millikin formula. I feel that we are making *real* progress in respect to 'reciprocity' in places where heretofore we have confronted total hostility. I hope these trends will not be discouraged by a refusal of *any* hospitality to *any* change in the administrative formula."[39]

Discussion on the Senate floor was partisan, but it lacked the intense protectionist sentiment voiced in the House. Republicans insisted that the bill would not cripple the reciprocity program, and Vandenberg argued that it would indeed be strengthened by eliminating some of the complaints against its administration. Among Republicans only Tobey, believing that the Millikin bill contradicted the commitment to economic recovery expressed in the Marshall Plan, urged extension of the act in its existing form.

38. Address in Omaha at the Reunion of the 35th Division, June 5, 1948, *Public Papers: Truman, 1948*, 295; *The New York Times*, May 28, 1948, p. 16, June 8, 1948, p. 1; U.S. Senate, Committee on Finance, *Extending the Authority of the President Under Section 350 of the Tariff Act of 1930, As Amended*, Senate Report 1558 to accompany H.R. 6556, 80th Cong., 2d sess., 1948, 3, 5–7.

39. Clayton to Vandenberg, June 8, 1948, Vandenberg to Clayton, June 9, 1948, Vandenberg Papers.

Democrats emphasized the resurgence of GOP hostility to reciprocal trade and saw in the bill a tendency to return to economic
nationalism and a threat to the objectives of ERP.[40]

At the insistence of Republicans Ives, Flanders, Cooper, Smith,
and Vandenberg, two amendments were adopted by voice vote.
The first changed the wording of the criterion upon which the
Tariff Commission was to base its recommendations; it would
consider possible injury not to "domestic producers" but to the
"domestic industry producing," which would make the criterion
apply to an entire industry rather than to individual and possibly
inefficient marginal producers. Secondly, the bill was changed to
require the Tariff Commission to report to the President within 120 days in order to avoid possible delay or obstruction of
negotiations.[41]

Before the final vote, Alben Barkley made three attempts to
obtain extension of the program without change. The closest vote
came on his amendment for a straight one-year extension, which
was defeated, 46 to 43. Only one Democrat, O'Daniel of Texas,
voted against it, while Republicans Cooper, Tobey, and Wilson
voted for it. After failing to obtain straight extension, many Democrats voted with the Republicans on final passage. Cooper was
the only Republican to vote No, along with 17 Democrats, including the minority leaders. The House accepted the Senate version without debate.[42]

Truman's foreign-policy advisers disliked the overemphasis on
protection of domestic industry, probable delays that would arise
from the procedural changes, and the uncertainty that the one-
year extension was bound to create among foreign allies, but they
believed the program to be workable and viewed the legislation as
a Republican commitment to the trade program. Moreover, a
presidential veto resulting in a lapse of the program would be
much more damaging to U.S. foreign policy than extending the
act on the terms demanded by the congressional majority. So,

40. U.S. *Congressional Record*, 80th Cong., 2d sess., 1948, XCIV, Part 6, pp.
8043–44, 8049, 8066, 8068–70.
41. *Ibid.*, pp. 8037, 8050, 8072.
42. *Ibid.*, pp. 8072–74, Part 7, p. 8335.

Truman signed the bill, and while he noted its shortcomings, his message was mild in comparison to his denunciations of the Republican measure later in the campaign.[43]

Congressional support for elements of the Administration's foreign policy depended primarily upon legislative estimates of a particular measure's usefulness in fighting the Cold War. Containment of the Soviet Union through Greek-Turkish aid, interim aid, ERP, and the Vandenberg Resolution appealed to conservatives in both parties and outweighed the undesirable domestic implications of these programs. Anticommunism was reinforced by Soviet actions in 1947 and 1948, as well as by Truman's rhetoric. Finally, the Administration capitalized on its strategy of involving GOP leaders through prior consultation and agreeing to Republican revisions.

These conditions did not prevail for all programs affecting foreign policy. While anticommunists supported the defense program, legislators in both parties hesitated to commit their constituents' sons and husbands to military service in an election year. Moreover, they believed that the military strength required to halt communism could be attained through air power, a conviction reinforced by some Administration personnel. Finally, the Administration's presentation of its defense program came as a shock to leaders of both parties. Since they had not been consulted in advance, they had no personal stake in the policy.

The same was true of the displaced-persons legislation. Although the Administration worked closely with McGrath, there was no consultation with the Republican leaders and thus no bipartisan approach. Furthermore, the disposition of displaced persons seemed to have no immediate relationship to the Cold War. Indeed, many congressmen opposed their admission because of their suspected communist tendencies. Most Democratic and many Republican restrictionists were consistent supporters of containment, but they considered domestic matters paramount,

43. Lovett to Clifford, June 16, 1948, Clifford Papers; Webb to Hopkins, June 23, 1948, U.S. Bureau of the Budget Files, Reports to the President on Pending Legislation; Statement by the President Upon Signing the Trade Agreements Extension Act, June 26, 1948, *Public Papers: Truman, 1948*, 385.

and saw no compelling reason to depart too much from traditional nativist attitudes.

Domestic considerations were equally important in determining congressional positions on the reciprocal-trade program. While Democrats united behind Truman's program, only a handful of Republicans supported it, not enough to ensure complete success. Traditional Republican protectionism and inveterate opposition to the concentration of executive power forced the Administration to accept substantial changes in its program. Partisan feelings on reciprocal trade were strong and were reinforced by attacks on the Republican bill by Democratic legislators and the President during the part of his campaign that preceded the Senate's action. Moreover, most Republicans did not believe that they were jeopardizing containment by altering the reciprocal-trade program.

Despite these shortcomings, the consensus on foreign policy established in the Eightieth Congress was remarkable. For the first time, the Republican party went on record in support of reciprocal trade, and members of both parties relaxed, though qualifiedly, their traditional opposition to peacetime military expansion and a generous immigration policy. Most important, the commitment of the United States to containment through massive foreign aid and a future alliance was unprecedented and steered U.S. foreign policy on a new course, one that it would follow for many years. The stability of the consensus was sufficient to withstand domestic partisan politics, for with the exception of the European Recovery Program, all the foreign-policy measures were enacted after Truman had begun in earnest his campaign against the "do-nothing," Republican-controlled Congress.

CHAPTER 8

"MY EXHIBIT A"

ALTHOUGH TRUMAN had carefully followed Clifford's strategy for arousing major voting blocs and had won popular approval for his militant stand against the Soviet Union, his political prospects appeared bleak as the Eightieth Congress neared adjournment. The Wallace threat appeared more ominous in February, when Progressive candidate Leo Isacson trounced both major party candidates for the House seat from the Twenty-fourth Congressional District in the Bronx. Truman had soft-pedaled the civil-rights issue since his February message, yet the possibility of a Southern revolt remained alive, and the Democratic coalition seemed in danger from defections of both liberals and conservatives. Liberals, urban bosses, and Southerners agreed on one thing—Truman had to go. Men as diverse as Claude Pepper, John Sparkman, James Roosevelt, Jake Arvey of Chicago, Frank Hague of New Jersey, and Kenneth McKellar opposed Truman's renomination, and there was a desperate scurry to find a replacement to head the Democratic ticket. A repeat of the 1946 debacle seemed certain, only this time the stakes would be higher. Yet Truman was not dissuaded. He had the New Deal record to run on, he had the record of the Eightieth Congress to run against, and there was still a lot of mileage available in both. Between June and November, he used it brilliantly: "It was my Exhibit A."[1]

The essential task for Truman was to reinvigorate former New Deal enthusiasts who were at this time apathetic. As one Democrat pointed out, it was "not that there is any hostility to Truman; rather, nobody seems to give a damn." In his November memorandum, Clifford had stressed the need to arouse particular interest groups, singled out the West as "Number One Priority," and

1. Irwin Ross, *The Loneliest Campaign: The Truman Victory of 1948*, 65–66, 72–75; McKellar to E. H. Crump, April 7, 1948, Kenneth D. McKellar Papers; Harry S. Truman, *Memoirs*, Vol. II, *Years of Trial and Hope*, 174.

suggested that Truman "find occasion to visit the West on business." The opportunity came when the University of California invited Truman to speak at its commencement exercises on June 12. Expanding the occasion into a fourteen-day trip across the country, the President found a chance to demonstrate his ability as a vigorous campaigner who was able to rally popular support and to spark his demoralized party.[2]

The tone of the trip and of the entire campaign was suggested on May 14, when Truman addressed a Young Democrats' Dinner. In a speech carried over nationwide radio, he spunkily dismissed the prophets of doom: "I want to say to you that for the next 4 years there will be a Democrat in the White House, and you are looking at him!" After calling the roll of the great Democratic Presidents, Truman directed his audience's attention to his main theme, the Republican record in the Eightieth Congress. He decried their catering to "special interests," deplored their indifference to rising prices and housing and their eagerness to emasculate the Labor Department and cut appropriations, and at the same time enumerated his repeated attempts to get Congress to act in the common welfare. Unfortunately, he said, there was not enough time "to tell you all the things that have taken place since this Republican Congress took control of this country."[3]

On his Western trip of June 4 through June 18, Truman pounded away at his theme. Covering fifteen states, he gave major speeches at Chicago, Omaha, Butte, Seattle, Berkeley, and Los Angeles and spoke informally at over sixty whistle stops along the way. His familiar, folksy, often corny manner seemed to please the crowds who gathered around the rear platform of the train, frequently exchanging remarks with the President and egging him on. The train stopped at all hours of the day, and twice Truman appeared in bathrobe and pajamas in order not to disappoint voters who had stayed up late to see him. While his formal addresses were more serious, the pattern of his remarks remained the same,

2. Bob Riggs to Alben Barkley, June 5, 1948, Alben W. Barkley Papers, Political File; Clifford, "Memorandum for the President," 38, Clark M. Clifford Papers.

3. Remarks at the Young Democrats Dinner, May 14, 1948, *Public Papers of the Presidents of the United States: Harry S. Truman, 1948*, 259–61.

and they increased in intensity as the journey progressed and the candidate warmed to his subject.

Truman repeatedly castigated the Republican Eightieth Congress as one of special interests, responsive only to various lobbies. To stir up the voters, he chided his audiences for the low turnout at the polls in 1946: "Two-thirds of you stayed home in 1946, and look what a Congress we got! That is your fault, that is your fault. . . . if you people want to continue the policies of the 80th Congress, that will be your funeral." The purpose of this trip, which he enjoyed calling a "nonpolitical, bipartisan" one, was to enable the people to get a look at their President while he told them what was good for the country. Moreover, Congress was still in session, and, he said, "I want to give them the opportunity to find out what the people think of those things they have not done. . . . They still have time." If Congress adjourned before doing "something about prices, and something about the welfare of the laboring man, and something about housing, it would be a disgrace to this country."[4]

Truman lambasted Congress for its record on every significant domestic issue except civil rights. At Los Angeles, he listed eight major pieces of legislation upon which Congress had refused to act or had acted in the interest of "special classes," including price controls, housing, labor, social security, health insurance, aid to education, agriculture, reclamation, and the "rich man's tax law." At other stops, he usually mentioned just one or two issues that were of particular interest to the people he addressed. In the smaller towns of Idaho, Montana, Washington, California, and New Mexico, he emphasized congressional cuts in public-power appropriations and especially its attacks on federal transmission facilities. In larger cities and in industrial sections of the Midwest and Pennsylvania, the President stressed housing, prices, labor and social security. Audiences in Nebraska and Kansas heard him prod Congress to enact legislation for agriculture. And, here and there, Truman blasted the Republican-controlled Congress for its tax-

4. Informal Remarks in Washington, June 10, 1948, *ibid.*, 317. See also 286, 305, 307, 309, 314, 317, 357, 358, and 372 for Truman's charges of "special interests" and warnings to the voters not to repeat their mistake of 1946. Address in Seattle Before the Greater Los Angeles Press Club, June 14, 1948, *ibid.*, 349.

cut bill. Vetoes of the Reed-Bulwinkle, social security, and Federal Security Agency appropriation bills came in the midst of the cross-country tour and embellished the President's liberal posture.[5]

Truman's failure to use the issue of civil rights in making his case against Congress indicated that his commitment did not outweigh practical political considerations. His only allusion to racial inequality came in the address to the Swedish Pioneer Centennial Association in Chicago on June 4, and his remarks were mild and innocuous. Referring to the threat of communism, he maintained that it arose primarily where people were denied adequate housing, wages, education, medical care, and basic constitutional rights: "If some of our people are arbitrarily denied the right to vote or deprived of other basic rights, and nothing is done about it, that is an invitation to communism." He then urged legislation to provide basic needs, and along with housing, education, medical care, and social security, he included "the full rights of citizenship, an equal chance for good jobs at fair wages." These general comments were the extent of Truman's appeal for his civil-rights program. He referred to no specific legislation and made no charges against Congress. Clark Clifford was concerned about Southern reaction to even these indirect references and asked William L. Batt, Jr., director of the Research Division of the Democratic National Committee, to assess the response and suggest a safe future course. Batt discovered that Southern party leaders and Southern newspapers made no mention of the remarks and learned from a former director of the Associated Press for the South that Truman "could make short statements like this about civil rights without arousing a bad Southern reaction, when the major emphasis of the speech was on something else." Concerned about Wallace's appeal in large cities, George Elsey and David Bell urged that Truman give some emphasis to congressional inaction on civil rights and specifically submitted one sentence for his Los Angeles speech: "They have not passed a single piece of legislation extending civil rights." But Truman made no more mention of civil rights on his Western trip, apparently agreeing

5. *Ibid.*, 296, 301–2, 307–9, 316–17, 321, 330, 347, 349–54, 357, 361, 367, 369, 372–74, 376.

with McGrath, who preferred criticism for neglecting civil rights to taking the chance "of arousing a bad negative reaction from the Southern wing of the Party."[6]

While not conceding that Truman's prospects for November were bright, many observers believed that the trip had been effective. They thought he had aroused the flagging spirits of the Democratic organization, demonstrated to his party that they had an effective weapon with which to attack the opposition, and presented a new fighting and determined image. Part of this evaluation rested on the increasingly larger crowds who came to see the President; part of it was based on the Republican reaction to Truman's blasts. A *New York Times* reporter wrote, "The very howls of outrage [from Republican leaders] bore testimony to the fact that he had drawn blood. Frantic late-hour gestures toward action on domestic problems the President said had been ignored gave further proof that Congress was not really oblivious to his barbs."[7]

Senator Taft was among those who howled loudest and vehemently retaliated, "He is blackguarding Congress at every whistle station in the West." In a formal response to Truman's charges, Taft defended briefly Republican accomplishments in the Eightieth Congress and then launched an attack on Truman's program. "We are still fighting the New Deal," he maintained, and he added up the expenditures that would result from the President's proposals. Truman's health program meant "the socialization and nationalization of medicine," and the President was advocating government controls "which in every country in Europe have so reduced production that our taxpayers are paying $7,000,000,000 a year to help support them." The Republicans were concerned with problems of housing, health, education, and social security, Taft said, but it would take time to examine the proper relationship of the Federal Government to the states in these matters. Moreover, since the President was completely uncooperative, it would do no good to remain in session to enact legislation that he

6. *Ibid.*, 289–90; Batt to Clifford, June 8, 1948, Bell to Clifford, undated, Clifford Papers, Speech File.

7. New York *World-Telegram*, June 11, 1948, Louisville *Courier-Journal*, June 13, 1948, Democratic National Committee Records; *The New York Times*, June 20, 1948, p. E4.

would only veto, for, Taft declared, "We had better adjourn now and appeal to the people in November."[8]

The Senator intended to lead that appeal to the people. The campaign was to be based on the Republican record since 1946, and who would be a more appropriate presidential candidate than the man who had so largely forged that record? The Republican convention thought otherwise and hedged its bets by nominating Governor Thomas E. Dewey, who had won re-election in 1946 by a big margin. Dewey had supported progressive legislation in New York and had avoided involvement in the congressional squabbling in Washington. Similarly, the Republican platform was equivocal about the record of the Eightieth Congress. It praised its "record of solid achievements . . . in the face of frequent obstruction from the executive branch" and listed its accomplishments. Yet the platform also contained commitments to a number of programs that Congress had rejected: "aggressive anti-monopoly action," federal aid for slum clearance and public housing where private enterprise or local government funds were inadequate, extension of social security, programs to improve the nation's health, promotion of educational facilities, and civil-rights legislation, including bills outlawing the poll tax and providing federal protection against lynching.[9]

Dewey seldom mentioned the work of Congress. Upon arrival at the convention, he expressed pride in Congress' "remarkable record in several major fields" but emphasized its accomplishments in foreign policy and national defense legislation. In his acceptance speech, which forecast the tone of his campaign, Dewey ignored the Eightieth Congress completely. Instead, he briefly endorsed the platform and devoted his address to the theme of unity: "Our people are turning away from the meaner things that divide us. They yearn to move to higher ground, to find a common purpose in the finer things which unite us. We must be

8. Taft, text of Address to the Union League Club of Philadelphia, June 11, 1948, in U.S. *Congressional Record*, 80th Cong., 2d sess., 1948, XCIV, Part 11, pp. A3831–32.

9. George H. Mayer, *The Republican Party, 1854–1964*, 470–71; Platform of the Republican Party in U.S. *Congressional Record*, 80th Cong., 2d sess., 1948, XCIV, Part 12, pp. A4661–62.

the instrument of that aspiration." His running mate, Earl Warren, governor of California and progressive Republican, similarly said little about the Eightieth Congress, noting only that under the circumstances, it made "remarkable progress." The attacks on the New Deal that had occupied many Republicans for the past sixteen years were missing from the platform and from the acceptance speeches of Dewey and Warren. Thus through its platform and the two men at the top of its ticket, the Republican party, dominated at the convention by its more liberal wing, conceded the unpopularity of much of the record of the Eightieth Congress and recognized the appeal of the Democratic social and economic reforms.[10]

These developments at the Republican convention threatened to undermine the President's strategy, which had looked promising in the first two weeks of June. By ignoring the record of the Eightieth Congress and pointing to the platform promises, the Republican candidates were depriving Truman of the issues around which he wanted to build his campaign. Still, the President had another gambit. Between the conventions, a memo calling for "bold and daring steps, calculated to reverse the powerful trend now running against us" circulated among his political advisers. Specifically, the President should call a special session of Congress to deal with major legislation that the Republican platform had endorsed.[11]

In June, Congresswoman Helen Gahagan Douglas had suggested that Truman threaten to call a special session if Congress failed to pass the comprehensive housing bill. At that time, William Batt and George Elsey opposed the idea. They argued that it would tie the President to the Capital during the session. Moreover, they feared that it would commit Truman to a fight against the Eightieth Congress. If the Republicans then nominated a progressive candidate who repudiated the record, Truman would be left "beating a dead horse." Finally, the aides were painfully conscious of Democratic disunity and recent failures of the mi-

10. *The New York Times*, June 21, 1948, pp. 1, 3; U.S. *Congressional Record*, 80th Cong., 2d sess., 1948, XCIV, Part 12, pp. A4657–58.
11. Unsigned memo, "Should the President Call Congress Back?" June 29, 1948, Samuel I. Rosenman Papers.

nority to support the President on legislation. Wrote Elsey, "The Democrats have splintered in all directions and at the moment I see little prospect of any early or happy family reunion."[12]

But the idea of a special session remained alive. Both Democrats and Republicans were bombarded with requests for Congress to reconvene and take up unfinished business. Other presidential advisers, including Charles Murphy and speech writer Samuel I. Rosenman, suggested a special session, Batt changed his mind about its political advantages, and Clifford, too, warmed to the idea. The unsigned memorandum, credit for which Batt later claimed for his Research Division, emphasized the political assets in such a move. It would focus attention on the Eightieth Congress and the more reactionary Republicans, force Dewey and Warren to defend its record, and reveal the inability of Republicans to make good their pledges. In addition, it would publicize the divisions within the GOP on such issues as housing, inflation, and social security. Finally, a special session would spotlight the President in action and give him a chance "to follow through on the fighting start he made on his Western tour."[13]

The call was issued at the Democratic convention in the course of Truman's acceptance speech. The contrast between the President's address and that of his opponent was striking: Instead of platitudinous appeals to unity and other vague ideals, Truman hit hard at specific issues and aroused a dispirited convention. He briefly noted the Democratic domestic and foreign record of the past sixteen years and devoted the rest of his speech to the Repub-

12. Batt to Clifford, undated, Elsey to Clifford, undated, Clifford Papers, Political File. The Batt memorandum was written on June 17, 1948, the day after the House Rules Committee refused a rule on the housing bill.

13. Demands for a special session came from labor, religious, farm, and other organizations, as well as prominent political figures and private citizens. *The New York Times*, June 22, 1948, p. 15, June 24, 1948, p. 7, July 9, 1948, p. 7; Public Opinion mail in Harry S. Truman Papers, OF 419–A; R. Alton Lee, "The Turnip Day Session of the Do-Nothing Congress: Presidential Campaign Strategy," *Southwestern Social Science Quarterly*, 44 (December, 1963), 256–67; Ross, *The Loneliest Campaign*, 134–36. Ross concludes that the unsigned memorandum was written under Batt's leadership by the Research Division of the Democratic National Committee. Richard O. Davies, *Housing Reform During the Truman Administration*, argues that Charles Murphy led the push for a special session, 84–85, 161n45. The unsigned memorandum has much in common with Batt's earlier memorandum and suggests his authorship.

lican record. Truman charged the GOP with serving special interests in its "rich man's tax bill" and its attacks on labor, and in its failure to act on inflation controls and a host of other measures, including civil rights. But, he noted, when the Republicans wrote their platform, they pledged action on "a lot of things I have been asking them to do that they have refused to do when they had the power," such as controlling inflation, promoting slum clearance, providing for low-rent housing and education, and extending social security. "I wonder if they think they can fool the people of the United States with such poppycock as that!" Action on two of the GOP promises—housing and inflation control—was necessary immediately. Because his "duty as President requires that I use every means within my power to get the laws the people need on matters of such importance and urgency," Truman was calling Congress back on July 26, called Turnip Day in Missouri, to enact legislation on these two problems. At the same time, Congress could act on other important bills which the Republican platform favored.

> Now, my friends, if there is any reality behind that Republican platform, we ought to get some action. . . . They can do this job in 15 days, if they want to do it.
> They are going to try to dodge their responsibility. They are going to drag all the red herrings they can across this campaign, but . . . Senator Barkley and I are not going to let them get away with it.
> Now, what that worst 80th Congress does in this special session will be the test. The American people will not decide by listening to mere words, or by reading a mere platform. They will decide on the record, the record as it has been written.[14]

Intense planning occupied the Administration during the two weeks preceding July 26. Truman called upon his Council of Economic Advisers to draw up anti-inflation legislation. Reluctant to endorse price controls and miffed at not being consulted before the call for the session, the council presented an extensive program, but with less than unanimous enthusiasm. Edwin Nourse believed that "no set of legislative measures could at this juncture

---

14. Address in Philadelphia Upon Accepting the Nomination of the Democratic National Convention, July 15, 1948, *Public Papers: Truman, 1948*, 406–10.

really stem the inflationary tide and stabilize prosperity." Agreeing with Nourse and admitting no possibility for a favorable congressional response, Leon Keyserling nevertheless insisted that the council still was obligated to advocate programs that, if adopted, "might put us in a better position than we would be without them." Despite their lack of faith in legislative remedies, the council urged Truman to avoid the debacle of the 1947 special session. Responsibility for the President's anti-inflation program "should be centrally located and forcefully exercised to develop a showing that the proposals being made here have been preceeded [sic] by study and reflection and that, if the authority requested were to be granted, it would be succeeded by intelligent and discerning action." To this end Paul A. Porter, former head of the OPA who had fought for the extension of price controls in 1946, was brought in to coordinate the program. Also, to guarantee unanimity among his advisers, the President called a full Cabinet meeting to read a draft of his message. If the Cabinet chiefs opposed any part of the program, they were to say so then and not later. None dissented.[15]

In other areas, Truman's aides prepared careful reports on the status of existing legislation to determine what specific requests should be made and to assign priority to various recommendations. Batt directed a concentrated effort to mobilize a wide array of interest groups behind all aspects of the President's program. Dozens of private organizations, including the National Public Housing Conference, the Americans for Democratic Action, the American Civil Liberties Union, the National Association for the Advancement of Colored People, the National Education Association, the American Veterans' Committee, labor and farm organizations, and religious groups were called upon to publicize their support of Truman's proposals, to lobby on the Hill, and to encourage their members to put pressure on legislators. Rickety bridges between Truman and Democratic congressional leaders

15. Nourse to Keyserling and Clark, July 18, 1948, Keyserling to Nourse and Clark, July 18, 1948, Clark to Keyserling and Nourse, July 17, 1948, Council of Economic Advisers to the President, July 19, 1948, Edwin G. Nourse Papers, Daily Diary; *The New York Times*, July 24, 1948, p. 1, August 1, 1948, p. E1; Joseph and Stewart Alsop, "Prices and the President," *Washington Post*, July 28, 1948, p. 11.

were rebuilt as the Administration rallied senators and representatives to battle for the President's program and established liaisons among Congress, the Administration, and the Democratic National Committee. Before addressing Congress, Truman read his message to Democratic leaders and invited their suggestions, providing a precedent for similar meetings to be held during the session to encourage a fighting spirit in the Democrats. Finally, during the week preceding the special session, White House Press Secretary Charles Ross fed to reporters details of the President's program piece by piece, thus making front page news every day and drawing attention to the session.[16]

Republican preparations for the special session were considerably less coordinated. Acknowledging the effectiveness of Truman's latest weapon, Marion T. Bennett of Missouri expressed the private reaction of the GOP: "The call of the special session is very distressing." Publicly, Republicans tried to discredit the President with vehement charges of playing politics. Vandenberg termed Truman's latest action "a last hysterical gasp of an expiring administration." Herbert Brownell, Dewey's campaign manager, reacted carefully but firmly, stating, "The Republican platform calls for the enactment of a program by a Republican Congress under the leadership of a Republican President. Obviously this cannot be done at a rump session called at a political convention for political purposes in the heat of a political campaign." Brownell said that Dewey had been consulted about the statement, but it was not to be taken as the nominee's. The Republicans would respond specifically upon hearing the President's message.[17]

Truman appeared before Congress on July 27, and Republicans greeted him with open hostility. His address recalled all the issues of which he had spoken on his Western trip and at the conven-

16. Unsigned memo, "Special Session, Legislative Program, Status," undated, Frederick J. Lawton Papers; Unsigned memo, "Proposed Legislative Program to be Submitted to the Congress on July 26, 1948," July 17, 1948, Charles S. Murphy Papers; Louis Brownlow to Webb, July 19, 1948, James E. Webb Papers; Batt to Clark Clifford, July 28, 1948, Clifford Papers, Speech File; Unsigned memo, "Conference with Phil Murray," July 22, 1948, Clifford Papers, Subject File.

17. Bennett to Walter C. Ploeser, July 16, 1948, Marion T. Bennett Papers; *The New York Times*, July 16, 1948, p. 1, July 21, 1948, pp. 1, 16.

tion, but reporters noted that the tone was one of "pleading and persuasion" that lacked the inflammatory rhetoric of the earlier speeches. The partisan jibes, at least, would not be carried to the floor of Congress. Truman devoted the first half of his address to inflation, a problem that would not "wait for the next Congress to act." The anti-inflation proposals repeated those of November, 1947, with the addition of an excess-profits tax to increase the Treasury surplus. The second major recommendation was for action on the Taft-Ellender-Wagner housing bill. Next in priority were requests for legislation for providing aid to education, raising the minimum wage, extending and increasing social security benefits, amending the displaced-persons act, authorizing a loan for the construction of United Nations headquarters in New York, and ratifying the International Wheat Agreement, which guaranteed farmers a minimum export market for the next five years. Congress should also restore cuts in appropriations for public-power projects, revise the federal pay-raise bill passed in June, and enact the President's civil-rights program. Finally, there were measures that Congress should take up if it had time—health insurance, replacement of Taft-Hartley with a "sound labor-management relations law," a "real" long-range farm program, a "stronger" reciprocal-trade act, universal military training, a national science foundation, strengthened antitrust legislation, and approval of the St. Lawrence seaway treaty. Here was every major proposal the President had made to the Eightieth Congress since January, 1947.[18]

Truman's strategy left Republicans in a quandary. Should they do nothing and adjourn immediately? Should they do all they could to build a record to take to the people? Or, should they select just a few measures for enactment? Strong leadership from their presidential nominee was not forthcoming. Despite pleas from Harold Stassen either to take complete charge or keep his hands off, Dewey attempted to take the middle road. Brownell announced that Dewey thought Congress should "give careful consideration to whatever is proposed in the President's message," but this was his only public comment. Private strategy meetings

18. *Ibid.*, July 28, 1948, pp. 1, 3; Message to the Special Session of the 80th Congress, July 27, 1948, *Public Papers: Truman, 1948*, 416–21.

were fruitless. Brownell tried to commit legislative leaders to a few measures requested by Truman and supported in the Republican platform. Vandenberg, too, pressed for passage of some legislation to demonstrate Republican sincerity and prepare a better case for the campaign. Brownell specifically pleaded for liberalization of the displaced-persons act, but Revercomb refused to consider it. Taft, as a matter of principle, was adamant against cooperating with any aspect of Truman's blatantly partisan maneuver.[19]

The official Republican response to Truman's message was written by Republican leaders in Congress; according to Taft, Dewey was "more or less" consulted but made no recommendations. The statement repeated the charge of presidential politics and pointed out that the middle of an election campaign was hardly the time to enact legislation. They could find "very little of an emergency nature" in the President's recommendations and wondered how he could blame Republicans for failure in the area of social-welfare legislation when the Democrats had had fourteen years to handle such problems. GOP leaders announced that the Senate would first consider the House-passed anti-poll-tax bill and that committees of both houses would study the anti-inflation proposals, although the President himself was responsible for much of this inflation. In any case, such "police-state methods" as price and wage controls and rationing would do more harm than good. Congressional committees would also study the housing problem, but the long-range program involved "serious complications and differences of opinion which [could not] be dealt with adequately at this special session."[20]

The Senate first considered the anti-poll-tax bill, with Republicans hoping to embarrass the Democrats and point the finger of blame at them for at least one failure of the Eightieth Congress. A motion to consider the bill, introduced by Kenneth Wherry, brought forth lengthy speeches from Southern Democrats and sanctimonious Republican demands that the minority support the President's program. On August 2, Wherry submitted a clo-

19. Jules Abels, *Out of the Jaws of Victory*, 124; Ross, *The Loneliest Campaign*, 136–37.

20. *The New York Times*, July 28, 1948, p. 3; U.S. *Congressional Record*, 80th Cong., 2d sess., 1948, XCIV, Part 12, p. A4671.

ture petition on the motion, but Vandenberg, as presiding officer, followed precedent and upheld Georgia Democrat Richard Russell's point of order that motions, as opposed to measures, were not subject to cloture. Taft appealed the ruling, but the appeal was also subject to unlimited debate, and on August 4 the bill was shelved. The Republicans made no attempt to kill the filibuster by keeping the Senate in continuous session. According to Wherry, this would have been hypocrisy in view of determined Southern efforts to prevent a vote.[21]

Meanwhile, the Banking and Currency committees had held hearings on inflation controls. On August 5, the House committee reported a bill with three provisions: (1) authorization for the Federal Reserve Board to reinstate consumer credit controls, (2) an increase of the reserve requirements of Federal Reserve banks by 3 per cent on demand and 1 per cent on time deposits (the Administration had asked for increases of 10 and 4 per cent), and (3) an increase of the gold-reserve requirement to 35 per cent against deposits and 40 per cent against Federal Reserve notes in circulation (the existing reserves of most banks were already near 50 per cent). The majority had previously pushed through, over vigorous Democratic objections, a resolution suspending the rules for the remainder of the session. This procedure limited debate to 40 minutes, prohibited amendments from the floor, and required that bills receive a two-thirds majority for passage. Thus, Democrats had to accept Republican-written measures or nothing.[22]

Alluding to the suspension of the rules, Truman intervened with a statement just before the House was to vote on the anti-inflation measure: "It would appear that the Republican leaders are unwilling to extend to the Congress an opportunity to vote on the issues of direct price control, the authority to impose allocations and priorities, and the other elements of a balanced program which I submitted to the Congress." The Republican leaders had refused to take up Truman's proposals in committee, and when the President urged them to reconsider, they paid no heed to Truman's charge and appeal. In the limited debate over the measure,

21. *Ibid.*, Part 8, pp. 9488–9509, 9554–87, 9597–9604, 9710, 9736.
22. *Ibid.*, pp. 9761–71, 9877–78.

Democrats expounded on the weakness of the bill while Republicans argued that Administration policies were the primary causes of inflation. Javits was the only Republican who opposed the measure in debate because he thought it inadequate. The bill passed, 264 to 97.[23] The Senate amended the House bill to eliminate increasing the gold-reserve requirement, to raise the reserve requirements by 1½ and 4 per cent on time and demand deposits respectively, and to extend the authorization to June, 1949. Before the final vote, Barkley introduced a substitute measure embodying the President's program. By a vote of 53 to 33, 47 Republicans, joined by 6 Southern Democrats—Byrd of Virginia, Eastland of Mississippi, McClellan of Arkansas, Robertson of Virginia, Stennis of Mississippi, and Stewart of Tennessee—quickly defeated it. William L. Langer was the only Republican to support the substitute. The Republican bill passed by voice vote, and the House promptly concurred in the Senate amendments.[24]

Housing legislation, the second major concern of the special session, presented many more difficulties to the GOP strategists. Realizing that the House leaders would not allow the Taft-Ellender-Wagner bill to reach the floor and anxious to prevent open dissension among Republicans, Taft worked out a compromise with important party members in the House. Both houses would support a bill to stimulate private construction of low-rent housing, but the T-E-W bill, with its provisions for slum clearance and public housing, would not be allowed to reach either floor.[25]

Taft, however, was unable to control liberal Republicans in the Senate. In the Banking and Currency Committee, Charles Tobey and Ralph Flanders voted with five Democrats to report a bill that included the public-housing and slum-clearance features. When the committee bill reached the floor, Senator Joseph R. McCarthy of Wisconsin, an inveterate foe of public housing, introduced an amendment eliminating slum clearance and public housing. In

23. The President's News Conference of August 5, 1948, *Public Papers: Truman, 1948*, 431; U.S. *Congressional Record*, 80th Cong., 2d sess., 1948, XCIV, Part 8, pp. 9877–90.

24. *Ibid.*, pp. 10159–60.

25. Davies, *Housing Reform During the Truman Administration*, 91.

the ensuing hassle among Republicans, Taft stuck to his agreement and spoke against his own bill, arguing that he could not persuade the House leaders to accept T-E-W and that a limited measure was better than none. He prevailed upon twelve Republicans who had previously voted for T-E-W to support the McCarthy amendment, and it passed, 48 to 36. The 12 Republicans who refused to support Taft were joined by 24 Democrats in voting against the amendment.[26]

The House leaders supported the McCarthy substitute, and it passed easily, 351 to 9. Although the Democrats could have prevented the bill from receiving the necessary two-thirds majority, they apparently thought the McCarthy substitute was better than nothing. The Republican managers were spared the embarrassment of an open fight in their ranks that their counterparts in the Senate had endured; only the liberal Republican Javits pleaded strongly for T-E-W, and a handful of Republicans from urban states expressed regret that slum-clearance and public-housing provisions were not included in the bill.[27]

Three of Truman's other proposals were considered during the "Turnip Day" session. The House with little debate passed, 164 to 27, the loan of $65 million for the United Nations headquarters, which the Senate had authorized during the regular session. In the Senate, Republicans sponsored an amendment to the displaced-persons bill that broadened eligibility requirements by extending the deadline date for having entered the camps. A Senate Judiciary subcommittee, however, voted it down, 2 to 2, with Revercomb and Donnell opposing and Cooper and McGrath supporting the amendment. Democrat McCarran of Nevada was absent, but he had taken a restrictionist approach during the regular session and had told Revercomb privately that he was opposed to revision of the bill. The third item considered was the International Wheat Agreement guaranteeing an export market of 185,000,000 bushels of U.S. wheat each year for the next five

26. *Ibid.*, 92–95; U.S. *Congressional Record*, 80th Cong., 2d sess., 1948, XCIV, Part 8, p. 9935.

27. *Ibid.*, pp. 10219–20. See remarks by Javits, *ibid.*, pp. 9375, 9899–9900, 10207, and by Wolverton (Republican, New Jersey), Hand (Republican, New Jersey), and Foote (Republican, Connecticut), *ibid.*, pp. 10213–15.

years. After holding hearings, the Senate Foreign Relations Committee voted unanimously to postpone action until the following session. Expressing full support for the program, the committee noted that technical difficulties necessitated a new treaty and promised to support one in the future.[28]

Truman could not have been more pleased with the outcome of the "Turnip Day" session. Aside from the anti-poll-tax disaster in the Senate—and he could charge that the majority made no vigorous effort to force a vote—the Democrats turned the special session to good account. The failure of Congress even to consider most of the President's requests was publicized by a White House score card of the special session released on August 12 and by Truman's observation to reporters that "it was entirely a 'do-nothing' session." Again, upon signing the credit-controls and housing measures, Truman sharply denounced Republicans in Congress for the feebleness of their response to his recommendations. The President had successfully focused attention on the discrepancies between the Republican platform and Republican action and had reinforced the framework upon which he would build the remainder of his campaign.[29]

The developments of the special session increased Dewey's dilemma, but he did not change the strategy outlined in his acceptance speech. He could not afford to lose the support of conservative congressmen during the campaign, nor did he wish to emphasize the split in his party. On the other hand, he was sensitive to the popular support for the extension of social and economic reforms, which coincided substantially with his own convictions. His only escape seemed to lie in avoiding specific issues and appealing to vague principles. Confidence in victory, which was reinforced by polls that consistently predicted Republican success, also permitted such a strategy. Since Dewey was ahead,

28. Ibid., pp. 9891–99, 9974–76; The New York Times, August 7, 1948, p. 3; Vandenberg to Dewey, July 14, 1948, Arthur H. Vandenberg Papers, William L. Clements Library, University of Michigan.

29. The New York Times, August 13, 1948, p. 1; The President's News Conference of August 12, 1948, Public Papers: Truman, 1948, 438; Statement by the President Upon Approving the Housing Act, August 10, 1948, ibid., 436–37; Statement by the President Upon Signing Resolution, "To Aid in Protecting the Nation's Economy Against Inflationary Pressures," August 16, 1948, ibid., 449–51.

the best course was to attempt to maintain his lead and not risk antagonizing various groups by discussing issues. Although Congressional leaders urged him to "talk about the constructive aspects of the Eightieth Congress and not let Truman get away unanswered, with his constant criticism of our record," Dewey chose for the most part to avoid the issue.[30]

His statement at Spokane that "the 80th Congress delivered as no Congress ever did for the future of our country" was exceptional. Occasionally the Republican candidate praised Congress for specific actions, such as the record appropriations for reclamation and rural electrification and the first long-range farm price-support program. In Pittsburgh, he talked at length about Taft-Hartley, crediting both parties for its passage and predicting that "wherever and whenever it needs change it will be changed."[31]

But more typical of Dewey's campaign was his kickoff speech at Des Moines: "Tonight we enter upon a campaign to unite all America." He discussed the general problems of peace, prices, housing, and discrimination and proposed that "with restoration of faith in ourselves, of competence in our Government, of unity of purpose among our people, there is nothing, as a people, we cannot do." By electing an Administration that could unite the people, voters would have taken "the greatest single step toward solving these problems." Alleged communists in government, an issue dramatized by the indiscriminate accusations of Elizabeth Bentley and Whittaker Chambers before the House Un-American Activities Committee, also occupied a considerable part of the Republican nominee's attention, and he promised to "faithfully and vigorously expose Communists." Charging Truman's Administration with mismanagement, inefficiency, confusion, and incompetence, he pledged that his Administration would restore unity, teamwork, integrity, and competence to government. Dewey scorned the "mud-slinging," "cheap wisecracking," and "ranting, boasting partisanship" of his opponent and de-

30. Joe Martin, *My First Fifty Years in Politics*, 195; *The New York Times*, August 13, 1948, p. 1, August 19, 1948, p. 15.

31. Abels, *Out of the Jaws of Victory*, 190; *The New York Times*, September 22, 1948, p. 21, September 28, 1948, p. 18, October 3, 1948, p. 42, October 12, 1948, p. 20, October 16, 1948, p. 7, October 27, 1948, p. 22.

nounced the Democrats for attempting to divide the people by setting class against class and for seeking to spread fear with uninformed predictions. He pledged support for the Republican platform but phrased his promises in general terms and set forth no specific means of achieving his goals.[32]

In sharp contrast, Truman's design for victory called for emotion-rousing appeals on the specific issues that the Eightieth Congress provided him. A typical speech began with Truman's calling up memories of the Depression, which he said was caused by Republican policies that favored the interests of Wall Street "gluttons of privilege." He then would point out Democratic contributions to ending the Depression and compare economic conditions of 1932 with the general prosperity of 1948. One had only to look at the record of the Eightieth Congress, according to the President, to see that Republican policies had not changed. In 1946 the Republicans began to "whittle away at New Deal laws. Now they have tasted blood and they are waiting for the time when they can go ahead with a Republican Congress and a Republican President and do a real hatchet job on the New Deal." Again, the President warned, "if you elect a Republican President to go along with a Republican Congress like the 80th, you can expect them to take you headlong back down the road that led to the great depression in the 1930's." Nor should the people be fooled by Republican campaign promises: "Actions speak louder than words. The record of the Republican party that really counts is the record of that good-for-nothing, 'do-nothing,' 80th Congress." To a Cleveland audience, Truman slyly recalled how "encouraged" he had been by the Republican platform and how by calling the special session he had given the party an opportunity "to show good faith by converting its platform promises into legislative performance." Point by point, he demonstrated how the Republicans had refused to act.[33]

32. *Ibid.*, September 21, 1948, p. 20, October 12, 1948, p. 20, September 25, 1948, p. 2, October 2, 1948, p. 9, October 29, 1948, p. 8, September 23, 1948, p. 18, October 15, 1948, p. 15, October 27, 1948, p. 22, October 31, 1948, p. 43; Abels, *Out of the Jaws of Victory,* 148, 188–89.

33. See, for example, Address at Dexter, Iowa, on the Occasion of the National Plowing Match, September 18, 1948, *Public Papers: Truman,* 1948, 504–5; Address in Buffalo, October 8, 1948, *ibid.,* 720; Address at the Armory, Springfield,

Time and again, Truman sought to link Dewey with the Eightieth Congress. This was not easy, for as Truman explained, the Republican nominee

> ... has treated it like a poor relation; he has shut it up in the backroom, so that its bad manners and terrible record won't frighten the voters he is entertaining in the parlor. . . .
>
> I am proposing to drag out [*sic*] the old reprobate of a Republican 80th Congress out of the backroom, and disclose him to the guests as the candidate's nearest and dearest relative.

The President frequently quoted Dewey's infrequent statements of praise for the Eightieth Congress, and he argued that the Republican candidate was "bound hand and foot by the record of the 80th Congress and he is running on that record and nothing else." Truman delighted in taunting the Republican candidate on the nature of his campaign; he maintained that a man could not win by "running away from the record or ducking the issues" and warned his audiences not to be lulled to sleep by "high-level platitudes." Referring to Dewey's appeal, Truman predicted that the only "unity" the Republicans would achieve was the "unity of the Martins, and the Tabers, and the Wherrys, and the Tafts."[34]

Besides interpreting the record of the Eightieth Congress as official GOP policy and a preview of what would come under a Republican Administration, the President also discussed specific issues. He equated the record of the Eightieth Congress with the behavior of the most reactionary Republicans. In the West he emphasized public power and reclamation. Pointing to the drastic budget cuts made in the House Appropriations Committee during the first session, he asserted that the partial restoration of those cuts was made only because of vigorous action by Democrats. Even the appropriations voted were "not aimed to benefit the

Illinois, October 12, 1948, *ibid.*, 761; Address in the Memorial Auditorium, Gary, Indiana, October 25, 1948, *ibid.*, 846; Address at the Armory, Akron, Ohio, October 11, 1948, *ibid.*, 743; Address in Indianapolis at the Indiana World War Memorial, October 15, 1948, *ibid.*, 802–3; Address in the Cleveland Municipal Auditorium, October 26, 1948, *ibid.*, 865–68.

34. Address at the Armory, Springfield, Illinois, October 12, 1948, *ibid.*, 764; Address at the Gilmore Stadium in Los Angeles, September 23, 1948, *ibid.*, 555–56; Address at Bonham, Texas, September 27, 1948, *ibid.*, 593.

people as much as to benefit the power interests," because Congress had eliminated construction of some transmission facilities and curtailed construction of others.[35]

Before farm audiences, Truman charged Republicans with cutting funds for rural electrification and soil-conservation payments. While grain prices were falling in September and October, he called attention to the bill that in rechartering the Commodity Credit Corporation, prevented it from acquiring additional storage facilities and thus forced farmers to sell their record wheat and corn crops below support prices and turned them "back to the speculators." Finally, he contended that the Republicans had threatened the farmers' export market by "crippling" the reciprocal-trade program and by "killing" the International Wheat Agreement.[36]

In urban areas, Truman called attention to the Taft-Hartley act, which he interpreted as a deliberate Republican attempt to make it harder "for organized labor to bargain for better wages and better living conditions." He also emphasized inadequate action on price controls and housing and told with relish how Taft "ran out" on his own housing bill in the special session. The tax cut was the "rich man's tax relief," and Truman frequently quoted from a Republican publication that urged party members to contribute some of their tax savings to the campaign fund. Less frequently mentioned were the Republicans' attacks on social security, failure to raise the minimum wage, failure to enact legislation for federal aid to education and national health insurance, and their part in passing the discriminatory displaced-persons bill and the Reed-Bulwinkle act exempting railroads from antitrust prosecution.[37]

35. Address at the Mormon Tabernacle in Salt Lake City, September 21, 1948, *ibid.*, 533–34; Address at Lakeside Park, Oakland, California, September 22, 1948, *ibid.*, 545–47; Address at Phoenix, Arizona, September 24, 1948, *ibid.*, 567; Address at El Paso, Texas, September 25, 1948, *ibid.*, 575–77.

36. Address at Dexter, Iowa, September 18, 1948, *ibid.*, 506–7; Address at Bonham, Texas, September 27, 1948, *ibid.*, 593–95; Address at Skelly Stadium, Tulsa, Oklahoma, September 29, 1948, *ibid.*, 636; Address at the Armory, Springfield, Illinois, October 12, 1948, *ibid.*, 762; Address at the State Fairgrounds, Raleigh, North Carolina, October 19, 1948, *ibid.*, 825–26.

37. Rear Platform and Other Informal Remarks in Michigan and Ohio, Sep-

Again Truman muted the civil-rights issue. Asserting that Negro votes in crucial areas would outweigh Southern losses, William Batt urged the President to "speak out frankly and fully" on his past record in the Senate, as well as in the White House, "to prove that he *acts* as well as talks Civil Rights." Truman rejected the advice. At the convention, the national party had gone too far in the area of civil rights. ADA Democrats, with the support of urban bosses, had upset the Administration's plans for a mild civil-rights plank when they wrote into the platform demands for legislation to protect minorities and end discrimination against them in political participation, employment opportunity, physical safety, and military service. The adoption of the amendments precipitated a Southern revolt: Two days after the convention, disaffected Democrats met at Birmingham, Alabama, formed the States Rights party, and endorsed a presidential ticket headed by J. Strom Thurmond, governor of South Carolina. Although most prominent Democrats disdained the Dixiecrat movement, it intensified the concern of Truman and his strategists for the national ticket.

Accordingly, while Truman issued the executive order for desegregation of the military on July 26 and listed civil-rights legislation on his agenda for the special session, he was unwilling to risk additional Southern defections by stressing civil rights in the campaign. Only three times—in Carbondale, Illinois, Chicago, and South Bend, Indiana—did Truman deplore racial and religious discrimination in general terms, and only twice did he refer to his own program and the congressional response. In Cleveland, he recalled his appeal to the special session to pass legislation protecting "basic rights of citizenship and human liberty" and accused Republicans of merely paying lip service to civil rights. Finally, in Harlem on October 29, he devoted an entire speech to

---

tember 6, 1948, *ibid.*, 471–72, 474; Address at the Gilmore Stadium in Los Angeles, September 23, 1948, *ibid.*, 557–58; Address in Charleston, West Virginia, October 1, 1948, *ibid.*, 673; Address in Wilkes-Barre, Pennsylvania, October 23, 1948, *ibid.*, 834; Address in Johnstown, Pennsylvania, October 23, 1948, *ibid.*, 836–37; Address in the Cleveland Municipal Auditorium, October 26, 1948, *ibid.*, 866–68.

civil rights, describing the work of his Civil Rights Committee and contrasting his own efforts with congressional inaction.[38]

Truman's campaign strategy was followed by vice-presidential candidate Alben Barkley, who as minority leader had witnessed firsthand the failures of the Eightieth Congress. He, too, derided Dewey for his ambiguity about the record of the Republican Congress and used that record to define the real objectives of the Republican party. Mentioning most of the domestic issues of the Eightieth Congress, Barkley stressed the Republicans' failure to enact effective inflation controls, their "rich man's" tax bill, and their attacks on social security, farm programs, and labor.[39]

On October 30, Truman summarized his campaign themes in St. Louis and rested his case. He returned to Independence to vote, with all the pollsters predicting defeat. But as the returns came in during the early morning hours of November 3, once-confident commentators began fumbling for explanations of the apparent Democratic upset. By midmorning the results were clear, and Dewey conceded defeat. When the final tallies were in, Truman had captured 303 electoral votes to Dewey's 189; the President won a popular vote of 24,105,812 (about 1.5 million less than Roosevelt received in 1944), while Dewey received 21,970,065. Wallace, the Progressive candidate, polled only 1,157,172 votes, and Thurmond on the States Rights ticket won 39 electoral votes and 1,169,063 popular votes. Democrats gained a 54 to 42 margin over Republicans in the Senate, and one of 263 to 171 in the House.[40]

38. Batt to Clifford, "Notes on the President's Campaign," August 11, 1948, Clifford Papers, Political File; Barton J. Bernstein, "The Ambiguous Legacy: The Truman Administration and Civil Rights" (MS, Truman Library, 1966), 18–20; Ross, *The Loneliest Campaign*, 120–26, 130–33; Address at the University of Southern Illinois, Carbondale, Illinois, September 20, 1948, *Public Papers: Truman, 1948*, 650; Address in the Chicago Stadium, October 25, 1948, *ibid.*, 852; Rear Platform and Other Informal Remarks in Indiana and Ohio, October 26, 1948, *ibid.*, 855; Address in the Cleveland Municipal Auditorium, October 26, 1948, *ibid.*, 868; Address in Harlem, New York, Upon Receiving the Franklin Roosevelt Award, October 29, 1948, *ibid.*, 924.

39. Reading copies of Barkley speeches at Springfield, Illinois, August 18, 1948, Wilkes-Barre, Pennsylvania, September 18, 1948, Bridgeport, Connecticut, September 22, 1948, New York City, September 23, 1948, Barkley Papers, Speech File.

40. Address at the Kiel Auditorium, St. Louis, Missouri, October 30, 1948, *Public Papers: Truman, 1948*, 936–39; Eric F. Goldman, *The Crucial Decade—*

Truman's energetic campaign failed to bring the people to the polls in large numbers, and the ratio of popular vote to its potential in 1948 was low. According to one analysis, neither candidate "was able to swing the independent vote in any significant way, attract any sizable number of defectors from the opposition party, or stimulate any important fraction of the in-and-out vote to go to the polls in his behalf. These are the marks of strong candidate appeal, and they were not present in the 1948 election." Truman was, however, able to hold a sufficient number of voters to their Democratic loyalties. Election analyses based upon representative sampling explain Truman's victory in terms of the 20 per cent of the voters who made their decisions in the last month of the campaign and thus upset predictions of pollsters, who stopped sampling early. This group of voters, which gave Truman his margin of victory, consisted largely of Democrats who failed to support their party's candidate until very late in the campaign. Their early disaffection was due to their unfavorable image of Truman as President and to new problems and issues that distracted them from the socioeconomic questions around which the Democratic majority had been built. Their rally to Truman in the last weeks of the campaign was the result of an increase in the salience of the older socioeconomic issues that had initially made them Democrats. Thus, Truman's hard-hitting discussion of the issues made a substantial contribution to his victory, and it was the Eightieth Congress that had provided him with an effective and dramatic framework in which to discuss those issues.[41]

Other analyses have interpreted Truman's victory in terms of various interest groups. Several stress the Democratic gains in the farm belt, which had been a traditional Republican stronghold except in 1932 and 1936. There, Truman shrewdly manipulated the record of the Eightieth Congress to convince farmers that a

---

and After: America, 1945–1960, 86–88; U.S. Department of Commerce, Bureau of the Census, *Historical Statistics of the United States, Colonial Times to 1957,* 682.

41. Angus Campbell, Philip E. Converse, Warren E. Miller, and Donald E. Stokes, *The American Voter,* 531–32; Angus Campbell and Robert L. Kahn, *The People Elect a President,* 7–8; Bernard R. Berelson, Paul F. Lazarsfeld, and William N. McPhee, *Voting: A Study of Opinion Formation in a Presidential Campaign,* 14–19, 254–70.

Republican Administration would mean a return to conditions of the 1920's. The Democratic upset in the Midwest—Truman won in Iowa, Wisconsin, and Ohio, which had gone Republican in 1944—enabled Truman to win despite Republican gains in the Northeast. Yet the campaign appeal to urban voters on the issues of housing, labor, and rising prices also contributed to Truman's victory by ensuring the electoral votes of Massachusetts, California, Ohio, Illinois, and Missouri.[42]

Predicting a Democratic victory on the eve of the elections, Senator J. Howard McGrath, chairman of the Democratic National Committee, concluded:

> The Republican 80th Congress may well have been the deciding factor in the election. Without the performance of the Republican Congress available to the voters to compare with Governor Dewey's glib promises, Governor Dewey might possibly have been elected on the basis of his generalities about efficiency and unity and his siren song to make the New Deal bigger and to administer it better than the Democrats have done.[43]

Discounting the partisan rhetoric, McGrath's statement aptly summarizes the role of the Eightieth Congress in the 1948 election. The basic reason for Truman's victory was the popularity of his party and its domestic program, but Truman himself focused the electorate's attention on the Democratic program. In a highly personal and emotional way, he sharply contrasted it with the least popular aspects of the Eightieth Congress and skillfully identified that Congress with the Republican party in general.

42. Allen J. Matusow, *Farm Policies and Politics in the Truman Years*, 185–86; Samuel Lubell, *The Future of American Politics*, 171–73; Louis H. Bean, "Forecasting the 1950 Elections," *Harper's Magazine*, 200 (April, 1950), 36–37; Abels, *Out of the Jaws of Victory*, 290; Goldman, *The Crucial Decade*, 90; Eugene H. Roseboom, *A History of Presidential Elections*, 503–4.

43. Quoted in *The New York Times*, November 1, 1948, p. 19.

CONCLUSION

COMPARISON OF THE Administration's legislative program with the record of the Eightieth Congress in domestic affairs invites the conclusion that Truman's legislative leadership was a failure. Such a view, however, ignores the *degree* to which the legislative record was at odds with the President's goals and fails to consider the extent to which circumstances that Truman could not influence contributed to the dearth of reform legislation and the attacks on New Deal programs. In fact, the unsatisfactory record in domestic legislation resulted from a combination of external circumstances and ineffective presidential leadership. Moreover, in view of the high priority that Truman placed on Cold War measures and his own re-election, it must be concluded that Truman was highly successful where he most wanted to be.

During the Eightieth Congress, Truman faced the same obstacles to success in domestic legislation that limited his predecessor and successors. The conservative coalition that had risen to plague Roosevelt in 1937 was even stronger after the Republican victory of 1946. War-based prosperity had transformed large groups within the Democratic coalition from "have-nots" into "haves," and congressmen of both parties reflected the views of satisfied constituencies. The dissatisfactions that existed—concern over rising prices and irritation at work stoppages—could hardly be channeled into public pressure for the expansion of reform. Finally, Truman had to operate in a postwar period characterized by an expanding economy, high employment, and serious inflation. In such an environment, the most skillful politician could have achieved at most only a small part of Truman's program.

This is not to say that Truman displayed the characteristics of a highly skilled politician. In many cases, he failed to unite the Administration behind a position and then energetically seek to translate that position into legislation. In part, this failure resulted

211

from the Administration's defensive position. Faced with the prospect of an unwanted portal bill and restrictive labor legislation, Administration leaders believed that positive proposals should be offered but could not put together a limited program that would quiet demands for harsher legislation. The problem was especially clear in the tax-cut legislation. During the first session, the Administration firmly opposed any tax reduction and succeeded in its opposition; Truman's offering his own tax-cut plan in 1948 surely contributed to the success of the Republican version.

The confusion within the Administration about presidential programs also showed itself when political expediency dictated the presentation of proposals before adequate groundwork could be laid. The request for selective service went up to Congress, by Elsey's admission, before the Administration had completely worked out its own position and before cooperation with congressional leaders had begun.[1] Failure to specify the details of Truman's anti-inflation program for the special session of 1947 resulted in considerable embarrassment when congressional questioning revealed glaring differences of opinion among Administration spokesmen. Truman's occasional inability to control his own appointees also contributed to legislative defeats, notably on rent control and the wool bill during the first session and again on the anti-inflation program of the special session.

Finally, the Administration cooperated poorly with congressional Democrats. There was no consultation before the presentation of Truman's tax and civil-rights bills in 1948 or before his major foreign-policy address to Congress in March, 1948. Draft bills incorporating Truman's objectives for legislation dealing with portal suits, restrictions on labor, and inflation controls in 1947, and tax reduction in 1948 either were not available at all for sympathetic congressmen or reached the Hill too late to do any good. Not until April, 1948, did Truman begin to work closely with party leaders in the legislature, but by then, much of the record of the Eightieth Congress was complete.

---

1. Elsey, notes on Truman's Saint Patrick's Day Address, March 15, 1948, George M. Elsey Papers, Speech File.

Truman's failure to exercise vigorous legislative leadership was consistent with his conception of presidential responsibility in domestic affairs. As President, he felt it his duty to set objectives before the nation. Anticipating a hostile response to his civil-rights program, Truman insisted, "But it needs to be said." Thus, he believed that he was discharging his responsibility by forcefully stating the requirements; in his view, he was not expected to pursue these objectives strenuously in the more mundane day-to-day operations of executive-legislative relationships. Truman expressed this limited view of his obligations as Chief Executive by stating, "What the country needed in every field . . . was up to me to say . . . and if Congress wouldn't respond, well, I'd have done all I could in a straightforward way."[2]

In addition, Truman believed that the disposition of the Congress would make energetic action on his part an exercise in futility. It is clear that by June, 1947, Truman anticipated few, if any, favorable responses to his domestic proposals. He abandoned hope for congressional action and saw no point in acting aggressively. Giving highest priority to Democratic victory in November, Truman had only to exhort forcefully, intensify his requests for liberal programs, meet every attack on reform programs with strongly worded vetoes, and thereby equate the Republican party with the most reactionary members of the Eightieth Congress.

Given the unhospitable atmosphere for reform and Truman's limitations as legislative leader, the record of the Eightieth Congress testified remarkably to the acceptance of a large role for the Federal Government in the promotion of economic stability and social welfare. The successful attacks on New Deal programs represented a limited curtailment of some programs, not a wholesale dismantling of reform legislation. Although important restrictions were imposed upon organized labor, the Taft-Hartley act did not destroy government protection of collective bargaining. While tax relief was granted in larger measure to higher income groups, the principle of progressive taxation prevailed. The Eight-

2. Quoted in Richard E. Neustadt, *Presidential Power, The Politics of Leadership,* 177.

ieth Congress overruled judicial interpretations expanding social security but made no cutbacks in current coverage and took a modest step toward expanding benefits. And, although budget requests were cut for a variety of programs, the substance of each was left intact.

A group of moderate Republicans and moderate Southern, Southwestern, and border-state Democrats held the balance of power and were largely responsible for the nature of much of the domestic legislation of the Eightieth Congress. Especially in the Senate, this group voted with Northern Democrats to weaken anti-Administration measures. After accomplishing these modifications, they voted with conservatives of both parties to ensure passage of such bills over presidential veto. This pattern obtained in the portal, Taft-Hartley, social security, and tax-reduction legislation.

Truman's willingness to exercise his veto power played an equally crucial role in diluting assaults against the Administration's domestic policies. Republican leaders were forced to modify considerably the two major measures of the Eightieth Congress —Taft-Hartley and tax reduction—in order to win Democratic support sufficient to override presidential vetoes. That Truman's stubborn defense of liberal policies was designed with an eye on the 1948 campaign should not obscure his personal commitment to those programs and his substantial contribution to blunting antireform legislation.

More remarkable than the domestic record of the Eightieth Congress was its mobilization of U.S. resources to implement the concept of containment of communism. Less willing to expend men than dollars, Congress rejected some of the Administration's requests for military expansion, but it did enact the first peacetime draft, support the enlargement of U.S. air power, and take the first step toward a permanent military alliance. Moreover, it marshaled large majorities in support of economic aid for Greece, Turkey, and Western Europe and passed legislation in substantial agreement with Administration requests. Congress demonstrated that concern over communist expansion was the principal motivation for its response to Truman's foreign-policy proposals when it watered down such Administration measures as reciprocal trade and admission of displaced persons—proposals that lacked the anticommunist appeal of containment measures.

Besides its central role in implementing executive proposals, Congress influenced the President's decision making in foreign policy in other ways. Republicans in Congress were chiefly responsible for the new emphasis in 1948 on bolstering the government of Chiang Kai-shek. Vandenberg's demands in 1946 and 1947 for a tougher policy toward the Soviet Union undoubtedly weakened Kennan's and Marshall's voices of moderation and strengthened the influence of Administration officials Harriman, Forrestal, Acheson, and Clayton, who were also advocating a tougher U.S. policy. Also, early in the Eightieth Congress, the Administration's uncertainty about legislative support for containment measures led it to embellish its request for Greek-Turkish aid with bold, crusading, ideological rhetoric and to exaggerate the threat to U.S. security in the Middle East. Finally, although Truman generally tried to keep foreign policy separate from domestic politics, one major reason for his militant speech of March, 1948, was his need to enhance his own prestige in the forthcoming elections, a need that overruled Marshall's pleas for temperance.

The Republicans' persistent hawkishness contributed to Truman's public presentation of U.S. foreign policy, but the containment policy was a product of Administration appraisals of the international situation. The Administration's emphasis on the vulnerability of U.S. security to Russian expansion, which it equated with communism—and noncommunist revolution— everywhere, certainly won votes for containment measures, but it also indicated precisely how Truman and his advisers viewed the situation. And this view helps to account for the disparity between Truman's legislative leadership in domestic and foreign affairs. Like Congress, Truman placed highest priority on measures to suppress communism and spent less effort on behalf of reciprocal-trade and displaced-persons legislation, but for his containment measures, notably Greek-Turkish aid and the Marshall Plan, the President supplemented public appeals with incessant efforts to obtain congressional approval. He exercised the full range of his presidential powers: With his aides, he carefully cultivated public opinion, provided draft bills for his proposals, and worked closely with congressional Republicans and Democrats at every stage of the bills' passage through Congress. In obtaining public support for containment, however, the Truman Administration allowed Congress to increase U.S. involvement on the losing side of the Chinese civil war, limited the possibilities for a *rapprochement* with the Soviet Union, and contributed to the hardening of public attitudes toward communism and a rigidity in foreign policy that continued into the next two decades.

Truman's ability to invoke a broad consensus on foreign policy was matched only by his skill in presenting the record of the Eightieth Congress as a foil for the 1948 campaign. From mid-1947 through the special session of 1948, by his vetoes and his escalating demands for reform legislation, Truman determined the issues upon which he would run for re-election. Although he was unable to rally voters to the polls as Roosevelt had, Truman shrewdly used the Eightieth Congress to demonstrate the public's continuing attachment to New Deal reform, assured his own and his party's ascendancy, and in so doing gained the admiration and support, if not the love, of liberals in the United States. In contributing to the reunification and reinvigoration of the progressive movement, however, Truman's victory helped to stifle pressures for more fundamental reform and a less hostile approach to the Soviet Union, and to ensure that anticommunism would tend to take precedence over domestic reform in the priorities of U.S. liberalism.[3]

Simultaneously, Truman established a popular mandate in support of his domestic objectives in his second term. The Eighty-first Congress translated this mandate into legislation for a comprehensive public-housing program, expansion of social security, an increased minimum wage, expansion of soil conservation, reclamation, rural electrification, and public-power programs, and liberalization of the displaced-persons act. To be sure, Congress rejected major elements of the Fair Deal: aid to education, federal health insurance, federal protection of civil rights,

3. Alonzo L. Hamby, "Harry S. Truman and American Liberalism, 1945–1948" (Ph.D. dissertation, University of Missouri—Columbia, 1965), 269–74.

and an agricultural program focused on abundance and the expansion of consumption.[4] However, Truman's dogged advocacy
of these measures during the Eightieth Congress and after kept
them alive as national goals and paved the way for acceptance of
most of them two decades later. The next generation would find
many of these programs inadequate as solutions to basic social
and economic problems, but such a judgment should not detract
from a generally favorable evaluation of Truman's domestic
leadership. Given the conservative nature of U.S. politics, which
the President himself symbolized, the general tendency of domestic reform to support the long-term needs of corporate capitalism,
and the limitations on presidential power, and taking into account
the long gestation period of many Populist-Progressive goals, Harry Truman's contributions to domestic reform were substantial.

4. Richard E. Neustadt, "Congress and the Fair Deal; A Legislative Balance
Sheet," *Public Policy*, 5 (1954), 366–67.

BIBLIOGRAPHY

MANUSCRIPT COLLECTIONS

Assistants, Aides, and Counsels to the President, Files. Harry S. Truman Library, Independence, Missouri.

Alben W. Barkley Papers. University of Kentucky Library, Lexington, Kentucky.

Marion T. Bennett Papers. Western Historical Manuscripts Collection, University of Missouri, Columbia, Missouri.

John W. Bricker Papers. Ohio Historical Society, Columbus, Ohio.

Hugh A. Butler Papers. Nebraska State Historical Society, Lincoln, Nebraska.

Clarence Cannon Papers. Western Historical Manuscripts Collection, University of Missouri, Columbia, Missouri.

Arthur Capper Papers. Kansas State Historical Society, Topeka, Kansas.

John D. Clark Papers. Harry S. Truman Library, Independence, Missouri.

William L. Clayton Papers. Harry S. Truman Library, Independence, Missouri.

Clark M. Clifford Papers. Harry S. Truman Library, Independence, Missouri.

Albert M. Cole Papers. Kansas State Historical Society, Topeka, Kansas.

Committee for the Marshall Plan, Records. Harry S. Truman Library, Independence, Missouri.

Thomas C. Connally Papers. Library of Congress, Washington, D.C.

Matthew Connelly Files. Harry S. Truman Library, Independence, Missouri.

Democratic National Committee Records. Harry S. Truman Library, Independence, Missouri.

Robert L. Doughton Papers. University of North Carolina Library, Chapel Hill, North Carolina.

Helen Gahagan Douglas Papers. Western History Collections, University of Oklahoma, Norman, Oklahoma.

Carl T. Durham Papers. University of North Carolina Library, Chapel Hill, North Carolina.

George M. Elsey Papers. Harry S. Truman Library, Independence, Missouri.

Warner W. Gardner Papers. Harry S. Truman Library, Independence, Missouri.

Ellen Clayton Garwood Papers. Harry S. Truman Library, Independence, Missouri.

John W. Gibson Papers. Harry S. Truman Library, Independence, Missouri.

Paul M. Herzog Papers. Harry S. Truman Library, Independence, Missouri.

Clifford R. Hope Papers. Kansas State Historical Society, Topeka, Kansas.

John H. Kerr Papers. University of North Carolina Library, Chapel Hill, North Carolina.

Harley M. Kilgore Papers. Franklin D. Roosevelt Library, Hyde Park, New York.

———. University of West Virginia Library, Morgantown, West Virginia.

Frederick J. Lawton Papers. Harry S. Truman Library, Independence, Missouri.

J. Howard McGrath Papers. Harry S. Truman Library, Independence, Missouri.

Kenneth D. McKellar Papers. Memphis Public Library, Memphis, Tennessee.

Frank McNaughton Papers. Harry S. Truman Library, Independence, Missouri.

Burnet R. Maybank Papers. South Carolina Department of Archives and History, Columbia, South Carolina.

Charles S. Murphy Papers. Harry S. Truman Library, Independence, Missouri.

Philleo Nash Papers. Harry S. Truman Library, Independence, Missouri.

National Security Committee Records. Harry S. Truman Library, Independence, Missouri.

Edwin G. Nourse Papers. Harry S. Truman Library, Independence, Missouri.

Sam Rayburn Papers. Sam Rayburn Library, Bonham, Texas.

Samuel I. Rosenman Papers. Harry S. Truman Library, Independence, Missouri.

Charles G. Ross Papers. Harry S. Truman Library, Independence, Missouri.

George B. Schwabe Papers. Western History Collections, University of Oklahoma, Norman, Oklahoma.

John W. Snyder Papers. Harry S. Truman Library, Independence, Missouri.

David H. Stowe Papers. Harry S. Truman Library, Independence, Missouri.

John Taber Papers. John M. Olin Research Library, Cornell University, Ithaca, New York.

Elbert D. Thomas Papers. Franklin D. Roosevelt Library, Hyde Park, New York.

Elmer Thomas Papers. Western History Collections, University of Oklahoma, Norman, Oklahoma.

Harry S. Truman Papers. Harry S. Truman Library, Independence, Missouri.

U.S. Bureau of the Budget Files. Record Group 51, Series 47.1 and 47.1a. National Archives, Washington, D.C.

———. Reports to the President on Pending Legislation. Harry S. Truman Library, Independence, Missouri.

———. Files Retained by the Bureau in the Executive Office Building. Executive Office Building, Washington, D.C.

U.S. Department of Labor Files. Record Group 174, John W. Gibson File. National Archives, Washington, D.C.

———. David A. Morse File. National Archives, Washington, D.C.

———. Secretary's File. National Archives, Washington, D.C.

U.S. Federal Security Agency (Office of the Administrator), Files. Record Group 235, File 011.4 (Health Insurance). National Archives, Washington, D.C.

Arthur H. Vandenberg Papers. William L. Clements Library, University of Michigan, Ann Arbor, Michigan.

John M. Vorys Papers. Ohio Historical Society, Columbus, Ohio.

James E. Webb Papers. Harry S. Truman Library, Independence, Missouri.

Kenneth S. Wherry Papers. Love Library, University of Nebraska, Lincoln, Nebraska.

UNPUBLISHED MATERAL

Berman, William C., "The Politics of Civil Rights in the Truman Administration." Ph.D. dissertation, Ohio State University, 1963.

Bernstein, Barton J., "The Truman Administration and the Politics of Inflation." Ph.D. dissertation, Harvard University, 1963.

———, "The Ambiguous Legacy: The Truman Administration and Civil Rights." MS, Truman Library, 1966.

Branyan, Robert L., "Antimonopoly Activities during the Truman Administration." Ph.D. dissertation, University of Oklahoma, 1961.

Hamby, Alonzo L., "Harry S. Truman and American Liberalism, 1945–1948." Ph.D. dissertation, University of Missouri—Columbia, 1965.

Hinchey, Mary H., "The Frustration of the New Deal Revival." Ph.D. dissertation, University of Missouri—Columbia, 1965.

Lorimer, Sister M. Madeline, "America's Response to Europe's Displaced Persons, 1948–1952: A Preliminary Report." Ph.D. dissertation, St. Louis University, 1964.

McClure, Arthur F. II, "The Truman Administration and Labor Relations, 1945–1948." Ph.D. dissertation, University of Kansas, 1965.

Poen, Monte M., "The Truman Administration and National Health Insurance." Ph.D. dissertation, University of Missouri—Columbia, 1967.

Pratt, James W., "Leadership Relations in United States Foreign Policy Making: Case Studies, 1947–1950." Ph.D. dissertation, Columbia University, 1963.

Street, Kenneth W., "Harry S. Truman: His Role as Legislative Leader; 1945–1948." Ph.D. dissertation, University of Texas, 1963.

Waltrip, John R., "Public Power During the Truman Administration." Ph.D. dissertation, University of Missouri—Columbia, 1965.

PUBLIC DOCUMENTS

U.S. Department of Commerce, Bureau of the Census, *Historical Statistics of the United States, Colonial Times to 1957.* Washington: Government Printing Office, 1960.

U.S. Congress, Joint Committee on the Economic Report, *Hearings on the Anti-Inflation Program as Recommended in the President's Message of November 17, 1947.* 80th Cong., 1st sess., 1948.

U.S. House of Representatives, Committee on Agriculture, *Providing Support for Wool.* House Report 257 to accompany S. 814. 80th Cong., 1st sess., 1947.

———, *Stabilization of Agricultural Prices.* House Report 1776 to accompany H.R. 6248. 80th Cong., 2d sess., 1948.

———, Committee on Appropriations, *Interior Department Appropriation Bill, Fiscal Year 1948.* House Report 279 to accompany H.R. 3123. 80th Cong., 1st sess., 1947.

———, *Department of Agriculture Appropriation Bill, Fiscal Year 1948.* House Report 450 to accompany H.R. 3601. 80th Cong., 1st sess., 1947.

———, *Government Corporations Appropriation Bill, 1949.* House Report 1880 to accompany H.R. 6481. 80th Cong., 2d sess., 1948.

———, *Interior Department Appropriation Bill, 1949.* House Report 2038 to accompany H.R. 6705. 80th Cong., 2d sess., 1948.

——, *Foreign Aid Appropriation Bill, 1949.* House Report 2173 to accompany H.R. 6801. 80th Cong., 2d sess., 1948.

——, Committee on Banking and Currency, *Housing and Rent Controls.* House Report 317 to accompany H.R. 3203. 80th Cong., 1st sess., 1947.

——, *Aiding in the Stabilization of Commodity Prices and to Aid in Further Stabilizing the Economy of the United States.* House Report 1160 to accompany H.J. Res. 273. 80th Cong., 1st sess., 1947.

——, Committee on Education and Labor, *Labor-Management Relations Act, 1947.* House Report 245 to accompany H.R. 3020. 80th Cong., 1st sess., 1947.

——, Committee on Expenditures in the Executive Department, *Reorganization Plan Number 1 of 1948.* House Report 1368 to accompany H. Con. Res. 131. 80th Cong., 2d sess., 1948.

——, Committee on Foreign Affairs, *Relief Assistance to the People of Countries Devastated by War.* House Report 239 to accompany H.J. Res. 153. 80th Cong., 1st sess., 1947.

——, Committee on the Judiciary, *Regulating the Recovery of Portal-to-Portal Pay and for Other Purposes.* House Report 71 to accompany H.R. 2157. 80th Cong., 1st sess., 1947.

——, *Emergency Displaced Persons Admission Act.* House Report 1854 to accompany H.R. 6396. 80th Cong., 2d sess., 1948.

——, Committee on Ways and Means, *Individual Income Tax Reduction Act of 1947.* House Report 180 to accompany H.R. 1. 80th Cong., 1st sess., 1947.

——, *Individual Income Tax Reduction Act of 1947.* House Report 795 to accompany H.R. 3950. 80th Cong., 1st sess., 1947.

——, *Revenue Act of 1948.* House Report 1274 to accompany H.R. 4790. 80th Cong., 2d sess., 1948.

——, *Maintaining the Status Quo in Respect of Certain Employment Taxes and Social Security Benefits Pending Action by Congress on Extended Social Security Coverage.* House Report 1319 to accompany H.J. Res. 296. 80th Cong., 2d sess., 1948.

——, *Extending the Authority of the President Under Section 350 of the Tariff Act of 1930, As Amended, and for Other Purposes.* House Report 2009 to accompany H.R. 6556. 80th Cong., 2d sess., 1948.

U.S. Senate, Committee on Banking and Currency, *Stabilization of Commodity Prices and the National Economy.* Senate Report 780 to accompany S.J. Res. 167. 80th Cong., 1st sess., 1947.

——, Committee on Finance, *Individual Income Tax Reduction Act of 1947.* Senate Report 173 to accompany H.R. 1. 80th Cong., 1st sess., 1947.

———, *Revenue Act of 1948*. Senate Report 1013 to accompany H.R. 4790. 80th Cong., 2d sess., 1948.

———, *Extending the Authority of the President Under Section 350 of the Tariff Act of 1930, As Amended*. Senate Report 1558 to accompany H.R. 6556. 80th Cong., 2d sess., 1948.

———, Committee on Labor and Public Welfare, *Federal Labor Relations Act of 1947*. Senate Report 105 to accompany S. 1126. 80th Cong., 1st sess., 1947.

U.S. *Congressional Record*. Vols. XCIII–XCIV.

ARTICLES

Aiken, George D., "Senator Aiken Warns His Party." *The New York Times Magazine* (March 22, 1947), 10, 70–71.

Alsop, Joseph, "Congressmen Heading Home from Europe." St. Louis *Post-Dispatch*, October 24, 1947, 1D.

Bean, Louis H., "The Republican 'Mandate' and 1948." *The New York Times Magazine* (January 19, 1947), 16, 52.

———, "Forecasting the 1950 Elections." *Harper's Magazine*, 200 (April, 1950), 36–40.

Brown, Charles C., "Robert A. Taft, Champion of Public Housing and National Aid to Schools." *Bulletin of the Cincinnati Historical Society*, 26 (July, 1968), 225–53.

Clayton, William L., "GATT, the Marshall Plan, and OECD." *Political Science Quarterly*, 78 (December, 1963), 493–503.

Coffin, Tris, "A Man of the Good Old Days." *New Republic*, 116 (February 17, 1947), 28–30.

Davies, Richard O., " 'Mr. Republican' Turns 'Socialist': Robert A. Taft and Public Housing." *Ohio History*, 73 (Summer, 1964), 136–43.

Galbraith, John K., "Who Needs the Democrats?" *Harper's Magazine*, 241 (July, 1970), 43–62.

Hamby, Alonzo L., "The Liberals, Truman and FDR as Symbol and Myth." *Journal of American History*, 56 (March, 1970), 859–67.

Hitchens, Harold L., "Influences on the Congressional Decision to Pass the Marshall Plan." *Western Political Quarterly*, 21 (March, 1968), 51–68.

Lee, R. Alton, "The Turnip Day Session of the Do-Nothing Congress: Presidential Campaign Strategy." *Southwestern Social Science Quarterly*, 44 (December, 1963), 256–57.

Mann, Seymour T., "Policy Formation in the Executive Branch: The Taft-Hartley Experience." *Western Political Quarterly*, 13 (September, 1960), 597–608.

Neustadt, Richard E., "Congress and the Fair Deal; A Legislative Balance Sheet." *Public Policy*, 5 (1954), 351–81.

———, "Presidency and Legislation: Planning the President's Program." *American Political Science Review*, 49 (December, 1955), 980–1021.

Reynolds, J. Lacey, "Taber: 'The Third House of Congress,'" *The New York Times Magazine* (February 15, 1948), 10, 57–60.

Wallace, Henry, "The Fight for Peace Begins." *New Republic*, 116 (March 24, 1947), 12–13.

NEWSPAPERS AND PERIODICALS

Congressional Quarterly, 1946–1949.
The New York Times, November, 1946–November, 1948.

BOOKS

Abels, Jules, *Out of the Jaws of Victory*. New York: Henry Holt and Company, 1959.

Acheson, Dean, *Present at the Creation: My Years in the State Department*. New York: W. W. Norton and Company, 1969.

Anderson, Patrick, *The President's Men; White House Assistants of Franklin D. Roosevelt, Harry S. Truman, Dwight D. Eisenhower, John F. Kennedy, and Lyndon B. Johnson*. New York: Doubleday and Company, Inc., 1968.

Bailey, Stephen K., and Howard D. Samuel, *Congress at Work*. New York: Henry Holt and Company, 1952.

Barnet, Richard J., *Intervention and Revolution: The United States in the Third World*. New York: New American Library, Inc., 1968.

Berelson, Bernard R., Paul F. Lazarsfeld, and William N. McPhee, *Voting: A Study of Opinion Formation in a Presidential Campaign*. Chicago: University of Chicago Press, 1954.

Bernstein, Barton J., ed., *Politics and Policies of the Truman Administration*. Chicago: Quadrangle Books, 1970.

———, ed., *Towards a New Past: Dissenting Essays in American History*. New York: Vintage Books, Inc., 1969.

Bohlen, Charles E., *The Transformation of American Foreign Policy*. New York: W. W. Norton and Company, 1969.

Bontecou, Eleanor, *The Federal Loyalty-Security Program*. Ithaca, N.Y.: Cornell University Press, 1953.

Campbell, Angus, Philip E. Converse, Warren E. Miller, and Donald

E. Stokes, *The American Voter*. New York: John Wiley and Sons, 1960.

Campbell, Angus, and Robert L. Kahn, *The People Elect a President*. Ann Arbor: Survey Research Center, Institute for Social Research, University of Michigan, 1952.

Carroll, Holbert N., *The House of Representatives and Foreign Affairs*. Pittsburgh: University of Pittsburgh Press, 1958.

Christenson, Reo M., *The Brannan Plan: Farm Politics and Policy*. Ann Arbor: University of Michigan Press, 1959.

Coffin, Tris, *Missouri Compromise*. Boston: Little, Brown and Company, 1947.

Crabb, Cecil V., Jr., *Bipartisan Foreign Policy: Myth or Reality?* Evanston, Ill.: Row, Peterson and Company, 1957.

Dalfiume, Richard M., *Desegregation of the U.S. Armed Forces: Fighting on Two Fronts, 1939–1953*. Columbia: University of Missouri Press, 1969.

Daniels, Jonathan, *The Man of Independence*. Philadelphia: Lippincott, 1950.

Davies, Richard O., *Housing Reform During the Truman Administration*. Columbia: University of Missouri Press, 1966.

Divine, Robert A., *American Immigration Policy, 1924–1952*. New Haven: Yale University Press, 1957.

Eccles, Marriner S., *Beckoning Frontiers: Public and Personal Recollections*. New York: Alfred A. Knopf, 1951.

Ferrell, Robert H., *George C. Marshall*. Volume XV of *The American Secretaries of State and Their Diplomacy*, Ferrell and Samuel F. Bemis, eds., New Series 1925–1961. New York: Cooper Square Publishers, 1966.

Flanders, Ralph E., *Senator from Vermont*. Boston: Little, Brown, and Company, 1961.

Forrestal, James, *The Forrestal Diaries*, Walter Millis and E. S. Duffield, eds. New York: The Viking Press, 1951.

Goldman, Eric F., *The Crucial Decade—and After: America, 1945–1960*. New York: Random House, Vintage ed., 1961.

Harnsberger, Caroline T., *Man of Courage*. New York: Wilcox and Follett Company, 1952.

Harris, Joseph P., *The Advice and Consent of the Senate; A Study of the Confirmation of Appointments by the United States Senate*. Berkeley: University of California Press, 1953.

Hartley, Fred A., *Our New National Labor Policy; The Taft-Hartley Act and the Next Steps*. New York: Funk and Wagnalls Company, 1948.

Hillman, William, *Mr. President; The First Publication from the Personal Diaries, Private Letters, Papers, and Revealing Interviews of Harry S. Truman.* New York: Farrar, Straus and Young, 1952.

Holmans, A. E., *United States Fiscal Policy, 1945–1959: Its Contributions to Economic Stability.* London: Oxford University Press, 1961.

Huthmacher, J. Joseph, *Senator Robert F. Wagner and the Rise of Urban Liberalism.* New York: Atheneum, 1968.

Javits, Jacob K., *Order of Battle: A Republican's Call to Reason.* New York: Atheneum Publishers, 1964.

Jewell, Malcolm E., *Senatorial Politics and Foreign Policy.* Lexington: University of Kentucky Press, 1962.

Johnson, Walter, *1600 Pennsylvania Avenue: Presidents and the People Since 1929.* Boston: Little, Brown and Company, 1963.

Jones, Joseph M., *The Fifteen Weeks (February 21–June 5, 1947).* New York: The Viking Press, 1955.

Kennan, George F., *Memoirs, 1925–1950.* Boston: Little, Brown and Co., 1967.

Kirkendall, Richard S., ed., *The Truman Period as a Research Field.* Columbia: University of Missouri Press, 1967.

Knipe, James L., *The Federal Reserve and the American Dollar: Problems and Policies, 1946–1964.* Chapel Hill: University of North Carolina Press, 1965.

Kolko, Gabriel, *The Politics of War: The World and United States Foreign Policy, 1943–1945.* New York: Random House, 1968.

LaFeber, Walter, *America, Russia, and the Cold War, 1945–1966.* New York: John Wiley and Sons, Inc., 1967.

Latham, Earl, *The Communist Controversy in Washington: From the New Deal to McCarthy.* Cambridge: Harvard University Press, 1966.

Lee, R. Alton, *Truman and Taft-Hartley; A Question of Mandate.* Lexington: University of Kentucky Press, 1966.

Lilienthal, David E., *The Journals of David E. Lilienthal.* Vol. I: *The TVA Years, 1939–1945.* Vol. II: *The Atomic Energy Years, 1945–1950.* New York: Harper and Row, 1964.

Lubell, Samuel, *The Future of American Politics.* 2d ed. rev. New York: Doubleday and Company, Inc., 1956.

Leuchtenburg, William E., *Franklin D. Roosevelt and the New Deal, 1932–1940.* New York: Harper and Row, 1963.

Martin, Joe, *My First Fifty Years in Politics.* New York: McGraw Hill, Inc., 1960.

Matusow, Allen J., *Farm Policies and Politics in the Truman Years.* Cambridge: Harvard University Press, 1967.

Mayer, George H., *The Republican Party, 1854–1964.* New York: Oxford University Press, 1964.

Millis, Harry A., and Emily Clark Brown, *From the Wagner Act to Taft-Hartley: A Study of National Labor Policy and Labor Relations*. Chicago: University of Chicago Press, 1950.

Millis, Walter, *Arms and the State: Civil-Military Elements in National Policy*. New York: Twentieth Century Fund, 1958.

Nourse, Edwin G., *Economics in the Public Service: Administrative Aspects of the Employment Act*. New York: Harcourt, Brace and Company, 1953.

Neustadt, Richard E., *Presidential Power, The Politics of Leadership*. New York: John Wiley and Sons, Inc., 1960.

Osgood, Robert E., *Limited War: The Challenge to American Strategy*. Chicago: University of Chicago Press, 1957.

Patterson, James T., *Congressional Conservatism and the New Deal: The Growth of the Conservative Coalition in Congress, 1933–1939*. Lexington: University of Kentucky Press, 1967.

Perkins, Dexter, *A History of the Monroe Doctrine*. Boston: Little, Brown and Company, 1955.

Phillips, Cabell, *The Truman Presidency: The History of a Triumphant Succession*. New York: The Macmillan Company, 1966.

Price, Harry Bayard, *The Marshall Plan and Its Meaning*. Ithaca, N.Y.: Cornell University Press, 1955.

Public Papers of the Presidents of the United States: Harry S. Truman. Washington: Government Printing Office, 1961–1966. 8 vols.

Rayback, Joseph G., *A History of American Labor*. New York: Macmillan Company, 1959.

Redding, Jack, *Inside the Democratic Party*. Indianapolis: The Bobbs-Merrill Company, 1958.

Rogow, Arnold A., *James Forrestal, A Study of Personality, Politics and Policy*. New York: Macmillan Company, 1963.

Roseboom, Eugene H., *A History of Presidential Elections*. New York: Macmillan Company, 1957.

Ross, Irwin, *The Loneliest Campaign: The Truman Victory of 1948*. New York: New American Library, 1968.

Rostow, W. W., *The United States in the World Arena*. New York: Harper and Brothers, 1960.

Schilling, Warner R., Paul Y. Hammond, and Glenn H. Snyder, *Strategy, Politics, and Defense Budgets*. New York: Columbia University Press, 1962.

Schmidt, Karl M., *Henry A. Wallace: Quixotic Crusade, 1948*. Syracuse, N.Y.: Syracuse University Press, 1960.

Seidman, Joel I., *American Labor from Defense to Reconversion*. Chicago: University of Chicago Press, 1953.

Smith, Merriman, *A President Is Many Men*. New York: Harper and Brothers, 1948.

Steinberg, Alfred, *The Man from Missouri: The Life and Times of*

228

Harry S. Truman. New York: G. P. Putnam's and Sons, 1962.
Steiner, Gilbert Y., *The Congressional Conference Committee: Seventieth to Eightieth Congresses*. Urbana: University of Illinois Press, 1951.
Truman, David B., *The Congressional Party*. New York: John Wiley and Sons, 1959.
Truman, Harry S., *Memoirs*. New York: Doubleday and Company, 1955, 1956. 2 vols.
Vandenberg, Arthur H., Jr., ed., *The Private Papers of Senator Vandenberg*. Boston: Houghton Mifflin, 1952.
Westerfield, H. Bradford, *Foreign Policy and Party Politics: Pearl Harbor to Korea*. New Haven: Yale University Press, 1955.
White, William S., *The Taft Story*. New York: Harper and Brothers, 1964.
Xydis, Stephen G., *Greece and the Great Powers, 1944–1947*. Thessaloniki: Institute for Balkan Studies, 1963.

INDEX

A

Abernethy, Thomas G., 119

Acheson, Dean, 116, 165, 215; and reciprocal trade, 51; and Greek-Turkish aid, 57–58, 59n18, 61–62, 61n20; and European aid, 104–6

Agricultural legislation, 20, 188, 197, 206, 208, 217; appropriations, 39; Truman's position on, 23, 130, 154–57. *See also* International Wheat Agreement

Aiken, George, 12, 142n23; opposition to Republican leadership, 15–16, 29–31, 104; and Lilienthal nomination, 35; and labor legislation, 43, 84, 149; and rent control, 94; and tax reduction, 96; voting behavior, 98–99, 157; and Reed-Bulwinkle bill, 146; and agricultural legislation, 155

Air Force, 170–71, 173

Allen, Leo E., 14

American Federation of Labor, 15, 103

American Veterans Committee, 114, 195

Americans for Democratic Action, 114, 195, 207

Andersen, H. Carl, 76, 79, 95, 119, 134, 136

Anderson, Clinton, 88, 91, 123

Antimonopoly legislation, 103, 156, 191; Truman's position on, 23, 130, 197. *See also* Reed-Bulwinkle bill

Appropriations, 46, 71, 103, 157, 214; Truman's position on, 24–25, 35–37, 39–40, 73–74, 102, 187, 188, 197, 205–6; legislative budget, 36–39; Department of the Interior, 38, 143; agricultural, 39, 154; for Tennessee Valley Authority, 143–45. *See also* Public power

Arvey, Jake, 186

Atomic Energy Commission, 31–35

Austin, Warren, 121

Austria, 109, 110, 116, 120, 175

B

Baldwin, Raymond E., 99, 114, 122–23, 145n28

Ball, Joseph H., 72, 84, 85, 141–42, 142n23, 162n4

Barden, Graham A., 82

Barkley, Alben, 103, 137, 194; relations with Truman, 17n25, 133; and Lilienthal nomination, 35; and labor legislation, 43, 44, 89–90, 149; and inflation, 126, 200; and social security, 139; and civil rights, 153; and agricultural legislation, 155–56; and reciprocal trade, 183; and 1948 campaign, 208

Batt, William L., Jr., 189, 192–93, 193n13, 195, 207

Bell, David, 189

M

MacArthur, Gen. Douglas, 163
McCarran, Patrick, 35n14, 43, 78n12, 96, 175–76, 201
McCarthy, Joseph R., 162n4, 200–201
McClellan, John L., 35n14, 77, 78, 89, 96, 135, 200
McCormack, John W., 18, 114
McGrath, J. Howard, 42, 43, 72, 73, 73n2, 137, 152, 176, 184, 190, 201, 210
McKellar, Kenneth D., 32, 34, 35n14, 43n27, 63, 78n12, 100, 153, 186
McMahon, Brien, 139
Malone, George W., 90, 99, 118, 118n29, 162n4, 174
Mansfield, Mike, 111, 127
Marshall, George C., 27–28, 51, 57, 59, 59n18, 64, 91, 105–9 *passim*, 112, 116,
    117, 119, 163–64, 168, 172, 173, 180–81, 215
Marshall Plan, 102, 108, 110, 116, 117, 120, 129, 159–67, 169, 182, 215;
    Truman's position on, 109–10, 159, 165. *See also* European aid; European
    Recovery Program; Interim aid
Martin, Joseph W., 10–12, 14, 57, 122, 148, 164, 180, 205
Maybank, Burnet R., 89, 153
Millikin, Eugene D., 15–16, 38, 51–52, 96, 179–80, 181–82
Minimum wage, 103, 123, 148–49, 150, 216; Truman's position on, 45, 103, 131,
    147, 148–49, 197, 206. *See also* Fair Labor Standards Act; Labor legislation
Molotov, Vyacheslav, 107
Monroney, Mike, 93, 125, 127
Moore, E. H., 32, 99, 162n4
Morse, David A., 71, 80
Morse, Wayne, 12, 29–31, 35, 38, 77, 96, 126, 139, 140, 141, 176; and labor
    legislation, 15, 81, 84, 89, 90, 142n23; voting behavior, 98–99, 157
Morton, Thruston, 136
Murdock, John R., 140
Murphy, Charles S., 71, 130, 141, 193, 193n13
Murray, James E., 42–43, 72, 84, 85, 100
Murray, Philip, 89, 103, 115
Myers, Francis J., 140

N

National Association for the Advancement of Colored People, 114, 195
National Labor Relations Act, 81. *See also* Taft-Hartley; Wagner act
National Labor Relations Board, 81, 83, 86, 87
National Science Foundation bill, 97–98, 197
National Security Committee, 170, 172
New Deal, 1, 2, 3, 6, 7, 13, 17, 22, 24, 27, 32, 34, 40, 46, 101, 142, 154, 155, 157,
    186, 204, 210, 211, 213, 216; and Republicans, 8–10, 11, 14, 25, 26, 36, 75,
    104, 179, 181, 190, 192
Nitze, Paul, 49
Norrell, W. F., 144
North Atlantic Treaty Organization, 159, 173–74. *See also* Vandenberg Resolution
Nourse, Edwin G., 116, 130, 194–95

3, 8–10; legislative program, 10–12; leadership in Congress, 12–16; intraparty
conflict, 15–16, 29–31, 32–35, 37–39, 46, 90, 104, 122–23, 132, 147,
200–201; and labor legislation, 15–16, 41–43, 83–86, 90, 148–49; and
foreign policy, 48–53, 56–58, 62–64, 65, 117–20, 159–67, 169–74, 179–84,
185, 215; and tax reduction, 74–79, 95–96, 132–36; members' voting
behavior, 98–101, 156–57, 213, 214; and elections of 1948, 187–91, 191–92,
194, 198, 202, 204–6, 208–10; and special session of 1948, 196, 197–202
Republican Steering Committee, 111, 180
Revercomb, Chapman, 162n4, 175, 176, 178, 198, 201
Rich, Robert F., 178
Richardson, Seth, 28
Rizley, Ross, 50, 172
Roberts, Owen J., 172
Robertson, A. Willis, 43n27, 100, 126, 200
Robertson, Edward V., 99
Rogers, Edith Nourse, 83
Roosevelt, Franklin D., 3, 8, 208, 211, 216
Roosevelt, James, 186
Rosenman, Samuel I., 193
Ross, Charles, 196
Rowe, James H., Jr., 16–17
Rumania, 23, 47, 67
Russell, Richard, 176, 199

S

Sabath, Adolph J., 31, 42
Saltonstall, Leverett, 35, 99, 145n28, 176
Schwabe, George B., 10, 36
Schwellenbach, Lewis B., 44
Selective Service, 159, 168–73, 212, 214. *See also* Defense program; Universal
military training
Seventy-eighth Congress, 7
Seventy-ninth Congress, 6–7, 8, 12, 21, 72, 113, 115
Smith, Frederick C., 93, 125, 127
Smith, H. Alexander, 12, 61, 72, 84, 85, 142n23, 176, 183
Smith, Lawrence, 65
Snyder, John, 74, 124, 132, 168
Social security legislation, 98, 103, 104, 131, 137–41, 156, 190, 191, 193, 208,
213–14, 216; Truman's position on, 22, 24, 25, 98, 103, 130, 138, 139, 141,
147, 188, 189, 197, 206
Soviet Union, 1, 48–65 *passim*, 105, 106, 159, 161, 167, 168, 169, 175, 176, 184,
186, 215, 216; and European aid, 106, 107, 108, 111
Spain, 107, 164
Sparkman, John J., 89, 153, 186
Special session of 1948. *See* Turnip Day session
Spence, Brent, 9, 125
Stalin, Joseph, 54, 56, 159
Stassen, Harold, 197